TUDOR AND STUART
LINCOLN

PUBLISHED BY
THE SYNDICS OF THE CAMBRIDGE UNIVERSITY PRESS
London Office: Bentley House, N.W. I
American Branch: New York
Agents for Canada, India, and Pakistan: Macmillan

Printed in Great Britain at the University Press, Cambridge
(Brooke Crutchley, University Printer)

THE STONEBOW

From a drawing by S. H. Grimm (1784) in the British Museum

TUDOR & STUART
LINCOLN

BY

J. W. F. HILL

C.B.E., LL.M., Litt.D., F.S.A.

CAMBRIDGE
AT THE UNIVERSITY PRESS
1956

TO

PAST AND PRESENT COLLEAGUES

OF THE

LINCOLN CITY COUNCIL

CONTENTS

ILLUSTRATIONS

PLATES

LIST OF ABBREVIATIONS

A.A.S.R.	*Reports and Papers of the Associated Architectural Societies*
A. & O.	*Acts and Ordinances of the Interregnum*
A.P.C.	*Acts of the Privy Council*
Birch	*Royal Charters of the City of Lincoln,* edited by W. de Gray Birch
B.M.	British Museum
C.J.	*Commons Journals*
C.P.R.	*Calendar of Patent Rolls*
C.S.P. [*D.*] [*For.*]	*Calendar of State Papers* [*Domestic*] [*Foreign*]
D.N.B.	*Dictionary of National Biography*
E.H.R.	*English Historical Review*
H.M.C.	*Historical Manuscripts Commission Reports*
L.A.O.	Lincolnshire Archives Office
L.A.S.R.	*Lincolnshire Architectural Society Reports*
L.J.	*Lords Journals*
L. & P. Henry VIII	*Letters and Papers of Henry VIII*
L.P.L.	Lincoln Public Library
Lincs. N. & Q.	*Lincolnshire Notes and Queries*
L.R.S.	Publications of Lincoln Record Society
M.L.	*Medieval Lincoln,* by J. W. F. Hill
P.R.O.	Public Record Office
V.C.H.	*Victoria County History*

PREFACE

LIKE its predecessor *Medieval Lincoln*, this book is the product of the residuary moments of a busy life, and its progress has been constantly interrupted by work which at the time seemed to matter more. If in consequence there are inconsistencies of viewpoint or form I hope they may be forgiven.

In writing both books I have had especially in mind two classes of readers: those who may be able to use the local evidence in treating of wider historical themes which are themselves beyond my scope and purpose; and those who, living mostly in or near Lincoln, or having associations with it, may find that the tale will aid their historical imagination and make the city a more interesting place to live in or to visit. I believe that local history is a stimulus to civic spirit, and I should like to think that the books have indirectly served the cause of local government.

The principal sources of evidence on which I have relied are the records of the Lincoln Corporation, and in particular the minutes of the common council. The earliest surviving council register begins in 1511, in time to make it possible to write Chapter II. No such survey could be written for any earlier period. Thereafter the minutes continue unbroken save for the period from 1638 to (except for a few entries) 1656. Detailed references to them would have so heavily incumbered the footnotes that I have had to abandon their citation. Students will readily identify the evidence gathered from this source. The minutes were calendared, but inadequately, for the Historical Manuscripts Commission by W. D. Macray in 1895, and a catalogue of the Corporation records, compiled by W. de Gray Birch, was published in 1906. The records are now in process of transfer to the Lincolnshire Archives Office. There are, in addition, the city quarter sessions records, the cordwainers' gild book and the Christ's Hospital minutes and accounts. I have drawn on the miscellaneous collections of the Lincoln Public Library, including a small group of Sir Robert Clayton's papers; a few more of them are in my own possession. There are a few manuscripts relating to the history of Lincoln School, and several of the city parishes have records of the period.

The scope for research has been vastly increased by the creation of the Lincolnshire Archives Office, which incorporates the Lincoln Diocesan Record Office, founded as a memorial to Canon Foster by the Pilgrim Trust. It is administered by a joint committee of the three administrative counties of Lindsey, Kesteven and Holland and the city and county borough of Lincoln. It includes the Lincoln Diocesan Registry, whose riches have been disclosed by Miss Kathleen Major's *A Handlist of the Records of the Bishop of Lincoln and of the Archdeacons of Lincoln and Stow* (1953). The episcopal registers, accounts, *libri cleri*, inventories and correspondence have all provided evidence for the history of the city. The Office also has custody of the muniments of the dean and chapter, which have thrown light on a number of matters, and many private collections, among which I have found those of the Earl of Ancaster and Lord Monson, the Whichcote papers from Aswarby and the Hatcher papers from Holywell of great value. The Lindsey quarter sessions records have also been consulted. The annual reports of the Office, beginning in 1948, give details of accessions, and are indispensable to all workers upon Lincolnshire history.

These sources have been supplemented on many points from the national collections: the State Papers Domestic in the Public Record Office; the books of the Staple Company, the summary of the depopulation returns of 1607 (for knowledge of which I am indebted to Mr J. D. Gould), and other papers at the British Museum; Archbishop Laud's papers relating to Bishop Williams in the Lambeth Palace Library; the local acts upon the statute roll and copies of the Braye MSS. at the House of Lords Record Office; abstracts of the letters of the Armynes of Osgodby among the Morrice MSS. in Dr Williams's Library; and the Treasury Letter Books and copies of the Peover MSS. at the General Post Office Record Office. At the Bodleian Library are Thomas Sympson's 'Adversaria' (see p. 32) and other volumes among the Gough MSS., the first account book of Christ's Hospital (p. 136), and a militia assessment of the Restoration period from the Waterford MSS., formerly at Doddington (p. 170); and at the Cambridge University Library is Sir Anthony Oldfield's Letter Book (p. 170). Other manuscript sources are acknowledged in the footnotes.

In the preface to *Medieval Lincoln* I gave some account of the collections made for the history of the city and county by Thomas Sympson (now in the Bodleian Library) and John Ross (now deposited by Lord Monson in the Lincoln Public Library). I did not then know of the collection made by Edward James Willson. The collection has not been preserved intact, but happily a large part of it has come into the possession of the Society of Antiquaries, who very generously deposited their volumes in Lincoln for my use.

Willson was born in Lincoln in 1787 and educated at the grammar school. He soon abandoned his father's calling of a builder and became an architect. He restored a number of parish churches, was county surveyor for Lincoln castle, and from time to time advised the dean and chapter on cathedral repairs. He contributed much to architectural publications, including those of Britton and the elder Pugin. For many years he was a member of the Lincoln city council, and he was mayor in 1851–52. There is a memoir in the *Gentleman's Magazine* for March 1855; and see now Mr H. M. Colvin's *Biographical Dictionary of English Architects 1660–1840* (1954). His portrait was presented to the city of Lincoln by his grandson, the Rev. E. H. Willson, O.S.B., in 1948; it hangs in the Inner Guildhall.

Another unpublished collection ought to be mentioned here. Mr C. L. Exley has spent many years in copying and abstracting documents relating to the history of the city, and has worked through the files of local newspapers. On many occasions he has been able to answer questions of mine from his vast stores of information, and I hope as I turn to a later period to benefit even more by his labours.

The printed sources on which I have relied mostly speak for themselves; the chief of them are listed in the table of abbreviations. There are several rare tracts and broadsheets relating to the city in the British Museum. The Lincoln Public Library and the Lincoln Cathedral Library have good collections of Civil War tracts. The Master of Emmanuel College, Cambridge, produced for me his college's unique copy of John Smith's tract on Psalm xxii, and the Librarian of Friends House the Martin Mason pamphlets. A copy of *The Prisoner against the Prelate* is in my possession.

I am grateful to the keepers of all the collections mentioned for the facilities they have given me; and to the Town Clerk and his staff, whom I have often plagued at short notice. For illustrations I am indebted to Lord Ancaster; Colonel C. F. C. Jarvis; the Mayor, Aldermen and citizens of Lincoln; the Bishop of London; Lord Monson; the Trustees of the National Portrait Gallery; the Dean and Chapter of Westminster; the Winchelsea Settled Trustees for the drawings from the Winchelsea Book of Monuments, now deposited by them in the British Museum; the Trustees of the British Museum for the use of the drawings by S. H. Grimm from his large collection of Lincoln drawings catalogued as Add. MSS. 15541 and 15542; and the Keeper of Western Manuscripts at the Bodleian Library for the drawing from Samuel Buck's notebook (MS. Gough Linc. 15).

The County Archivist, Mrs Joan Varley, and her colleague, Miss D. M. Williamson, have called my attention to sources, and indeed I cannot thank them too warmly for all their manifold services. The Principal of St Hilda's College, Oxford, has read the typescript and made valuable suggestions, and Mr G. S. Dixon has saved me from a number of mistakes. For books I have been able to use the Lincoln Public Library, the Lincoln Cathedral Library (where the Chancellor and the Librarian kindly gave me special facilities), the Nottingham University Library, the London Library, the Society of Antiquaries and the Institute of Historical Research. The Lindsey County Council, with a true regard for the wishes of Canon Foster, has transferred the Foster Library to the Lincolnshire Archives Office, but I used it constantly when it formed part of the Lindsey and Holland County Library. To the keepers of all these libraries and their staffs I am indebted for much friendly aid.

Mr A. W. Mawby and Mr F. E. Leafe have helped with the maps, and Mr Gerald Sharpe and Mr Brian Webb with arithmetic and in other ways. My secretary, Miss W. O. Hunt, has made the final typescript and has lightened the work at all stages. The index has been made by Miss F. E. Thurlby.

I wish to thank the officers and staff of the Cambridge University Press for their courtesy and care in seeing the book through to publication.

J. W. F. HILL

LINCOLN
Michaelmas 1955

CHAPTER I

COUNTRY BACKGROUND

IN the political geography of the sixteenth century Lincolnshire was the most north-easterly county directly governed from London, for the shires beyond the Humber were administered from York by the Council of the North. The area between Humber and Wash was not only remote, it was and is vast, for it is as far from Stamford on its southern tip to Barton-on-Humber as it is to London. It was isolated too, and more so than a small-scale map would suggest. To the north-west were the dreary wastes of Thorne and Hatfield, which in wintertime became an inland sea. To the west was the wide and unbanked river Trent. Geologists credit the flood waters of the Trent basin with having cut the gap in the limestone ridge in which Lincoln stands, and in times of flood they still seek to resume their ancient course across the sandy level between the modern river Trent and the Lincoln gap, and so to flood the lower city and cut it off from the west. Even when it was not in flood the Trent was a physical and psychological barrier. It had no bridge below Newark until Gainsborough bridge was built in 1790. There were only ferries, as at Gainsborough, Dunham, Littleborough and Stockwith. No main roads led to them. The county of Lincoln was virtually a peninsula, whose neck to the south was narrowed by the fens.

The coast was lonely and long, guarded to the landward by

Wide and wild the waste enormous marsh

of Tennyson. It was opened to the seaward by small creeks, sixteen in number, in which landings could be made unobserved or cargoes smuggled in or out. Throckmorton, the plotter against Elizabeth, had a plan of 'the havens and places easily to land in', which Sir Edward Dymoke asked to have, as an aid to the view of the sea coast in the Marsh and Holland.[1]

The county lay on the eastern flank of the north road. It was a long and dreary way from London, generally taking three days on horseback,[2] through Waltham, Ware, Royston and Huntingdon; the old north road had not yet been supplanted by the present road through Baldock and Stevenage. The miry clay lands of Bedfordshire all too often broke the spirit of the traveller on horse or foot. Walsingham's secretary told Lord

[1] *H.M.C. Rutland*, I, 176.
[2] During the Civil War messengers made the journey in two days. See, for example, *C.J.* II, 606.

Rutland that the ways to Grantham were foul and long;[1] and more than a century later Defoe reported to Harley from Leicester that the country was very deep and wet, and that he hoped to make more haste when he got over the Trent, the ground being harder.[2] If Defoe had gone to Huntingdon he might have found that the waters were out, and that he could not get through. The traveller who succeeded had then a choice of routes to Lincoln. He could keep on the north road to Newark, skirt the Trent there, and reach Lincoln by the Roman Fosse Way. He could turn right at Stilton to Peterborough, Crowland and Spalding and so to Boston, and reach Lincoln through Heckington and Sleaford, though if the season were late or early part of the road would almost certainly be drowned.[3] More likely he would go through Peterborough to Market Deeping, cross the Welland and enter Lincolnshire there, and keep the fenland on his right through Bourne and Sleaford. The decayed bridge at West Deeping and the Lincoln–London road were reported to be very foul and dangerous in 1621,[4] and the inhabitants of the towns along the road petitioned for repair of the Lolham bridges in the parish of Maxey by which the Ermine Street crossed the Welland, the decay whereof was causing great danger and damage.[5] Other ways there were for the adventurous traveller. He might go from Bourne along the Nordyke causeway between the East and West fens. Although it was the duty of the abbot of Revesby and his lay successors to maintain the causeway people were drowned there every year; and it was small comfort to know that in default of repair the abbey lands might be seized by the sheriff.

The other roads of the county were no better, and may have been worse. Bridge Dyke, the causeway from Kesteven to Boston, was the liability of Sempringham priory. It was complained in 1575 that no repairs had been carried out since the dissolution of the religious houses, as the lands charged with repair had come into the possession of Henry VIII. Money had been appropriated for repair, but not enough, and the inhabitants asked that lands should be granted for its maintenance.[6] The road from Fiskerton to Horncastle was a very cruel ill way, and from the west end of Langworth lane to Wragby town was a high passage and not passable by reason of the

---

[1] *H.M.C. Rutland*, I, 192.

[2] *H.M.C. Portland*, IV, 332.

[3] John Ogilby noted that Crowland was 'seated very low, and amongst deep fens, almost after the manner of Venice, its three streets being separated from each other by water-courses, the banks whereof are preserved by piles; the lowness of its situation admits of no carriages to come at it' (*Britannia* (1675), p. 72).

[4] *H.M.C. Rutland*, IV, 217.

[5] *A.P.C. 1623–25*, p. 65.

[6] *H.M.C. Salisbury*, XIII, 128.

deep miry way; and similarly from Dunholme to Faldingworth on the way from Lincoln to Market Rasen, which led through Caistor to Grimsby.[1]

A few notable travellers can be followed as they journey through the county. In 1541 Henry VIII entered it at Stamford, and went to Grimsthorpe as guest of his brother-in-law Charles Brandon, duke of Suffolk; thence to Sleaford and Lincoln, and so to Gainsborough, where he crossed the Trent by ferry. On his return from York he crossed the Humber from Hull to Barrow, and went south to Caenby and South Carlton, where he stayed with Sir John Monson. He must have passed through Lincoln to Nocton, and on to Sleaford and Grimsthorpe.[2] His servant John Leland also came in by Stamford, Bourne and Sleaford to Lincoln and out by Gainsborough ferry.[3] During the rising of the northern earls in 1569 munitions for the royal forces were sent to Barton-on-Humber for despatch by boat to Hull, whilst Sir Ralph Sadler went to York by way of Burton Stather. One of the rebels passed south over the Humber to Barton, and Lord Rutland had to wait for the tide there.[4] James I went from Grantham to Lincoln and returned by Newark; no Humber crossing or even Trent ferry for him.

In August 1634 three 'voluntary members of the noble military company' in Norwich marched to King's Lynn, and thinking it not fit to pass the Washes, which were neither firm nor safe for travellers, especially because of the new-made sluices and devices for turning the natural course of the waters, they chose to go by Wisbech, and thence over Tydd sluice and the rich fat level of ground of Spalding. The next day they went through Threekingham. From there to Sleaford they found the way for the most part 'pleasant, healthy and champion [champion land is uninclosed], a good sociable way for travellers, but such as notably deceive them that be weary. For when we first espied the high towers of the cathedral, we thought it near, but it proved to our pains and patience a full jury of miles, in the passing whereof we lost the sight of those high-topped colossuses at least 16 times.'[5] After their inspection of the city they intended to see Hull and Beverley, 'but that neither the day nor way over Humber would neither seasonably nor safely admit'. They therefore made for Newark.

[1] *H.M.C. Rutland*, IV, 217. Even outside the fen area the carriers and other travellers were often held up by water. See W. A. Massingberd, *History of Ormsby* (n.d.), p. 178.
[2] *Proceedings of the Archaeological Institute, 1848*, pp. 145–56.
[3] *Itinerary*, ed. L. Toulmin Smith (1907), I, 23–33.
[4] *C.S.P.D. Add. 1566–79*, pp. 123–5, 231.
[5] *A Relation of a Short Survey of Twenty-six Counties*, ed. L. G. Wickham Legg (1904), pp. 1–11, quoted in J. Simmons, *Journeys in England* (1951), pp. 104–5, 107. The old road over the heath probably followed the same route as the present, which gives the same impression.

In 1640 Sir Henry Slingsby and his family crossed the Humber to be farther from the Scots army which had taken Newcastle. They went from Hull to Barton (a six-mile journey) in a passage-boat, in a cross-wind and rough water; and after having trouble in getting clear of the boats in Hull harbour, they ran foul of another ship coming in, which bore them under her, and broke a little of the forepart of their boat.[1]

John Evelyn also crossed the Humber in bad weather and reached the north road by Lincoln and Grantham;[2] and John Loveday crossed it southwards and out by Newark.[3] Defoe had unpleasant memories of an ill-favoured dangerous passage by ferry in an open boat carrying about fifteen horses, ten or twelve cows and seventeen or eighteen passengers called Christians, from Barton to Hull, lasting four hours, and 'whether I was seasick or not is not worth notice, but that we were all sick of the passage anyone may well suppose', and on the return journey he preferred to go round by York.[4] Travellers from London to Hull had little choice, however, without a wide detour, and a judge going there had to inquire what time the tide would serve him from Barton, and ask for an officer to guide him from Lincoln.[5]

William III came in by Grantham to Lincoln, and thence by Dunham ferry to Welbeck.[6] Celia Fiennes elected to enter from the north road by Grantham to Lincoln, and retired by Belton to Newark.[7] Southey entered the county by Dunham ferry and went out by Newark.[8] They did not go north or east of Lincoln. Indeed, the wilder and remoter parts beyond the city were seldom penetrated save by those who went because they must. John Woodward, geologist and physician, was an exception. When about 1680–90 he visited his friend the incumbent of Nettleton near Caistor, he wrote that from Lincoln he had 15 such solitary miles, an Arabia Deserta, through wild fields and moors, as he had never ridden before. Below the town, which stands on the side of the Wolds, he saw the Nettleton sands, a mile by half a mile, which puzzled him. But the townsmen told him that aged people there had known it as excellent meadow, until a gentleman, rather than abate his rents, turned it into a warren; where the rabbits finding such easy delving threw out great heaps of sand

[1] *Diary of Sir Henry Slingsby*, ed. D. Parsons (1836), pp. 58–9.
[2] Diary, 19 August 1654.
[3] *Diary of a Tour in 1732*, ed. J. E. T. Loveday (Roxburghe Club, 1890), pp. 203, 210.
[4] *Tour*, ed. G. D. H. Cole (Everyman ed. 1927), II, 94.
[5] *Calendar of Ancient Deeds and Charters, Hull* (1951), L 744.
[6] *C.S.P.D. 1695*, p. 91.
[7] *Journeys of Celia Fiennes*, ed. C. Morris (1947), pp. 70, 71.
[8] *Letters from England*, ed. J. Simmons (1951), pp. 265–8. He noted that the Trent was the largest fresh-water river he had seen in England.

which the wind blew away, and the wind getting into the rabbit holes tore them up also and so made the waste. Six houses had been destroyed by the sand, and it would encroach farther but that the beck carried it away as fast as the wind brought it. 'So much of Arabia Araenosa.' The towns-men had eight-score cows and 1600 sheep, and there were three-score houses in the parish. The town was all thatch and mud and stud, except that the rectory had brick and tile in part. They had good turnips, and he was per-suading them to sow turnips first and then clover on their sandy heath in order to swerd it, but they were not forward to any point of improvement that was new. He was quite angry to see them 'keep a dingy fire with turves, when they might have seacoal for 16s. a chaldron, and fetch them but 7 miles off'.

Woodward's attempt to record the dialect of the natives shows that it has not much changed with the years. 'I have allmost learnt', he wrote, 'to speake to them in their own language, for instance, if any should ask me the way to Lincoln I could say, Yaw mun een goo thruft yon Beck, then yaw'st com to a new Yate, then turr off to th' raight, o're a Brig that lays o're a hoy Doyke, and than Yaw'st not hove ore a maile to th' next Tawn.'[1]

All roads had their perils, and the heath between Lincoln and Sleaford, whose undulations so misled the Norwich volunteers, was typical of the many expanses of gorse and rabbit warrens in which it was all too easy for the traveller to lose his way. Charities for the tolling of the church bell in the evening for the guidance of wayfarers were endowed at Blankney and Potterhanworth by folk who had themselves been rescued; and the Leasingham parish register records the burial of passing strangers. Within four miles of Lincoln, Dunston pillar was to stand in the eighteenth century, the only land lighthouse in the country. Highwaymen provided an added peril. Tradition said that Leasingham mill house was once the rendezvous of a desperate band of robbers who were connected with Dick Turpin, and that they were aided by the sons of respectable farmers in the neighbour-hood. Dunsby hill on the same heath was so notorious a haunt of robbers that in effecting insurances the 'accidents of Dunsby heath' were specially excepted.[2]

Then, as now, the traveller on the north road generally did not diverge from the main route at all. A tourist in the early eighteenth century describes his journey from Stamford to Grantham and Newark and so to

---

[1] Lindsey County Council B.R.A. 866. Abraham de la Pryme made the same Arabian comparison of the sandy commons in the north-west of the county, with poor barren land worth from 2s. to 4s. an acre (*Diary*, ed. C. Jackson (Surtees Society, 1870), pp. 58–9).
[2] G. Oliver, *Holy Trinity Guild at Sleaford* (1837), p. 8 n.; E. Trollope, *Sleaford* (1872), p. 3.

Doncaster and York; and later he refers to a journey from Boston 'over the Down of Lincoln' where they hunt the bustard, 'a bird as big as a turkey, and known no where else but here'. He adds that it lies in a cheap country 'which I would not give you a description of in my way through Stamford, it being a great way off my road, and therefore I take the opportunity of mentioning it here'.[1]

Travellers from Glasgow to London in 1739 found no turnpike road until they reached Grantham. Up to that point they travelled on a narrow causeway, with an unmade soft road on each side. They met strings of packhorses, thirty or forty in a gang; they had to leave the causeway to make way, and plunge into the side road from which they sometimes found it difficult to get back.[2]

His knowledge of the north road enabled Sir Walter Scott to place part of his story *The Heart of Midlothian* between Newark and Grantham. At York Jeanie Deans was warned to 'have a care o' Gunnerby Hill. Robin Hood's dead and gone, but there be takers yet in the Vale of Bever.' Her adventures in the village to which Scott gave the Lincolnshire name of Willingham (usually identified with Syston) show how familiar he was with the district.[3] Yet there is no sign that Scott ever left the north road to penetrate the county farther. When, after some years of making the journey from Scotland by sea, he returned (1828) to the road he found it, as it still is, the dullest in the world. 'Nothing seems to have altered in this twenty or thirty years, save the noses of the landlords, which have bloomed and given place to another set of proboscises as germane as the old were to the *very welcome—please to light—*'*Orses forward* and *ready out*. The skeleton at Barnby Moor has deserted his gibbet, and that is the only change I recollect.'[4]

The isolation of Lincolnshire, and the ignorance of the outer world about it, partly account for the fact that it has often been held in low repute. Henry VIII referred to it as 'one of the most brute and beastly' in the realm; but as he had been held in defiance by it he was a prejudiced witness.[5] Better evidence of common repute comes from the plea of a prisoner to the Lord Admiral in 1592: 'If I am grievous in your honour's hearing or sight let

---

[1] *A Journey through England in Familiar Letters from a Gentleman here to his Friend abroad* (2nd ed. 1724), II, 212, 262–3.

[2] Oliver, op. cit. p. 46 n.

[3] He describes in the rectory parlour prints of Sir William Monson, James Yorke the blacksmith and (in full armour) Peregrine, Lord Willoughby de Eresby, all Lincolnshire worthies, which he must have seen or at least heard of and remembered. See G. G. Walker's paper on 'Sir Walter Scott and Lincolnshire' in his *Tales of a Lincolnshire Antiquary* (1940).

[4] *Journal of Sir Walter Scott*, Preface by D. Douglas (1890), II, 195, and see ibid. I, 272.

[5] Below, p. 45 n.

me be banished in the Brill, Flushing, Lincolnshire, or in the worst place of her Majesty's dominions, or to some vile war without pay, so I am not left in this cage of misery....'[1] Thomas Cromwell was told by the future Lord Williams of Thame that he had seen nowhere 'such a sight of asses so unlike gentlemen as the most part of the gentlemen of Lincolnshire'.[2] Thomas Wilson, himself hailing from a remote part of the county, and rising to be Secretary of State, treats his countrymen as the very type of rustic: 'It is much better to be born in Paris than in Picardie: in London than in Lincoln for that both the ayre is better, people more civill, and the wealth much greater, and the men for the most part more wise';[3] and the typical bucolic appears in the saying 'fowls of the choicest kinds are to be had there [in Northumberland] enough to make a Lincolnshire man sick at the second course....'[4] He is also thought gullible:

> From olde famous Lincolne that's seated so hye,
> Well mounted and furnisht, with gold did I flye,
> To London's fam'd Citie some wit for to buy,
> Which cost me so deare, makes me sigh, sob and crye,
>   For this is the cheating Age,
>   For this is the cheating Age.

After various misadventures in the metropolis,

> Now Leonard of Lincolne with griefe bids adiew:
> My journey to London long time I shall rue:
> I ne're in my life met with villaines so vilde,
> To send a man home like the Prodigall Childe.
>   For this is the cheating Age,
>   For this is the cheating Age.[5]

The inhabitants at large were no doubt unaware of all this prejudice and ignorance, and had they known they would not have been much concerned to dispel it. Foreigners were not highly thought of: the natives' first inclination was to throw a stone at them; and they were only accepted and absorbed into the community after a lengthy probation. It was the magnates who were conscious of the isolation of the county and found it irksome. That they did so is indicated by the way in which they settled in

[1] *H.M.C. Salisbury*, IV, 221.
[2] *L. & P. Henry VIII*, XI, no. 888.
[3] *Arte of Rhetorique* (1560), f. 7.
[4] *H.M.C. Var. Coll.* VII, 432. Dr Birkbeck is supposed to have said that Lincoln was only remarkable for its fat cattle, and the difference between men and cattle was just the difference between bipeds and quadrupeds. Ross Collection, *Scrap Books, Lincoln*, I (L.P.L.).
[5] 'The Cheating Age: Leonard of Lincoln's Journey to London to buy Wit' (printed before 1626). See *A Pepysian Garland*, ed. H. E. Rollins (1922), p. 244.

the south and especially in the south-west. The earls of Rutland, with their seat at Belvoir, established themselves also at Newark, and, halfway from there to Lincoln, at Eagle; another of the family, Roger Manners, lived at Uffington near Bourne. Lord Burghley had his mother's property near Stamford. Lord Clinton secured seats at Tattershall and Sempringham. The Willoughby de Eresbys deserted their ancestral home at Spilsby in favour of Grimsthorpe. The relation of most of these seats to the north road is obvious. At Stamford, Grantham and Newark were the points of contact between Lincolnshire and the outer world. Here were seen the messengers who travelled between London and York, Berwick and Edinburgh, and who could tell the news of the Court and the wars with the French and the Scots, or the threat of invasion from Spain. Great men were entertained in the mansions of the district as they passed north or south on state affairs. The duchess of Suffolk was bidden receive Mary Queen of Scots at her house at Stamford in 1551.[1] The child of Lord Seymour and Queen Katharine Parr was with her at Grimsthorpe in 1549.[2] The Protector Northumberland was expected at the house of Cecil's father in June 1552,[3] and he and others wrote to the privy council from Lord Clinton's house at Sempringham on 21 June.[4] The advent of Sir Francis Walsingham was announced on his way to Scotland by the postmaster of Grantham to Rutland, and after being the guest of Roger Manners at Uffington Walsingham reported upon the honourable entertainment given by Manners to all passengers of quality who travelled northwards.[5]

When they could, the gentry followed the nobility in settling in the south-west. The Custs moved from Pinchbeck to Stamford. Welby built at Denton, Brownlow at Belton, Thorold at Marston and Syston, all near Grantham. The countryside is dotted with manor houses and parks, though their inhabitants have often in these days departed.

By contrast there are few great houses in Holland. The lack of gentry there was a serious matter to deputy lieutenants concerned with the musters. 'The want of gentlemen here to inhabit', they noted in 1580.[6] The reason is not difficult to guess. Here were the fens, a district not likely to appeal to those who knew conditions elsewhere and could make comparisons.

---

[1] *A.P.C. 1550–52*, p. 406.   [2] *C.S.P.D. 1547–80*, p. 21.
[3] Ibid. p. 41.
[4] *H.M.C. Salisbury*, I, 96.
[5] *H.M.C. Rutland*, I, 152, 163. Manners had a house in Lincoln also (ibid. p. 180).
[6] Joan Thirsk, *Fenland Farming in the Sixteenth Century* (1953), p. 44, quoting P.R.O. SP 12, 138, f. 8. For the fenland gentry see W. Moore, 'On the Great Level of the Fens', *A.A.S.R.* I, (1851), 335.

Nevertheless there was a case for the fens. Professor Darby has pointed out that the ill-name of the fenland derives in part from the descriptions in various itineraries, written by travellers with an eye for the unusual and without sufficient knowledge of the facts. He distinguishes between the marsh itself, the intermediate zone of grazing, flooded for part of the year, and the arable lands permanently above the water-level.[1] The arable fields raised large crops of barley, beans and peas in the sixteenth century, and later, it seems, of oats and coleseed (the latter for oil); and on the pasture grounds oxen and sheep were bred for the London markets. From the water came wildfowl, principally duck, mallard and teal, decoyed and sent to London; fish, especially pike, and goose feathers and quills, the birds being plucked four, five or six times a year for feathers, and three for quills, and some men having 1000 birds or more, kept at little or no charge, except in snowy weather when they were fed with corn. The soil was rich and the farmers prosperous; since drainage they are still more so. The drier parts of Holland supported a larger population.[2]

But water—fresh or salt—was an enemy as well as a friend.[3] The perils, the hardship and discomfort of flood and tempest were real enough, and the ague and malaria which attacked strangers did not always spare the natives. There was heavy mortality among sheep, which often died of the rot in great numbers. From the national point of view the produce of the undrained fen bore no comparison to that of the fenland after drainage; it was the national need during the Napoleonic Wars that accelerated the drainage in Lincolnshire.

It was not for nothing that the fenland proper had a bad name, and that the inhabitants were believed to walk on stilts.[4] Dugdale, a sober observer, gives a vivid picture of conditions in the fenland:

in the winter-time, when the ice is strong enough to hinder the passage of boats ...and yet not able to beare a man; the Inhabitants upon the Hards and Banks within the Fenns can have no help of food, nor comfort for body or soul;...

[1] H. C. Darby, 'The human geography of the Fenland before the drainage', *Geographical Journal*, LXXX (1932), 420–35.

[2] See Mrs Thirsk, op. cit.; and for the description of the fens in 1696 by Christopher Merrett, Surveyor to the Port of Boston, *Fenland Notes and Queries*, IV (1898–1900), 176–8.

[3] Cf. *C.S.P.D. 1603–10*, p. 521.

[4] The fens had a special use when stiltmen were required for service in the Low Countries under Leicester: twelve or sixteen of the most expert that could be found, with each two pairs of the highest stilts and the longest poles that might be used with them, were sent for in 1586 (*A.P.C. 1586–7*, p. 75). When Christopher Wordsworth became bishop of Lincoln he gained his first impression of his see from Camden, who represented the natives as obliged to walk on stilts; and the Rev. T. Mozley sent him a sketch of a Lincolnshire landscape consisting of a horizontal line with the motto *nil nisi pontus et aër*. (J. H. Overton and E. Wordsworth, *Christopher Wordsworth, Bishop of Lincoln* (1888), p. 206.)

And what expectation of health can there be to the bodies of men when there is no element of good, the air being for the most part cloudy, gross and full of rotten Harrs, the water putrid and muddy, yea, full of loathsome vermin, the earth spungy and boggy, the Fire noysome by the stink of smoaky Hassocks?

And while he notes the results of drainage works in the crops in the Isle of Ely and Whittlesey, in corn and grass at Thorney, he finds Deeping Fen under water, and in the Lincolnshire fen his descriptions of improvements cease.[1]

In the early years of the eighteenth century a rhymer living in Gainsborough wrote to a friend in Wolverhampton a humorous description of conditions in the Trent valley which might have been written of the fens:

> Sir, Happy are you that breathe the 'Hampton Air,
> And drink of rapid streams, as Chrystal clear!
> While wretched WE, the baleful influence mourn
> Of cold *Aquarius*, and his weeping Urn.
> Eternal Mists that droping course distil,
> And drizzly Vapours all the Ditches fill;
> The swampy Lands a Bog! the Fields are Seas!
> And too much Moisture is the Grand Disease.
> Here e'ery Eye with brackish Rheum o'erflows,
> And a fresh Drop still hangs at e'ery Nose.
> Here the Winds rule with uncontested Right,
> The wanton Gods at pleasure take their Flight.
> No shelt'ring Hedge! no Tree! or spreading Bough
> Obstruct their Course, but unconfin'd they blow!
>   ...   .
> All Dogs here take Water, and we find
> No Creature but of an amphibious Kind;
> Rabbits with Ducks, and Geese here sail with Hens,
> And all for Food must paddle in the Fens,
> Nay when provision fails, the hungry Mouse,
> Will fear no Pool to reach a neighb'ring House:
> The good old Dam clucks boldly thro' the Stream,
> And Chickens newly hatch'd assay to Swim;
> All have a Moorish taste, Cow, Sheep and Swine,
> Savour of Fens, and still on Frogs you dine:
> Bread is your only Sauce, a Barley Cake,
> Hard as your Cheese, and as the D-l black.
> Our choicest Drink (and that's the greatest Curse)
> Is but bad water made by brewing worse.

He thought housing conditions desperately bad:

> And soon the Waves possess'd their old Domain;
> They scorn'd the Shore, and o'er the Marshes round

---

[1] *History of Imbanking* (1662), Introduction; H. C. Darby, *Historical Geography of England* (1936), p. 454.

> Our Mud-walled Cotts were levell'd with the Ground;
> Tho' the coarse Building is so homely low,
> That when the House is fall'n you hardly know.
>
> ...   .
>
> Thus as in the Ark, here in one common Sty,
> Men and their Fellow-Brutes with equal honour lie.

After describing the odious cry of the hoarse sea-pye, the night raven and the owl, and above all the humming drone of the gnats who wound in every human part, the agues and coughs that

> as constant reign
> As *Itch* in Scotland or the *Flux* in Spain,

he turns to the natives:

> The Goths were not so barb'rous a Race,
> As the grim Rusticks of this Motly Place;
> Of Reason void, and Thought; whom Interest rules
> Yet will be *Knaves*, tho' Nature made them *Fools*!
> A strange half Human and ungainly Brood,
> Their Speech uncouth, as are their Manners rude!
> When they would seem to *speak* the Mortals roar;
> As loud as Waves contending with the Shore!
> Their wided Mouth do in a Circle grow,
> For all their Vowels are but A and O!
> The Beasts have the same language, and the Cow,
> After the Owner's Voice, is taught to low![1]

This facetious epistle to one who was no doubt accustomed to the elegant speech of the west midlands has enough in it of truth to conjure up an impression of life in fenland areas. Like conditions were all too often present in Lincoln below hill and on its borders. On the south-east the Witham fens came up to the city, and in winter swelled into a sheet of water covering everything east and south of the Sincil dyke and sometimes washing the east side of High Street. To the south-west the upper Witham drained about 200,000 acres of land, the water from which must all pass through the funnel of the Lincoln gap; and the gap might at any time be reappropriated by the Trent flood waters, converting a chain of pools into a vast inland sea. The water from the ridge to the north-west was gathered by the Till and brought into the Fossdyke, and so either to the Trent or to Brayford and the Witham. It was of this area that Dugdale wrote in his diary:

On the North west side of Lincoln, beyond the Hill, lyeth a large Fen, which extendeth to Torksey; through which, there is an antient drayne made, called

---

[1] *A Satyr on Lincolnshire, in a Letter from a Gentleman in Lincoln[shire] to his Friend in Wolverhampton, Staffordshire* (2nd ed. 1736). From a copy in the British Museum.

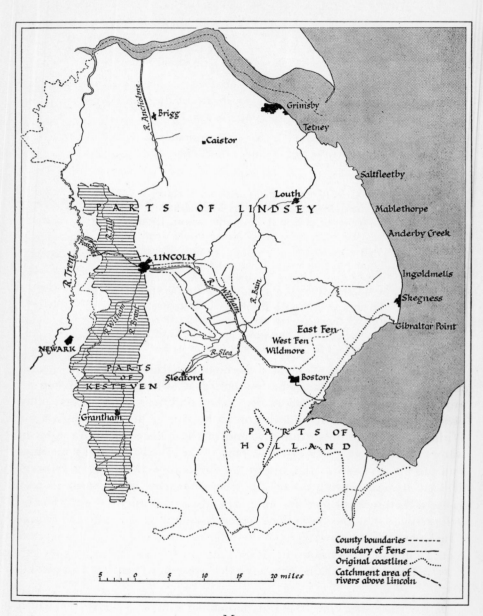

Map 1

Fosse dike: but the water coming into this drayne from Saxelby, south east wards, passeth into Witham, and soe runneth away to Boston: soe yt *Saxelby* seemeth to be the highest ground in all that Fen in regard yt from thence, part of the water comes to *Lincoln*; and part, the contrary way to *Torksey*. They say, that in digging of this Fen, after the first spade grasse they come to moore, about 18 inches thick; then to sand.[1]

Against these incursions of flood the various authorities were helpless. In the surviving minutes of the Lincoln Court of Sewers, which begin in 1760, the greatest of floods pass unrecorded; the only thing to do was to wait until the water subsided, and then resume the patching of banks and the cutting of weeds.[2] The first Witham Drainage Act was passed in 1762.[3] It brought some relief, but fen drainage had to wait for a series of local acts for separate parishes.

It was in this watery world that lower Lincoln lived. Miss Hatfield noted that its prevailing character was plain and marshy ground, studded with its genuine offspring the willow, mostly pollard.[4] Farmers commonly came to market in *shouts*, little narrow cock-boats holding two persons;[5] little fleets of them could be seen on Fridays on the river, though the building of the lock at Stamp End was to prevent their nearer approach. Fishing and fowling were an important occupation. Godwits lived at Washingborough in Gough's time, and on the east fen wild duck, wild geese, garganeys, pochards, shoveller and teal.[6] There were duck decoys below Burton Hall, and at South Carlton, Nocton and Skellingthorpe. Corporation tenants paid part of their rents to the mayor in fowl, and distinguished visitors were generally presented with pike, bream, eels or other fish. The judges of assize were commonly invited to spend a day fishing on Swanpool.

There is no doubt that the ill-fame of the low-lying lands gave the county a bad name. Thomas Stone in his *General View of the Agriculture of the County of Lincoln* (1794) is clear on the point. In a section headed 'Prejudices against the County' he says that estates had lately been sold there for half their real value. Gentlemen having landed property in the county and residing elsewhere had, without examining the state and condi-

---

[1] Printed in H. C. Darby, *The Draining of the Fens* (1940), p. 280.

[2] This helplessness is illustrated by the remark of an old Lincoln woman who lived in the danger area and was accustomed to retiring upstairs with her belongings as the floods approached: 'You can put fire out wi' watter, but you can't do nowt wi' watter.'

[3] 2 George III, c. 32.   [4] *Terra Incognita of Lincolnshire* (1816), p. 3.

[5] E. J. Willson MSS. v, 55. They are still used on Cowbit Wash.

[6] See his edition of Camden's *Britannia* (1786), II, 271. Major Cartwright, after vigorous campaigning for parliamentary reform, was grateful, on a visit to Lincoln, for two nights' rest on a double featherbed, 'in the land of goosefeathers' (*Life and Correspondence of Major Cartwright*, ed. Miss F. D. Cartwright (1826), II, 235).

tion of their property, accepted the idea that it was low and liable to flood, and had sold it with a view to purchase in another county; in one instance an estate was sold for nearly £100,000 less than it afterwards proved to be worth. Only since the American war had this prejudice been in any degree dispelled. It was well known to conveyancers in London that in advancing money upon mortgage securities Lincolnshire was formerly specially excepted. Because part of the county was low and its drainage for years neglected, it had been concluded in remote places that in winter the whole district was a duckpool; and the information that two-thirds of it was high and dry would have been little credited.[1] The foundation of agricultural progress was laid by Sir Joseph Banks during the wars with France, but it was only in the middle years of the nineteenth century that Lincolnshire became one of the foremost farming counties.

But in Tudor and Stuart times it was yet a far cry to the days of improvement in agriculture; and so it was in roads and transport. The deterrents to travel, physical, economic and psychological, were so great that small men moved about hardly at all, but stayed where God put them. Merchants went to fairs and markets, or round the farms to buy wool; lawyers went on circuit of the assize towns; magistrates went to sessions and clergy to visitations; country lads were apprenticed in neighbouring towns, and a few adventurous spirits went further afield, perhaps to London to try their fortunes. Of the citizens of Lincoln the recorder, who was often one of the city's representatives in parliament, and his parliamentary colleague, were taken by public duty to London. So occasionally was the mayor, but 'to ride up' was a serious matter, to be evaded if possible, and at the least to be postponed until the summer reduced the hardships of the journey. It is more difficult now than it was a generation ago to realise that ordinary folk seldom went farther than they could walk in a day, and that their turn did not come until the age of the railways; in Lincoln the 'foundry trips' with their reduced holiday fares began in the 1870's.[2]

Towns on the north road were liable to have their horses taken to ride post upon royal business; Grantham complained about 1578 that the practice had so increased as to become intolerable.[3] When Newark became a post town it made a virtue of necessity by using the fact as an argument

[1] Pp. 10, 11.

[2] When John Disney travelled from his house beyond Lincoln to London as a commissioner for the surrounded marshes in 1614 he spent four days on the journey each way at 6s. 8d. a day (L.P.L. MS. 5039). A special messenger sent post from London to Lincoln with diet and lodging cost £5. 10s. od. (A.P.C. 1615–16, p. 510). The city of Lincoln paid 40s. for a horse which Richard Sutton rode to London in 1542, and two years later William Yates was allowed 2s. a day in London.

[3] C.S.P.D. 1547–80, p. 612.

for incorporation (1626); it was claimed as a cause of prosperity and growing population.[1] Increasing traffic pointed to the growing importance of Anglo-Scottish relations.

In times of emergency Lincoln had to provide post-horses for the king. This happened several times in the latter years of Henry VIII. It was not until the beginning of the seventeenth century that regular posts were established, one of them being to Scotland.[2] There was a plan in 1635 for a post from London to Edinburgh in six days instead of two months, with a by-post to Lincoln, and the cost was to be met by the carriage of private letters. A statute of 1660[3] mentioned Lincoln and Grimsby as entitled to a weekly post, and within a few years Lincoln was receiving a regular service three times a week. Its letters came from Newark, dropped by the north mail.[4] By 1672 the Lincoln postmaster was Ralph Burnett, and he it was who set up riding stages from Lincoln to Wragby, Horncastle, Louth, Spilsby, Alford, Market Rasen, Caistor, Grimsby and Brigg: Boston and Wainfleet were served directly from Newark. 'By consent of the gentlemen and traders' of the county Burnett was allowed 3d. for every letter coming to or going from any of those places. For the service of such long stages by dirty ways he required an establishment of ten horses and four postboys. Even so, the farther towns were visited only twice a week. The attorney Dymoke Walpole of Louth told his London agent on 4 January 1676 that he had just received a London letter of 29 December, and could not have done sooner, 'for if you write by Thursday post it stays two days at Lincoln, and the Saturday letters come as soon. Tuesday and Saturday letters come without delay.'[5]

Burnett was soon in trouble with his Lincoln neighbours for charging a penny a letter carried about the city, which he was not entitled to charge, and they appealed to their representatives in parliament;[6] and he was refusing to deliver the franked letters of members of both Houses of Parliament according to their privilege. Perhaps it was because of all this trouble that an interloper began to carry letters, and had to be reminded of the post-office monopoly and threatened with penalties.

[1] *V.C.H. Notts.* II, 285. Prices to travellers were higher at Stamford and Grantham than in Lincoln, which was 'much the cheaper quarter' in 1685 (*H.M.C. 3rd Report*, p. 100). Stages in despatch south from Berwick were Northallerton, Boroughbridge, Wetherby, Ferrybridge, Doncaster, Scrooby, Tuxford, Newark, Grantham, Huntingdon, Caxton (*C.S.P.D. 1580–1625*, p. 278). Presently there was a postmaster at South Witham or Post Witham, between Newark and Stamford.

[2] Tuke's service was an emergency service. See below, p. 44.

[3] 12 Car. II, c. 35.

[4] B.M. Harleian MS. 7365.

[5] Clayton MSS. in my possession.

[6] Sir Thomas Meres was described as being very much Burnett's friend.

As in so much else, Lincolnshire was thought to be behind the rest of the country in its postal services, some towns having no post at all, and other towns having to pay an extraordinary tax above the common postage. In 1705 the county posts were farmed out.[1] Burnett had died, and the Lincoln post-office was carried on by his daughter Frances and her two successive husbands. Already some of the stages had been taken from them; and in 1705 they lost their 3d. for outgoing letters, and 2d. out of the 3d. for incoming letters, receiving instead a salary of £20 a year. By 1715 they were heavily in debt to the postmaster-general, complaining bitterly of their losses, and petitioning for relief; their complaints were held to be largely justified, and most of the debt was remitted.[2]

It was only the 'gentlemen and traders' who were much concerned with the posts; other folk neither sent nor received letters. But the gentlemen and traders found three posts a week inadequate, and in 1762 the common council were pressing for a daily post. By 1786 Palmer's improved mail-coach plan was in operation, reducing the time from London to Edinburgh from eighty-five to sixty hours.[3] It was probably then that Lincoln secured a daily post, which it was enjoying in 1791.[4] The Lincoln mail was still carried by postboys to and from Newark: in 1807 the common council asked that they and the postboys carrying mail to the eastern parts of the county should be armed.

By the middle of the seventeenth century there were stage-coaches on all the main roads, including regular services between London and York and Newcastle. Even the main roads had their perils, however: in November 1694 the York coach was being ferried over the Trent near Newark, when it upset the boat, and its three passengers were drowned.[5]

It was hardly to be expected that stage-coaches would directly serve the city until the local roads were taken over by turnpike trusts; though a stage-coach plying between London and the Angel at Lincoln twice a week, taking three days on the journey, was announced in 1729, there is nothing to show whether it prospered. In 1756 the road over the heath from Dunsby Lane and the main roads through the city were turnpiked; and the Newark road to the county boundary was added in 1777. Advertisements in the Lincoln Gazetteer of 1784 show a coach travelling from Louth

---

[1] The farmers were Richard Bigg of Winslow, Bucks., and Richard Dixon of Bourne, Lincs.

[2] General Post Office Record Office: Treasury Letter Books, 1699–1705, pp. 116, 256; 1715–24, pp. 2–6, 14, 19–20; transcripts of Peover MSS. I, 26; II, 208, 547, 688; III, 407, 414, 484.

[3] H. Robinson, Britain's Post Office (1953), p. 139.

[4] Universal British Directory, III (1791), 559.

[5] Joan Parkes, Travel in England in the Seventeenth Century (1925), p. 241.

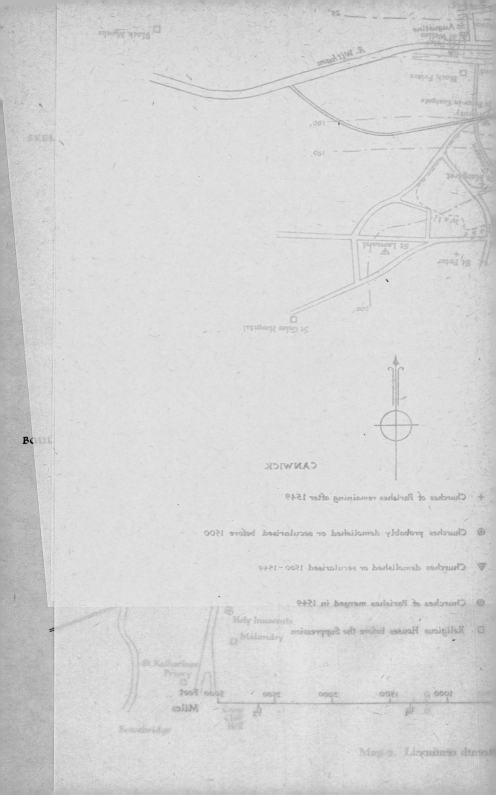

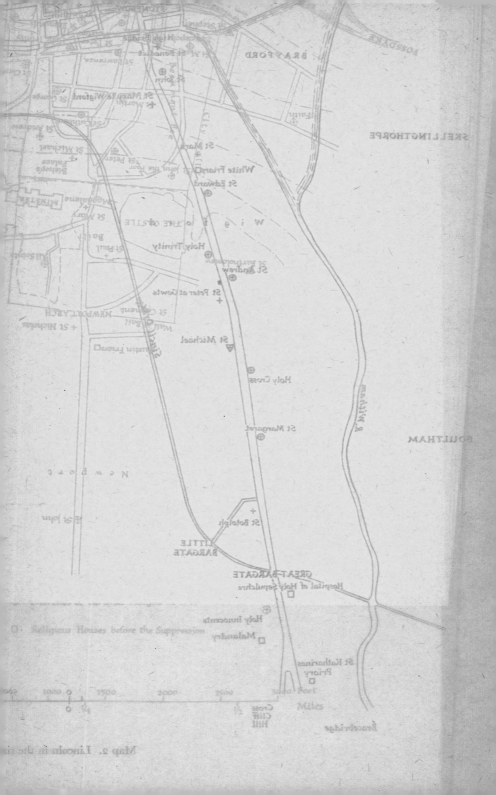

every Tuesday, and one leaving Lincoln for London every Wednesday at 4 a.m. and returning every Monday evening at 9 p.m. In 1785 a coach left London every Sunday, Tuesday and Wednesday night at 9 p.m., reached Newark the next night at 10 p.m., and left for Lincoln the next morning at 4 a.m. One left Lincoln every Monday, Tuesday, Thursday and Friday at 9 a.m. and reached London the next day at 6 p.m. The fare from Lincoln to London was £1. 11s. 6d.; outside seats half-price. By 1791 a stage-coach left for London every morning. But these advances in regularity, speed and comfort still lay in the future when Queen Anne died.

CHAPTER II

THE EARLY TUDOR CITY

IF John Leland had lived to write his projected 'Description of the Realm of England' he might have given a connected account of the city of Lincoln. The notes in his *Itinerary*[1] do, however, give the purport of his observations and of the information supplied to him. The things that he took for granted are naturally not mentioned, nor are they referred to, save obliquely, in the records of the common council. There were the dirt streets and lanes, churned in dry weather into dust and in wet weather into mud by the cattle driven daily to and from the commons, the sheep moving from one pasture to another or to market, and the horses of the well-to-do. There were the open sewers, the dunghills and middens, the dogs roaming the streets, the pigstyes behind or beside the houses built of stone and timber, or mud huts, the open commons and the pinfolds, the stalls and booths which encumbered the highways, the smells appropriate to the shops of the butcher, the baker, the tippler, the shoemaker and the rest. The urban scene was little different from the rural. 'Nothing doing, and no money stirring', said one of Thomas Cooper's characters in Chartist days, to which another replied, 'No, nor won't be, till after harvest'. Life moved in accordance with the cycle of the seasons, and thought and speech were slow.

But Leland notes some of the principal features. Approaching from the south, he must have passed between St Katharine's priory and the Malandry hospital, entered the suburb of Wigford by Bargate, which he mentions, and travelled along the high street—Ermine Street—across the gap in the limestone ridge. It was a long ribbon-built causeway, flanked and defended on the west by the river Witham, and on the east by the *old ea*, the Sincil Dyke. He comments that this lower part of the city was 'al marisch and won by policy, and inhabited for the commoditie of the water'. The road crossed the Witham (as it turned east) by the twelfth-century High Bridge, on which stood the chapel of St Thomas of Canterbury, and entered the walled city by the Stonebow. It is curious that he does not mention this gatehouse, then lately completed; it must have looked clean and new in its Tudor Gothic, with its figures of St Mary, patron saint of city and Minster, and the Angel Gabriel, facing south. Here, and on the hillside, was the medieval city proper, the lower Roman enclosure 'on the souther part of the hill'. Above it, on the hilltop, entered

[1] Ed. L. Toulmin Smith (1907), I, 29–32.

by the Bailgate, was the earlier and upper Roman enclosure, detached from the liberties of the city and annexed to the castle as an outer Bail under the manorial jurisdiction of the duchy of Lancaster. Partly within the Bail, and partly outside it to the east, was the Minster Close, an enclave governed and mostly owned by the dean and chapter. Newport Arch, the northern gate of the Bail, Leland notices, with Eastgate and Westgate, but he does not mention the Close. North of the Bail, straggling along the Ermine Street, was the medieval suburb of Newport. He thought it to be British, but he was not the last to make that mistake.

Some evidence of decay in the city is recorded by him, and other signs he cannot have failed to notice. Many houses were empty and falling for want of repair, a process watched with such anxiety that the common council had strictly forbidden private persons to pull down houses or export building material from the city, even though the houses were empty and there was no money to repair them. The rule had been laid down in 1515[1] that chief constables of the wards should suffer no houses to be taken down, but should give monition to the owner to cease; though if it were taken down for rebuilding or were in danger of falling, then on licence by the mayor and council the penalty was remitted. The tile, stone and timber of Mr Welby's house by the Waterside was inspected to see what might be sold within the city, and as a favour Sir Edward Burgh was allowed to buy 10 or 12 loads of stone and take it away. When Thomas Crygg took down a house in Northgate his plea that he acted on the orders of the clerk of the Works Chantry at the Minster did not save him from being committed to ward; when the dean and chapter took down some houses, the mayor and several aldermen were bidden commune with the dean and ask what answer he would make; but when Mr Monson took out tile without licence his plea of ignorance was accepted. Presently it was reported to the mayor and aldermen in secret council that the house of the abbots of Revesby had been taken down and the tile carried away during the mayoralty of Robert Alanson. Alanson replied that as soon as he had knowledge he made arrestment of the same, and commanded the carriers to leave the tile in the city until he could confer with the aldermen. When he had gone, the carriers went off with the tile. On a vote five were in favour of fining him, and five against. It was then resolved that if he should restore to the city a like quantity of tile he would be acquitted. Later the device of making the tiler or labourer taking tile off houses himself responsible was adopted. On report in 1540 that Edward Dawson had taken down a decayed cross-house and cut down one apple tree and one pear tree and built a turf house, it was decided that he should abide by the award of the mayor and

[1] Pursuant to statutes 6 Henry VIII, c. 5, & 7 Henry VIII, c. 1.

his brethren. As the century went on, the prohibition of the taking down of houses and sale of tile continued to be enforced, and in 1570 the common council rather tardily resolved to comply with their own rules and repair tenements and cottages belonging to the city.[1]

Though Leland ignored the housing question he took especial note of the parish churches. He found eleven in Wigford, of which he saw one in clean ruin. In the rest of the city were thirteen. He was shown a roll in which he counted thirty-eight churches, and 'common fame' carried the tale to fifty-two. He was also told some stories about suburbs. Some held that there were two to the east of the city, one towards the late cell of St Mary of York (known in modern times as 'Monks Abbey') which he called 'St Beges', wrongly thought to be the Icanhoe of Bede, and the other stretching towards Canwick village. The first of these was Butwerk, which had once had four parish churches; the other never existed, for the area east and south of Sincil Dyke flooded regularly. There was another suburb to the north-west, towards Burton, much of which, he was told, was destroyed by king Stephen, no doubt in the first battle of Lincoln. Another suburb had lain south of Bargate towards Bracebridge. Clearly the moral to which all his informants were pointing when they talked of vanished churches and suburbs and a blocked Fossdyke—to be mentioned later—was the decay of the city and the urgent need for financial relief. Leland was a royal commissioner and he might be able to bring a report of the city's plight to the proper quarter.

He may well have heard much more than he recorded about parish churches, for just before his visit their demolition had been proceeding apace;[2] and he might have been surprised to find that the process was directed by the common council, apparently without ecclesiastical challenge. The city's claim was based on the doctrine of escheat: if a church was disused it escheated to the king, whose title to escheats in the city had been granted by charter to the citizens, who were therefore entitled to 're-enter' on the king's behalf. The claim was asserted tentatively in the first instance. In January 1523 the council recorded that the precentor of the cathedral—the patron of the living—had felled the ash trees in the

---

[1] A rental of lands of Christopher Wymbisshe, 1537, refers to sundry properties in the city paying no rents: in St Martin, a house turned into a garden, two houses empty, a plot of land laid waste; in St Cuthbert, a plot of land laid waste; in St Margaret in Wigford, a garret chamber and a house laid waste; in St Swithin a house laid waste (Lancs. Record Office, D.D.To 1/11, per Mr C. L. Exley).

[2] The dean and chapter had set the example. In 1496 they had leased to one of the canons the site of All Saints within the Close (earlier called 'within the Bail'), and later gave him leave to take stone from the old church for the building of his house (L.A.O., D. & C., A/3/1, ff. 109 v., 176 v.).

churchyard of Holy Trinity at the Gresefoot, 'which is not now used as a sanctified place, whereby it is supposed that the king hath re-interest into the same'. It was agreed that seizure should be made thereof on the king's behalf to the use of the city, and that any action at law brought by the precentor should be defended. In the following May the mayor reported that whilst he was at the parliament he 'had communicated with my lord of Lincoln' [Bishop Longland] about the ashes the precentor had felled in divers churchyards in the city; and it was resolved that a reasonable answer should be given 'when that my lord chancellor cometh to Lincoln'.

This was Wolsey, on whom the city had reason to rely. Whether he came, and if so what happened, is not recorded; but ten years later the common council were dealing freely with the fabrics of disused churches. In January 1533 the 'stone and ramell' of All Hallows was sold to Mr Grantham, and in June St Augustine was ordered to be taken down 'as all other churches decayed shall be', and put in safe custody to the profit of the common chamber. The next year St Augustine was again ordered to be taken down, with Holy Trinity at the Gresefoot, and some of the stone was to be given to St Swithin, the proceeds of sale of the bells being divided between that church and the common chamber. The warden of the Grey Friars was promised some of the stone, and St Swithin was at last allowed to buy the walls of St Augustine on condition that no stone was sold out of the city, and no headstone put to any limekiln; though later the abbot of Bardney was allowed to buy stone.

The process went further in 1535. Holy Trinity at the Gresefoot, St Bartholomew, Holy Trinity at the Grey Friars and St Michael at Gowts were all condemned, except for their chancels. St Leonard was being demolished at the same time. Stone went towards the repair of St Peter at Gowts, the mending of roads and pavements, the chamber over Newland Gate and the wall against Brayford; Holy Trinity at the Grey Friars gate was allotted for dyking and setting the commons between the city and Burton. The timber roof of St Bartholomew was granted to the warden of the Grey Friars for the maintenance of his house. This extensive demolition of consecrated buildings on lay initiative may well have meant that the impending suppression of religious houses would not come as so great a shock as might have been expected.

In pleading for financial relief the common council declared that in the time of Henry VII, who had granted it, well understanding 'the great and unrecupable decay of the city', Lincoln was eight or nine parts clean fallen to ruin. At another time the city revenues were set out: every house a penny, called the land-toll penny, 'which draws not to the number of 300', amounting to 24*s.*; market tolls 20*s.*; tolls of the two fairs £16 and £17; amercements for affrays and blood and profits of the court were uncertain; the weavers fee farm £6; letting of enclosed common lands £13. 1*s.* 8*d.*; profits of the leets 40*s.* The tronage and pesage of wools in the days of the staple had been worth £100.

Broadly the picture presented by Leland and the common council was true: the city revenues insufficient to meet the overhead charges inherited from better times; the ranks of the citizens and potential civic officers depleted, with difficulty in filling the offices; gilds so dwindled that they could not control their trades; the pressure of a local magnate against which the support of clergy and gentry was sought as a counterweight; and all these troubles aggravated by the rise in prices. It was a city which could no longer sustain its medieval organization. Its old prosperity, founded on wool, had gone, and with it the great merchants and their wide connections with the sheep farmers of the east midlands, the merchants of Hull and Boston, and the cloth towns of France and Flanders. There were no longer doughty citizens who could quarrel with the lords of the castle and the Minster and hold offices in the county administration. Some of them, like the Dalderbys and the Blytons, had vanished altogether, leaving only their chantries behind; others had put their money into land and become gentry, like the Suttons at Burton and the Granthams at Goltho. They had left the fortunes of the city in the hands of tradesmen of little weight and experience, mercers and drapers and an occasional goldsmith, or tanners, butchers and braziers. Having lost its staple trade, Lincoln perforce lived on its markets and fairs. It was a sleepy little city, straggling along its great street, aroused into life on Mondays, Wednesdays and Fridays by the markets, occasionally filling up with sheep and cattle and their drovers at fairtime, and now and then assuming the air of a provincial capital with all the hum of activity that accompanied the judges of assize, the bishop at his visitation, a view of the trained bands or an election of knights of the shire.

It is no wonder, therefore, that the records are full of the most desperate expedients for raising money: loans voluntary and enforced; rents anticipated and reversionary leases granted; sales of exemption from office; payment of mayors and sheriffs by allowing them to give or sell the freedom of the city; sales of the fabric of disused churches; the felling of ashes and walnuts in the town ditches and on the common lands; the enclosing and letting of the common lands themselves. Some hint of the decline of population from the figure of perhaps 6000 at the Conquest is given by the yield of the land-toll penny. Allowing the conventional five persons to a house, 300 houses means 1500 persons, not including the Bail and Close.

With them the total might reach 2000. In the thirty years 1512–41 there were on an average nine apprentices enrolled every year, and eight freemen admitted. It may well be wondered whether the freemen were maintaining their numbers.

The council books bear eloquent witness to the lack of civic leaders. The mayor and his brethren leaned heavily on their recorder, a learned counsel of their own choice who gave much of the advice that would later be given by the town clerk; he was generally drawn from the local gentry, and served as one of the burgesses in parliament. Robert Sutton, a member of a notable merchant family, now an esquire and seated at Burton, was a freeman and served as an alderman and justice of the peace, though he seems to have escaped other civic office. Robert Alanson, a goldsmith, was also an alderman and justice. He was returned to parliament with the recorder in 1512; and they were returned again in 1515 when the king directed that the same burgesses should be elected so that they should be familiar with an act already passed.[1] Alanson had been sheriff in 1493, and was mayor in 1502, 1511 and 1524, and was relied upon in delicate negotiations with Lord Roos; and although by 1535 he was of great age and his wife, being crippled, could not oversee his housekeeping or even stir, and they were so poor that they had neither wheat nor malt, he was elected mayor again and given a tun of wine because he had many acquaintances whereby he was like to have much resort to his house to put him to cost. Aldermen attach importance to mayoral hospitality.

There are various hints that the patronage of Thomas Wolsey, Henry VIII's great minister, meant much to the city. He had been installed dean of Lincoln by proxy in 1509 and in person in 1511, and he was bishop in 1514 until he became archbishop of York in 1515; in this latter year he was made a cardinal, and it was no doubt in his honour that the inn in St Martin's parish belonging to the Welborne Chantry was named 'the Cardinal's Hat'.[2] He must have been instrumental in getting a new charter for the city in 1515, which was followed by the overhaul of gild charters. When Lincoln had to find ten soldiers for the royal forces in 1514 they were sent up to be in the retinue of 'my lord of Lincoln', who was content that they should have revytts or jackets and white fustian doublets, with yellow hose and horses to ride upon. Even when he became lord chancellor the common council looked to him for help about disused churches, and in 1531 they resolved to ask him to appropriate four benefices

[1] The minutes record the king's direction that the same burgesses should be elected; Mr M. G. Price kindly informs me that the royal letter survives at Wells and Shrewsbury.
[2] This handsome half-timbered house was restored in 1953, and is now the headquarters of the St John Ambulance Brigade.

to the Church of Lincoln in satisfaction of £80, part of the city fee farm due to the dean and chapter. His may have been the impetus that set on foot a modest attempt to tidy up the city about the time that he was bishop. High Bridge, Gowts bridge and Bargate bridge were repaired, roads were mended and the river cleaned out and frontagers called on to mend their banks. A great effort was made to complete the building of the Stonebow in 1520, when a contract was signed with William Spencer, freemason, and his fellows, to that end, and provision was made for the employment of carpenters, who were no doubt engaged in putting on the timber roof.

Especially can there be little doubt that Wolsey encouraged the attempt to reopen the Fossdyke, the canal which connected the Witham at Lincoln with the Trent at Torksey, and so gave access by water to the midlands, the Humber and much of Yorkshire.[1] It had been of vital importance to Lincoln in the Middle Ages, and its silting up had been one of the factors in the city's decay. The effort began with the appointment of a commission of sewers by the king in 1518, the cost of obtaining the commission being borne by the common chamber of the city. The mayor was a member, and so also was William Atwater, bishop of Lincoln, who probably owed his preferment to Wolsey and who became the moving spirit of the enterprise. The commission was 'for the district between the bridge of Torksey and the water of Brayford near Lincoln'.

The common council resolved to raise 100 marks in the city, every man to give of his goodwill, and those not present to be sent for. Officers were appointed to survey the Fossdyke and oversee the dykers. The bishop had other ways of raising money: he issued a letter of indulgence to all in his diocese. It referred to the decline of the city and to the Fossdyke project, and granted forty days' indulgence to all who would help.[2] He himself gave £100. Citizens were sent out to collect money—one of them lost his horse, and had to be given 40s. to buy another—and the aid of the archdeacons of Lincoln and Stow was invoked. There were men at work in May 1520, but some of the citizens had not yet paid half their assessments; the second half was called for, and the collections extended to York and elsewhere. By 27 June funds gave out, and attempts to borrow failed. The work had to cease.

A new effort was made in July, aided by Peter Effard, elected mayor when the mayor died in office. He hired workmen and raised a great sum of money. The following April, the Torksey men having promised help, it was suggested that their share should be to sewer the dyke between Fossbridge and Trent sluice; later the towns of Torksey and Fenton were asked

---

[1] *M.L.* ch. xv.
[2] *Registrum Antiquissimum*, ed. C. W. Foster (L.R.S. 1933), II, 135–7.

PLATE 1

MEMORIAL BRASS OF HENRY SAPCOTE AND JANE HIS WIFE
formerly in Lincoln Cathedral

By permission of the Winchelsea Settled Trustees

to make the Fossbridge itself. That winter a programme was prepared for the following summer, including a call on the 'four towns' in the county of the city to pay voluntarily if they were willing, compulsorily if they were not. But Atwater died in February 1521, and without him there was nobody—not even the vigorous Effard—to provide the leadership needed. The effort was abandoned.

There was much else that Effard could do. He was a native of Guernsey, and a notary public. He was evidently in legal practice in Lincoln, where there was a considerable volume of ecclesiastical business to be done. He became chapter clerk in 1522, and he married the daughter of Richard Laverock, constable of the Close. At Michaelmas 1518 he became an alderman, and by December was busy collecting for the Fossdyke. He was elected mayor over the heads of his seniors on a casual vacancy in 1520, and re-elected in Michaelmas in that year. He put through a great deal of business, taking twice as much space in the minutes as other mayors, and he evidently pulled together an easy-going administration. The Stonebow building was completed; he redrafted the Mayor's Cry; he made searching inquiry into the leases of common land; he summoned the parish constables to return the names of all who sold and tippled ale in their parishes; he had the weights and measures tested. His energy aroused much opposition. An alderman was convicted of seditious opposition to his worship, and a victualler sent to gaol for a scandalous suggestion that any of his kind could buy immunity from interference by a gift of fish to the mayor, otherwise he 'monnbe pollyd and tollyd'. It was no doubt at Effard's bidding that an act of common council preventing the mayor from commanding any of his brethren to ward without the consent of six of them was rescinded. It must have cramped his style. He was mayor again in 1531 and 1540 and died in 1541.[1]

Much the most serious problem which confronted the city was the fee-farm rent. This annual payment to the Exchequer in exchange for which the city farmed the royal revenues receivable in Lincoln, had been fixed at £180 in the twelfth century. For this huge payment first the bailiffs and

---

[1] Effard lived in Deancourte Hall, which had been the property of Lord Hussey and on his attainder was (inter alia) granted to Lord Clinton for services against the Scots (*C.P.R. 1547–48*, p. 218). The house was probably in Northgate. His widow Joan lived in a house belonging to the Fitzmartin chantry (*C.P.R. 1548–49*, p. 332). Effard's tombstone with its notary's mark is still to be seen in St Peter in Eastgate church. See *Chapter Acts 1520–36*, ed. R. E. G. Cole (L.R.S. 1915), p. xiii, and *Chapter Acts 1536–47*, ed. R. E. G. Cole (L.R.S. 1917), p. 44; and K. Major, 'Office of chapter clerk at Lincoln in the Middle Ages', in *Medieval Studies presented to Rose Graham* (1950), p. 188. For his will see A. R. Maddison, *Lincolnshire Wills 1500–1600* (1888), no. 61. Part of his probate inventory survives, recording altar furniture, images and candlesticks (L.A.O. Inv. 17/112).

then (under the charter of Henry IV) their successors the sheriffs were personally liable, and it was of such importance to the city that they should not default in their payments and so imperil the city's liberties, that they had to find sureties for the due performance of their duties. Already in the Hundred Rolls in the thirteenth century there are complaints, perhaps exaggerated, that those who had been bailiffs of Lincoln never rose from poverty and misery.[1] The burden upon the two bailiffs in office every year became so heavy that in 1378 three were appointed; and in 1401 the three asked that by reason of the burden they might have a fourth colleague assigned to them, to which the commonalty assented. The charter of Henry IV in 1409 created the city a county of itself, and the bailiffs were succeeded by sheriffs, two in number. The existence of a shire court for the city and other provisions of the charter may have brought some financial relief; and in 1466 the addition to the county of the city by Edward IV of the 'four towns' of Branston, Waddington, Bracebridge and Canwick enlarged the area from which revenue could be gathered. Even so, the resources of the sheriffs had become so inadequate that by the sixteenth century it had become the custom to indemnify the sheriffs against claims for the fee-farm rent, and the burden was borne by the common council.

Meanwhile the Crown had alienated the fee-farm rent. The sum of £100 per year had become payable to Lord Roos, and £80 to the dean and chapter for the Burghersh Chantry. The ninth Lord Roos was a Lancastrian, and after the Yorkist victory at Towton in 1461 he was attainted; and Edward IV released to the city the fee-farm payment to which Roos had been entitled. After the accession of Henry VII in 1485 Roos's son Edmund obtained the reversal of his father's attainder, and so recovered the fee-farm rent. This heavy blow was followed by some remission, for in 1492 parliament adjudged Edmund Lord Roos incapable of managing his own affairs, and vested his governance in Sir Thomas Lovell, who had married one of his sisters. Lovell seems thus to have acquired a life interest in the fee-farm rent, and he accepted an annual payment of 20 marks in lieu of the full payment of £100.

In 1520 the common council, foreseeing and dreading a return to the full burden on their benefactor's death, instructed the recorder to seek Lovell's aid and influence in dealing with the then Lord Roos. Lovell died in 1524. The mayor and aldermen, full of apprehension, consulted the recorder on how best to approach their new creditor; and knowing that there were difficult times ahead decided that they needed a discreet man as next mayor, and that they must take special care in drawing up the

[1] *Rotuli Hundredorum*, I, 317 a.

calendar for election. It was decided also to send representatives to 'make labour' to Roos, and to insist that those chosen should go willy nilly. Mr Burton, a draper, was sent to join the recorder, and the council gave them power to settle at any figure between 20 marks and £100. But the authority was revoked that same day, and Burton was told not to go beyond the 20 marks paid to Lovell, and to find out how the citizens of York in a like plight had fared.[1] After much coming and going the recorder reported that he had spoken with Roos, and 'hath good answer of him in the same', and that the mayor and his brethren might forbear coming to London until the summer. The matter dragged on throughout 1525 (in which year Roos was created Earl of Rutland), and the mayor paid 18 months' arrears on the basis of 20 marks a year and was given a receipt on account. In the following spring it was resolved to send two of the most discreet men to pursue the matter next term: Mr Alanson and Mr Burton were chosen. Meanwhile Rutland was sent 200 tons of stone to repair his river banks at Boston.[2]

There was delay because Rutland was not in London; and the common council bravely resolved that if his counsel came for any money they should have nothing unless they gave a full acquittance; no more receipts on account. This was in November 1526. The following April the visitors were expected, and twenty-eight of the common council determined that nothing should be paid until terms were reached. It was a recorded vote: those who so voted were 'pricked on their heads', a mark being placed over their names in the minutes. Only two aldermen were in the majority, which included all the sheriffs' and chamberlains' peers. But the aldermen, who were 'the sadder and more discreet men', resolved in secret council to have 'favourable communing' with Roos's counsel, and to point out that £10 worth of stone had been delivered, and the balance of the 20 marks was ready.

In these difficulties the council looked round again for a leader, and found one in Vincent Grantham, like Sutton of merchant stock but now an esquire. He was sworn to the liberties of the city and later elected an alderman and mayor, having the votes of fifty of the common congregation and ten of the aldermen. As he was not present two aldermen were sent to ask him to nominate one of the sheriffs according to custom. He made his own terms, nominating one sheriff, John Alaley, and asking that the council elect Harry Sapcote, a notary public, to be the other. Sapcote,

---

[1] According to A. L. Rowse, *The England of Elizabeth* (1950), p. 162, Rutland consented to forgo more than half his annual rent from York, and it was excused part of its remaining annuities to the Crown.

[2] The price quoted for carriage was 9*d.* a ton.

perhaps the first citizen of whose personal appearance there is any evidence,[1] was elected by a large majority. Grantham was voted a tun of Gascony wine to spend in his house for strangers, and 'he to call my Lord Ros' counsel to him when they come to the city, and he to have communication with them for the city matters within his house and in no other place'. The mayor and sheriffs were as usual allowed to admit a number of men as freemen—probably taking the fines themselves—and Harry Sapcote was promised that he should not be elected mayor for ten years save by his own free will. Whether counsel came does not appear, but in April 1528 the mayor and Sapcote were going to join the recorder in London; in June the mayor was going up again with power to settle. By the autumn Rutland's receiver was at Wragby, and two aldermen were sent to reason with him.

Matters dragged on until in 1530 Richard Clerk, the recorder, died. Rutland then gave a new and sinister turn to the negotiations by writing to the mayor and his brethren asking to be given the nomination of his successor. Perhaps Rutland was thinking more about the parliamentary seat that usually went with the office than he was about putting a nominee into the secret counsels of the city, though doubtless it was this latter aspect which most alarmed the city. The sorely tried common council first decided that the mayor and his brethren should devise an answer, and then resolved to postpone replying. On 11 July 1532 Thomas Moigne was elected, there being no other candidate. He was a member of a family seated at North Willingham in the Lincolnshire Wolds, and there is no hint that he was nominated by Rutland.

In 1534 Anthony Mussenden, a member of a Healing family, one of Rutland's counsel, sent word to say that he was coming to collect the fee-farm rent, to which reply was made that the mayor and his brethren would go to see his lordship themselves; they invoked the aid of Sir William Ayscough, who was asked to join them on the way; and they sent John Dyon the town clerk to London to consult counsel. The next year Moigne was asked to take proceedings in the Exchequer Court, and Dyon was sent up again. In May 1535 the parties agreed to go to arbitration.

[1] His memorial brass in Lincoln Minster perished in the Civil War, but there is a drawing of it in the Winchelsea Book of Monuments, here reproduced at p. 24. He came from a family settled at Elton, Hunts., and was practising as a notary in Lincoln by 1513; he was granted the reversion of the office of chapter clerk in 1530, and was admitted to the office in 1541 on Effard's death. He became also registrar of the diocese. He was mayor in 1535 and 1544, and died in 1553. He bought a house in St Stephen in Newland in 1520, and the manor of Bracebridge in 1546 for £300 (Lincoln Corporation Muniments, White Book, ff. 81 d, 101 d). See Major, op. cit. p. 188; *Chapter Acts 1536–47*, ed. Cole, xv, 126n. His son Edward Sapcote was also a notary, and registrar of the diocese. He presented the mayor's ring to the city.

Affairs were still dragging on when attention was distracted by the disastrous Lincolnshire Rising, which wrought havoc on the city side. Moigne was hanged, Dyon vanished, and Lincoln lay under a cloud. Mussenden, Rutland's agent, was submissively elected recorder. The question of the fee-farm rent was to haunt the city for a long time yet.

The civic community, some of whose problems and expedients have been described, was based on a distinction between those who were citizens, 'free' of the city, and denizens who were not free, aliens in the midst. Only freemen could hold civic office, follow any craft or trade in goods made by the crafts, and they had greater rights of pasture than unfree denizens. The freemen alone enjoyed the city's privileges, acquired by charter and custom, which they were not prepared to share with any who had not qualified in one of the ways prescribed.

No man could be admitted to the liberties who was not of full age and a true English subject; and when the horrid rumour spread about that William Robson, actually an alderman, was a Scot and no true Englishman born, he was put to the proof. One of the sheriffs was sent with him at his own expense to his country where he was born to bring back evidence of his town and parish. The weaver John Alanson, no doubt of suspiciously northern speech, produced a certificate from Newcastle on Tyne that he was an Englishman born. Nicholas Brught, a hatter, was examined by the secret council, and declared that he was born at Arras in 'Burgon land', and that several London hatters would vouch for him. He was therefore an alien, but not one of the king's enemies.

There were four ways in which an eligible man might become a freeman. If his father was a freeman at the time of his birth then he could claim by patrimony. Apprenticeship for seven years to a freeman in a craft gave title to the freedom on completion of time and coming of age. The common council could and frequently did sell the freedom; the price in this period was generally 20s. paid over 10 years. The freedom might also be given if it was to the city's interest to give it; a plumber might be induced to come to Lincoln to look after the conduit pipes which brought the water supply, or a fuller made free so long as he lived in Lincoln and employed workmen, though perhaps without the right to take apprentices.

The craftsmen were organised in gilds, and apart from the weavers and cordwainers who claimed royal grants, the other gilds were under the full control of the council. It was from the city that their powers derived, and their charters could be revoked or varied at will. Perhaps because of difficulties of enforcement of gild rules the council resolved to seek letters patent in confirmation of the city's liberties, and it appears from the proceedings of 1515 that the new royal grant was thought to involve the grant of new craft charters. The graceman (or master) of every occupation was called before the mayor and asked what his occupation would give towards the cost of the new grant. After it had been received, the occupations were ordered to submit drafts of the articles they wished to include in their new charters. Then when the mayor had seen all the drafts, divers occupations were 'annexed' together under the city's common seal. The reason for compulsory amalgamation was stated to be that each combined fraternity might be able to maintain itself to the pleasure of God and the ancient laudable custom of the city. Some of the crafts were no longer numerous enough to support the organization and expense of a gild alone.

The first gilds to get their new charters were the smiths, the tilers and the tailors, each paying a fee of 1 mark, followed by the shoemakers. The other gilds delayed, but charters for the mercers, bakers, and tanners were passed in 1522, and the painters' and stainers' draft was approved in 1526, The draft for the carpenters was sent to a committee with power to seal it. The mercers' charter was examined with a view to amendment in the light of experience.

The food trades were of especial importance to the whole community, and they were watched the more closely at times when prices were rising. Every year the mayor fixed the assize of bread and ale for the protection of the citizens. Between 1513 and 1518 the assize given to bakers varied between 5s. and 8s. 6d. a quarter of wheat; in June of 1520 it was 12s. 6d.; by Michaelmas it was 15s. 6d. On 10 February 1521 the secret council wrote to an unnamed member of the privy council that certain men of Lindsey had complained in open market that their corn which they would have brought to the king's market at Lincoln was stopped, as they said, by the sheriff of the county and his officers; and asking by what authority this was done, and whether the city was in any way to blame. There was great scarceness of corn that year, and a quarter of wheat was above the sum of 24s. a quarter, and malt above 12s.[1] After harvest the price of wheat fell to 7s. 6d., and in 1522 to 5s.

The bakers' gild was being overhauled at that time. Bakers' marks were allotted in 1522, and their new charter sealed in 1523. The next year it was called in and examined, and the late graceman of the gild acknowledged that the city had been misused in the serving of bread among the commons of the city, and on behalf of his fellowship he submitted to correction.

Corn was dear again in 1527 and 1528, and no assize was recorded until 1530. In 1527 Thomas Clerk of Newark was accused of buying up corn in the country and creating scarcity, and it was ordered that any corn brought

[1] 'Three Lists' in *A.A.S.R.* xxxix (1929), 242.

PLATE 2

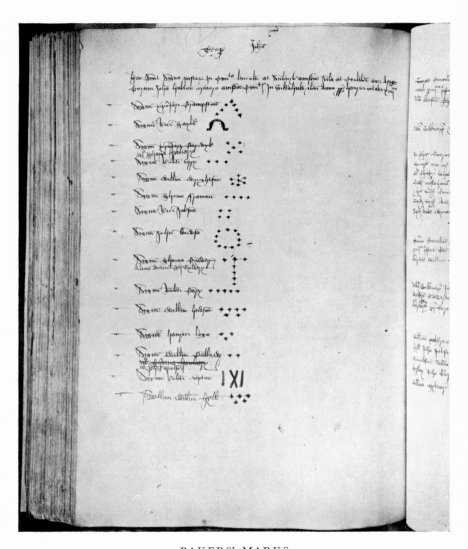

BAKERS' MARKS

From the Common Council Minutes

through the city by him and others should be detained for sale in the market; and for restraint upon badgers buying corn in the market a toll of ½d. per horse load was laid upon corn so bought.

After the harvest of 1531 the assize—previous year 6s.—was fixed at 13s. 6d., by February at 12s. and March 11s. 6d. These changes show how serious the increases were. It is notable that prices in Lincoln were sometimes higher and sometimes lower than prices in London and elsewhere. Transport was costly and slow, and markets were mostly local and dependent on the crops in their own area.

This excursus on prices illustrates the importance of control of the food trades, and especially of the bakers. As their charter was enrolled, it may serve as a specimen. The gild was founded in honour of St Clement. It was given a graceman and two wardens, who must enforce the assize of bread given by the mayor, both in men's bread and horse bread. The fellowship must at the mayor's command, without obstinacy or fraud, serve the inhabitants of the city with wheat bread, both of the more coket and the less coket (that is, hard or soft baked), and other bread, under penalty of forfeiture of the charter and a fine of 100s. to the common chamber. None might practise the trade of a baker unless he were a freeman and had agreed with the gild for a payment towards its sustentation. An apprentice or journeyman could not trade on his own account until he had become free and paid a setting-up fee, and a journeyman must serve the art of bakecraft for three years before he might set up. No innholder or hosteler might bake horse bread, and no woman baker or petty baker of white bread, cakes or brown bread might bake to sell without admission by the mayor, agreement with the gild, and a sign or seal given to her or him and registered at the gildhall. The members of the gild might within reason bake white bread in the lenten season without correction, provided that they served the inhabitants with wastells, crakenells, symnells and coket bread of good, sweet and well-seasoned paste according to the pureness of each of the said breads.[1]

The gilds were continuously supervised. When a poor tailor set up who could not afford the setting-up fee, the graceman was bidden to give him time to pay. Searchers were appointed to report the defaults of butchers, fishers, cordwainers and tanners to the mayor and justices. For every craft gild auditors were appointed by the mayor, and it was no doubt in view of complaints that it was resolved that chartered fellowships should not elect to office any but freemen of good conversation.

Most of the gilds (or companies, as they came to be called) died out in

[1] A wastell was a cake of the finest flour; a cracknel was a light crisp biscuit; a simnel was a rich currant cake.

the seventeenth century. Only the weavers and the cordwainers remained when Thomas Sympson wrote in 1738;[1] and the fortunate survival of the cordwainers until 1786 ensured the preservation of their gild book.[2] It gives a picture of gild life from within. On the edge of the gild, so to speak, are the outbrothers and sisters who, though members, do not follow the craft. They are classified as priests, aldermen, sheriffs (that is, those who have borne that office) and others. The outbrother promises to be a true brother of the gild founded for the honour of God's most blessed mother St Mary, St Blaise and all the saints. He will pay his brotherhood yearly, and soulscot on the death of a brother or sister, except for reason of poverty; and save for good cause will go yearly in procession with the graceman brethren and sisters from the chapel of St Thomas on the High Bridge to the Minster, and there offer a farthing according to custom. He is concerned only with the religious side of gild life and will therefore disappear at the Reformation.

The craftsman brother also promises brotherhood and soulscot, and further to obey the graceman and fraternity, and observe the charter; he does not promise to go in procession.

The graceman is the chief officer. He must provide for the obits of deceased brethren and sisters and attend them himself. He must personally supervise the preparation of the pageant of Bethlehem for St Anne's day, and (not so interesting) help to undress it afterwards. He must account yearly for gild moneys. The two wardens must obey him, collect soulscot, and help with the pageant. The dean must obey and help the graceman, and in particular give warning to the brethren, being masters, of the four mornspeech days in the year, and other days fixed by the graceman.

There are glimpses of the relations between masters and journeymen, who seem generally to have been of about equal numbers, some masters having no journeymen, some having one or two or three, and one having five. In 1527, in the presence of the graceman and ten masters, rules were laid down for the control of journeymen. Evidently the latter had a gild of their own, for they were forbidden to have a journeyman as graceman. One of them coming to the city and working with a master must at a fortnight's end pay (or his master for him) a penny to the gild light, swear on the charter to be a true brother, and pay 12d. a year. No master might work with another master's journeyman. Man must not be enticed from master, and if being froward he leaves a master willing to keep him, no other master may set him on work; he is blacklisted. William Brewster,

---

[1] 'Adversaria' (Bodleian Library, MS. Gough, Linc. 1), p. 290.
[2] It came into the Lincoln Stock Library, and thence to the Lincoln Public Library, where it is MS. 5009.

NORFOLK

CAMBS

Kings Lynn

Tydd

Wisbech

Thorney

Peterborough

Whittlesey

Stilton

Market Deeping

Crowland

Massey

Lolham

Spalding

Gedney

Moulton

Finchbeck

Surfleet

Sutterton

Boston

Swaton

Heding

Heckington

S.Kyme

Langrick

Sibsey

Asfby cum Fenby

Grantiby

Somercoates

Granthorpe

Wainfleet

Revesby

Louth

Tattershall

Thimbleby

Wraghby

Horncastle

Winceby

Bolingbroke

Spilsby

Burgh le marsh

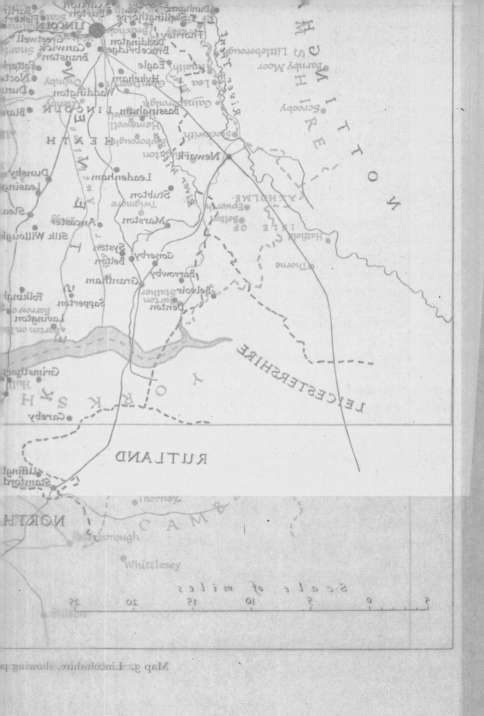

Map 3. Lincolnshire, showing p

a journeyman, caused his master to be falsely indicted; for such an offence all masters were forbidden to employ him, and he was expelled from the city for ever. A master later found employing him in defiance of the gild was fined two pounds of wax. Later it was ordered that no master should give work to any journeyman to do at home unless he dwelt far from his master, and if then he took it overnight he should bring it in the morning. A journeyman sick or in prison might have work taken to him. Maximum prices for payment of journeymen were fixed. They were piecework prices; a fact which suggests that the rule to be laid down by the Statute of Artificers in 1563 of a yearly wage would have a prejudicial effect on the earnings of the industrious worker.

Apprentices were directly controlled by the common council. In 1515 it was declared that the old ordinances for the profit of the common chamber were abused, and that if any master took an apprentice and failed to enrol him within a year, he was free to go to any other master by the advice and order of the mayor and his council. It seems that the rule was indifferently observed, for it was resolved in 1526 that any master who had not enrolled his apprentice within the year should have licence to enrol him by grace; though this concession to realism appears only as an addendum to a rule that apprentices must be enrolled within fourteen days, else they shall be free and the masters fined. The city had a double interest in the matter: the right to the freedom of the city by servitude and main-tenance of the body of freemen, and the enrolment fee.

The gild of St Anne has been mentioned. It was so closely united with and controlled by the common council that it was really the whole body of citizens organised for the purpose of religious pageantry. By custom the outgoing mayor became graceman of the gild, and it was added in 1523 that those who had been his sheriffs should be his gild wardens, and oversee the collection of money. If the ex-mayor died the common council chose the graceman, but they might hold the executors of the ex-mayor liable for the annual pageant; thus its production became one of the burdens of mayoralty, to be relieved as far as possible by public collection. When Mr Fox, late mayor, died in 1520, having received the usual aid during his mayoralty, his executors were bidden bring forth the gild;[1] and when Mr Taylbois died in office his widow was warned to bring forth the gild next year.

St Anne's priest was chosen by the council. In 1517 Robert Denyas was appointed for life while of good and lawful bearing at an annual salary

---

[1] In his will, 1 February 1520, he left 20s. to the Fossdyke 'if it goo forthe in castyng', and 20s. to the common hall for the reparation and building thereof (L.A.O., D. & C. A/3/3).

of £5. His duty was to sing for the brethren and sisters and all the benefactors of the gild, and to help to bring forth the gild procession and pageants. His services could be procured on payment to the gild. Mr Chambers promised to give his land and jewels to have the priest sing at St Mark's, and Mr Dighton made a grant on condition that he sang at St Michael on the Hill.

Every man and woman who could was required to be of the gild, and pay the customary brotherhood of 4d. at least for man and wife. Two collectors for each parish were appointed by the mayor and graceman, and when the result was inadequate the bishop's authority to collect outside the city was sought. Sometimes the device of farming the gild was tried; the highest bidder rented it, and made a profit if he could, though he was not allowed to receive windfalls like bequests.

The chief function of the gild was to produce a procession on St Anne's day. There might also be a play, as in 1521, when it was the Paternoster play. Every gild had to bring forth its pageant, part of the procession, according to custom. Each alderman provided a gown of silk for the kings and a man in a rochet with a torch to wait on the sacrament. Each sheriff's peer found a man in an honest cloth gown to walk among the prophets. Every constable waited on the pageants, and every man in his degree attended on the mayor.

All the city's resources were mobilised. The parish churches lent 'stuff' for furnishing the pageants, and it was matter for indignation when the parishioners of St John in Wigford refused to lend any of their 'honorments'. The gentry also lent gowns, though they showed some reluctance to do so in time of plague. When in 1515 the knights and gentlemen in the country declined for this reason, increased calls were made on the leading citizens. Plague reigned again in 1521, when an effort was made to borrow a gown from Lady Powes for one of the Maries, and the other was to be arrayed in the gild's own velvet gown, the prior of St Katharine being asked to make his usual loans. The gilds had each a special task: the tilers had to find men to wear the gowns for the kings, and the cordwainers contributed the pageant of Bethlehem.

There were other processional gilds. The Corpus Christi gild was brought forth by the contributions of everyone, and the mayor and his brethren supervised the bringing forth of St George's gild. Ascension day had its procession, when freemen were required to wait on the mayor, failure to do so being regarded as a breach of their oath.

The Great Gild of St Mary had fallen on evil days. It had been the gild of the leading merchants, and it occupied the gildhall which still stands near St Peter at Gowts church. It could no longer meet its expenses, and an attempt was made to restore it:

Where the great gild of this city called Our Lady Gild is fallen in decay and almost desolate for lack of good order, and for reformation of the same there is a paper drawn by Mr Taylbois, one of the aldermen of this city, for keeping and reforming the said gild here in this present brought forth and shewed hereunto annexed, the said act shall by assent of all present stand in effect and established and be of authority from this day forward.

The promised paper is not forthcoming, and henceforth the gild is known only in its end.

The pomp and circumstance of the processions and pageants helped to gild the burdens of civic office. The mayor was attended by swordbearer and macebearer, and the sheriffs by two axebearers. There was the great or best sword, no doubt the one associated with Richard II, and the second sword must have been in possession for some years before 1540, by which time it needed a new scabbard. In 1533 it was decided to buy a hat for the swordbearer, and the next year Vincent Grantham brought down from London the hat of maintenance; clearly it was from the first as it still is, associated with the sword. In addition there were the waits, with their liveries and chains of office, who went out nightly singing in winter.

On formal occasions those aldermen who had not passed the chair, and their wives, wore gowns of crimson; those who had been mayors added velvet tippets and their wives velvet heads. Great importance was attached to these marks of dignity, not least among the ladies. Aldermen and sheriffs' peers were entitled to have the Christmas girth (or feast) and the fairs proclaimed outside their houses by the waits. The compliment seems to have been continued to an alderman's or an ex-sheriff's widow, as was an invitation to the mayor's feast, but when it was proposed to extend it to the aldress's or sheriff's lady's second husband it was time to draw the line.

The lower ranges of the civic ladder had to be climbed before these dizzy heights were reached. The first step was that of chamberlain. Four were appointed yearly, one for each ward. Their chief duty was to collect the city revenues. They must of course be freemen, and they were probably appointed then, as later, by the mayor. When they went out of office they retained the rank of chamberlains' peers, and at one time they were exempted from jury service in civil causes unless the claim was large.

Only chamberlains' peers were eligible for the common council. The powers of this body were small, and seem to have been confined to giving assent to measures handed out to them from the Inner Chamber by the mayor and aldermen, and voting for election to the various offices. The number of the council was variable. In 1511 it was ordered that for all acts to be made by the common council twenty-four persons should be

chosen by common assent with the twelve aldermen to have full authority
to make ordinances for the common weal of the city; in 1514 'twenty two
and no more' were sworn, and in 1520 the number fell to sixteen.

Also from among the chamberlains' peers were chosen the two sheriffs,
one nominated by the mayor and the other elected by the council. It was
their duty to impanel juries and execute royal writs and other processes,
and to preside in the county court. Their chief burden, responsibility for
the fee-farm rent, has already been described. A past holder of the office,
having become a sheriff's peer, was eligible for election as an alderman.
The aldermen had long been twelve in number, though in 1550 it was
noticed that there were sixteen, and it was ruled that no more should be
elected until the number had fallen. They were the mayor's brethren,
deliberating with him in secret council in the Inner Chamber, and were
the real holders of civic power. They were elected for life by the common
council. The depressed state into which the city had fallen made it difficult
to maintain an active bench of aldermen, and perhaps in consequence
mayors had been disposed to act without them. To check such a danger
it was resolved in 1512 that the twelve aldermen should yearly thenceforth
assist Mr Mayor in everything he had to do for the well-being of the city.
The next year two new aldermen took the oath; three years later the number
was down again, and three more were bidden to be sworn. As they held
office for life there were generally some who were diseased or decrepit, and
who could not attend the mayor in procession and at other times according
to old honourable custom. Occasionally a bedridden or crippled alderman
was discharged and if in need was given a dole. Four of their number were
annually elected justices of the peace by the common council.

Only aldermen were eligible for the mayoralty. The secret council of
mayor and aldermen prepared a calendar of four names from which the
common council chose two, and of them the secret council chose one. It
was not always easy to fill the office, and the efforts that were made to
induce men of standing and education to come in from outside shows how
conscious the council were of their own incapacity to cope with the many
and difficult problems that beset them. It frequently happened that when
the mayor went out of office he had in his hand moneys belonging to the
common chamber, or at least owed money, and there was great difficulty
in getting it in. In 1544 several ex-mayors and the executors of another
were threatened with imprisonment for non-payment. To avoid this
trouble a chest with three locks was bought. It was to be kept in the
mayor's house, and the mayor, one alderman and one sheriff's peer were
each to have a key.

Although some of the functions of the mayor and citizens come within the modern concept of local government the concept itself was unknown to them. They thought of their functions in terms of property and privilege, mostly having a monetary value to the community or the individual citizen, and either positive or negative in the sense of being exempt from someone else's right to receive payment. The most valuable assets were the two fairs, but to the citizens the markets mattered most. Rules for their control were contained in an ancient proclamation known as the Mayor's Cry, in which 'Mr Mayor and his brethren do in His Majesty's name strictly charge and command all manner of persons who are in any wise concerned in the laws and ordinances now to be proclaimed, that they truly observe and perform the same' upon specified penalties. It controlled the times and places of the markets, and was specially concerned with the victualling and allied trades—fishermen, alehouse keepers, butchers, poultry women, corn, hide and skin dealers, tallowchandlers, bakers, horse and pig dealers. It also made rules against the fouling of the streets. Most of the rules went on from year to year, though controlled prices varied according to supply and demand.[1]

The right to collect tolls on produce brought into the city was important, but still more important to citizens trading elsewhere was exemption by charter from tolls in other towns. There were constant disputes about liability to pay. In 1550 a 'writing testimonial' was sealed for certain persons who took it with them when they traded elsewhere. The charter of Edward IV was ordered to be produced at Stourbridge fair, Doncaster, Newark, Cambridge and other places, and a dispute with Nottingham went on for a long time.

It was a cherished privilege, not to be measured in terms of money, that citizens might not sue outside the city in any action pleadable within it, and no freeman must ever sue another outside the city court. When Martin Hollingworth, an alderman, sued John Wylson, a mercer, in the court of Common Pleas at Westminster for debt and trespass he was disfranchised by a secret council. The record is signed by the mayor, recorder, and the other aldermen, and their act was confirmed in open council.

The gaols were in the custody of the sheriffs, who were fined if prisoners escaped. The pillory also was their affair. Robert Bishop, having been taken for petty larceny and abjured the city, returned; whereupon the sheriffs were commanded to set him in the pillory and nail his ear to it. One of the sheriffs brought him to the pillory, but confessed that he did not do execution upon the offender as the mayor, Master Peter Effard, had commanded, for which undue squeamishness he submitted to such fine as the mayor and his brethren imposed.

[1] See App. I.

The grammar school had long existed. It was situate near to St Rumbold's church in Skolegate, which can leave little doubt that the Skolegate of the period is the present Rumbold Street. In 1518 the mayor was collecting for purchase of a schoolhouse for the master, evidently because the old house was ruinous; the north end of it was taken down and the tile and timber laid up in safety. Towards the new house the chancellor of the cathedral gave the tile and Mr Dighton the schoolmaster the lime. Dighton then took the adjoining house on a lease on condition of repairing it, and he agreed to set an able learned man to keep the school, to be assigned and admitted by the chancellor. He was soon in disgrace and ordered to appear in court to answer to such action as should be laid against him, and the lease did not take effect.

There were some duties that the mayor and his brethren had to carry out at the royal command, especially those of defence. When musters of the militia were ordered the parish constables had to bring in the names of all able persons in their parishes; the parishes were assessed to pay for the harness; and the musters were taken by the mayor and his fellow commissioners in St Hugh Croft. Armour was sent for from London, and butts were set up for archery practice: perhaps the Shooting leys were so named for that reason.

The problem of the poor existed at the time when the surviving minutes of the council begin, and there is nothing to suggest that it was a new one. In 1517 the council, in pursuance of the king's command that the statute against vagabonds be put in execution, directed every chief constable within his ward to command the under constables of every parish to search and certify before the mayor and his brethren the names of idle men and women who would not work. The next year all such idle folk were ordered to be haled before the mayor in St Hugh Croft, to be made to work or leave the city. On reports of robbery by vagabonds a watch was set in the parishes. A man from Burgh le Marsh taken among vagabonds and valiant beggars was put in the stocks and then let go; a London butcher claimed that he had come to see his grandam, and there being no trespass proved against him he was discharged and commanded to the stocks; a London haberdasher who said he came to keep an alebooth, a London shearman said to be seeking work, and a Southwark haberdasher, come to the fair to sell pins and laces, were all clapped in the stocks as vagabonds. Another man without a dwelling said he was a saffron-seller who had wares to sell when he came to the city, but in nine weeks was spent up; his fate is not recorded.

In 1531 a statute enacted that impotent beggars should have licences issued by justices of the peace allowing them to beg within prescribed areas.

Vagabonds without licences, and all persons fit for work found begging, were to be whipped or set in the stocks and sent to their usual places of residence; the impotent were to be relieved and the able-bodied set to work.[1] Twice under this statute the common council ordered a search for vagabonds, and later the parish constables were bidden to bring the poor of their parishes before the justices and aldermen, have their names recorded, and those authorised to beg had an 'ensign' provided for them. They might collect their alms weekly, but alms were not to be given to others. Here was the beginning of a national poor law seen in operation.

[1] 22 Henry VIII, c. 12.

CHAPTER III

RELIGIOUS AND SOCIAL CHANGE

By 1533 Henry VIII had quarrelled with the pope, obtained his divorce from his Queen Katharine of Aragon, and married Anne Boleyn. The succession to the throne was limited by parliament to the children of Henry and Anne, and in July 1534 a royal commission was directed to the mayor, recorder and several aldermen ordering them to take the oaths of all persons spiritual and temporal within the city and suburbs to maintain the succession and not to bear obedience to any foreign authority. The significance of the order was no doubt explained to the citizens by their representatives in parliament, Vincent Grantham and alderman Sammes. The return made to the commission two months later declared that the mayor took the oath of the recorder, the recorder that of the mayor, and the commissioners the oaths of all residents.[1]

The feeling aroused by the king's measures was great. Lord Hussey of Sleaford, who acted as the king's lieutenant in Lincolnshire, told Chapuys, the imperial ambassador, that almost everyone would welcome the emperor's intervention, and that he 'ought first of all to make the said war, which might at once remedy everything, by the insurrection of the people, who would be joined immediately by the nobility and the clergy also, which is powerful and half in disorder'.[2] The king took precautions. A commission of array was issued on 6 October 1534 and received in Lincoln on 8 December. The constables of every ward in the city and of the 'towns' in the county of the city, and also the constable of the Close and the bailiff of the Bail were ordered to certify to the mayor and sheriffs the names of all persons over 16 years of age at St Hugh's Close, and to view the harness within their wards, and to report how much harness was in every man's house; and all men over 16 were to parade with their harness at the time and place appointed.

In November there was passed the Act of Supremacy declaring the king to be the Supreme Head of the Church of England, and on 24 March 1535 the royal proclamation to that effect was made by the mayor in the Bail, at the Stonebow, and in the marketplace at the church of St Mary le Wigford. There followed a number of anti-papal statutes which brought home to ordinary people the significance of the breach with Rome. The

---

[1] The mayor took the oaths of inhabitants of the Bail, which brought on him the wrath of Lord Burgh, who was steward of the duchy of Lancaster, to whom the Bail belonged.
[2] *L. & P. Henry VIII*, vii, no. 1206.

name of the bishop of Rome was ordered to be erased from all service and mass books, and all papal bulls and faculties were declared void. In March 1536 there followed an act for the suppression of monasteries with an income of less than £200 per year, and in June the king published his Ten Articles defining religious belief. It was perhaps a realisation of the need to step delicately that made the common council choose for that year an old and trusted alderman (Robert Alanson) as mayor.[1]

The discontent aroused by these changes was augmented by new taxation. Furthermore, there had been bad harvests for nine years, and the inclosure of land and the conversion of arable to pasture may have created some unemployment. Surviving returns to Wolsey's commission of inquiry into inclosures in 1517 record the inclosure of only 417 acres in the county, evicting forty-one persons. These returns, however, relate only to the neighbourhood of Horncastle, and there is no way of estimating the total for the county.[2] More land was affected after that date: in 1531 the abbot of Wellow inclosed the whole lordship of Weelsby.[3]

Professor Tawney recalls that laggards among the Lincolnshire men who rose in 1536 were spurred forward with the cry 'What will ye do? Shall we go home and keep sheep?' This can hardly be regarded as evidence of hatred of sheep farming; it sounds like the offer of a choice between action and quiescence. He also points out that the rebels embroidered their banner with a ploughshare.[4] But it was not the only emblem. There were the Five Wounds of Christ and a chalice with the Host; and it cannot be doubted that the causes of the rising were largely if not mainly religious. Besides these emblems there were the plough and the horn; and if the plough stood for husbandry, the horn must surely have stood for animal farming, including sheep farming. It can hardly be dismissed as referring to Horncastle or the tax on horned cattle.[5] It does not seem possible, without further evidence, to decide how far the causes of the rising were agrarian. There is no such suggestion among the formal demands of the rebels, and having staked their all on rebellion

[1] See above, p. 23.

[2] I. S. Leadam, *Domesday of Inclosures* (1897), pp. 243–60. Mr Beresford has lately pointed out that no prosecutions followed upon the inquiry in Lincolnshire, and his examination of deserted village sites leads him to the view that the main peak of the depopulation movement in the county had been passed by 1485 (Maurice Beresford, *Lost Villages of England* (1954), p. 241).

[3] Pleadings of Duchy of Lancaster, DN 1 VIII, no. R 4, quoted in C. Brears, *Lincolnshire in the seventeenth and eighteenth Centuries* (1940), p. 131.

[4] *The Agrarian Problem in the Sixteenth Century* (1912), p. 318.

[5] M. H. and R. Dodds, *The Pilgrimage of Grace, 1536–37, and the Exeter Conspiracy, 1538* (1915), I, 129. The banner of Robert Aske, the Yorkshire leader, bore only the Five Wounds.

they would not be likely to show reticence in saying what it was that they sought.

Religious discontent did not extend—certainly in the city—to solicitude for individual religious houses. Lincoln's relations with its two monastic foundations, the cell which belonged to the Benedictine house of St Mary of York, and the Gilbertine house of St Katharine, were limited to disputes about rights of pasture upon the fields surrounding the city. On 4 May 1536 the common council sent their recorder, Thomas Moigne, to London to see whether he could get a grant of any chantries within the city; and assuming that the Black Monks cell must be involved in the suppression of the smaller religious houses, they asked their burgess in parliament, Vincent Grantham, to see if he could get the city a grant of any of the Black Monks' lands, promising as a reward of success that he should have a 30 years' lease of them for himself. Grantham bestirred himself, and the council were called on to find £60 for the purpose. There was no such sum in the common chamber, and, living as usual from hand to mouth, the council resolved to pawn the Great Gild plate to the mayor for £28, and send this up with £12 from the common chamber. The parliamentary lobbying failed, for the cell was not yet to be suppressed, and when it was, the city failed to secure its lands.

Since June a body of royal commissioners had been at work dissolving the smaller monasteries. They were followed by two more such bodies, one to assess and collect the subsidy (which was a new tax on land and goods), and the other to inquire into the condition of the clergy and their fitness in morals, education and politics. The complaints of that summer were accompanied by dark hints of impending trouble. Men from Lincolnshire were reporting in other counties that 'anyone who would go thither at Michaelmas should have honest living for dyking and fowling', and some took the hint and set off as soon as the harvest was over.[1]

News of the coming of the clerical commission to Louth was the signal for a rising of the townsmen. On Monday, 2 October, when the registrar of the diocese attempted to read Thomas Cromwell's commission, his book was torn to pieces by the crowd and he barely escaped with his life. The next day a party set out for Caistor to seize another body of commissioners. They found the birds had flown, but they were joined by hosts of recruits, including many priests and dispossessed monks. Local gentry were sent for, brought in, and made to take the oath. The same day there was a muster at Horncastle, which was joined by many of the gentry, headed by the sheriff, Dymoke of Scrivelsby. The abbot of Barlings attended, with his canons in full armour.

[1] *L. & P. Henry VIII*, xi, no. 543; Dodds, op. cit. i, 78.

The demands of the rebels were six in number: that no more religious houses be suppressed, except (according to one report) 'such houses as the king has suppressed for his pleasure only'; that the subsidy be remitted; that the clergy be released from payment of tenths and firstfruits to the Crown; that the Statute of Uses be repealed; that villein blood be removed from the privy council; that five heretic bishops, including Cranmer, Latimer, and Longland, bishop of Lincoln, be deprived and punished.[1] The demands point clearly to clerical inspiration.

Moigne, the recorder of Lincoln, who was one of the commissioners for the subsidy at Caistor, got away from the commons and went to his bailiff's house at Usselby. There, on Tuesday, 3 October, he wrote to Hussey at Sleaford. Hussey wrote back, asking for further news, and whether Lord Burgh and others would meet him. He said he was going to Lincoln, and wrote to the mayor and other citizens, saying that he had heard from the dean that a company of false rebellious knaves had risen in Lindsey. He ordered the mayor to see the city securely kept, so that no such evil disposed rebellious persons could pass through it; to be ready with such company as he could make to suppress them; and to take up the bows and arrows in the bowyers' and fletchers' hands at a reasonable price. The mayor was to handle matters secretly, and if he thought he was unable to resist, send word to Hussey, who would come to his aid.

On Wednesday, 4 October, Hussey reported to Cromwell that 'a company of light persons' had risen in Lindsey. The same day a number of the gentry who were with the rebels—among them Moigne, who had been taken at his house at Willingham—sent to Hussey to know if he would join them; if not, 'the commonalty will in all haste come and seek you as their utter enemy'. Hussey sent on their letter to Cromwell, adding that the country was becoming more and more rebellious. The rebels, he said, were coming towards Lincoln, though he thought not in such numbers as was noised. His countrymen had for the most part promised to defend him, but he would not trust them to fight against the rebels.

An interesting report on the early stages of the rising was sent by Chapuys to his master the Emperor Charles V. He wrote that the number of rebels must be very great, and was apparently increasing. There was not a gentleman or a man of influence whom the king had not ordered to be ready with his power. The rebels, he thought, were not likely to hold out long, owing to want of money and an experienced head. Their leaders were an abbot, a secular priest and a shoemaker. The king was dejected and, according to Cromwell's nephew, in great fear.

[1] The Yorkshire rebels' proclamation even said that 'we think the beginning of all this trouble was the bishop of Lincoln'.

On the same 4 October (Wednesday) the rebels wrote to the mayor of Lincoln bidding him prepare the town to receive them on Saturday night. They arrived on the Friday evening, having been preceded by a party of forty men to prepare lodgings for them. There was a report that they numbered 40,000, of whom 16,000 were in harness, and 700 or 800 monks and priests. During their stay they broke up the bishop's palace, no doubt a demonstration of their dislike for Bishop Longland, who happily for him was not there.

On the Saturday parties were sent out to bring in the gentry. Five hundred men went to bring in Hussey, but he had escaped. Moigne and others were sent to bring in Robert Sutton of Burton, his brother Sir John Sutton, and the Disneys. The gentlemen of Horncastle and Louth, with representatives of the commons, then held a conference at Mile Cross, towards Nettleham. Articles prepared by 'the Horncastle side' were discussed, and the following day, when Moigne had rejoined the 'men of worship', the articles as amended were approved, and it was decided that they should be read to the commons, who were to be asked to go no further until they had received the king's reply to the articles. A meeting of gentlemen and some of the commons was then held in the chapter house of the Minster. During the meeting there arrived messengers from Beverley, escorted by a body of the commons, bearing a letter under the common seal of the town, saying that on hearing news of Lincolnshire the commons of Beverley had also risen, and asking for the grounds of the Lincolnshire rising. Thereupon a copy of the articles was sent to Beverley. Before the meeting ended another part of the commons came to the chapter house, with two Halifax men, bringing a message that Halifax had also risen. The commons were all for an immediate advance, but at the risk of their lives the gentry persuaded them to wait until they had the king's reply, urging that it would be high treason to advance before they had it. The following morning, Monday, the articles were copied and sent to the king.

Meanwhile feverish preparations were being made in London to suppress the rising. Lord Chancellor Audley wrote to Cromwell that he would devise a commission to suppress it. Sir Brian Tuke, treasurer of the king's chamber, who organised the king's posts, addressed letters on 6 October to the mayors and head officers of Waltham Cross, Ware, Royston, Huntingdon, Stilton, Stamford, Sleaford and Lincoln, ordering them to appoint horsemen to carry the king's letters from post to post. The Lincoln letter was entered in the minutes on 9 October, and the next day Robert Dyon was named as post to Sleaford. Cromwell's messengers had reached Ancaster by the 6th, and reported that further provision was needed to subdue the rebels than the strength of those parts. That day another correspondent reported that 'they are to-night at Lincoln and there prepared for'. Cromwell's servant had been hanged, and Hussey, who dared not stir, would probably be taken. Hussey himself was writing piteously to Lord Shrewsbury from 'my poor cabin at Sleaford' that he dared not leave his house.

The king had originally intended to take the field in person, but instead had chosen the duke of Suffolk, who by his marriage with Katharine Willoughby had become a great Lincolnshire landowner. Suffolk set off at once, and by Monday had reached Huntingdon, though he was far from ready to fight. He wrote to the king that he had no ordnance or artillery, and not enough men to do anything. He begged for guns, sufficient horsemen and a thousand or two of harness. He was told that the traitors were well horsed and harnessed, and he thought that the success of a battle would be doubtful. He expected the rebels to reach Stamford that night. If the royal forces there under Sir William Parr could hold them, Suffolk would repair thither; but if not he would concentrate at Huntingdon and make a determined stand. Clearly Suffolk was doubtful of the issue. His chief hope lay in the hesitancy of the gentry, and he asked for instructions in the event of their submission. His hopes were quickly fulfilled.

On Tuesday afternoon there came to the gentlemen assembled in Lincoln chapter house some 300 of the commons with a messenger bearing letters from the king and the duke of Suffolk. The commons insisted on hearing the letters. Moigne thereupon read the king's letter; but as there was a clause in it which might stir the commons he omitted it.[1] The omission was detected by the parson of Snelland, who said that the letter was falsely read, and Moigne's life was in danger. Some of the commons withdrew into the cloisters, and gave expression to their distrust of the gentry. After much debate it was decided to kill Moigne and his fellows as they came out of the west door of the Minster. They were, however, brought out by their servants through the south door, and later to the chancellor's house.

The only available account of the scene is that given by Moigne after his surrender, when his memory was likely to be coloured by his anxiety about his own fate. He said that he advised the gentlemen that if they

---

[1] The letter ordered the rebels to return home, deliver up their leaders, and submit to punishment. It contained the famous sentence: 'How presumptuous, then, are ye, the rude commons of one shire, and that one of the most brute and beastly of the whole realm, and of least experience, to take upon you, contrary to God's law and man's law, to rule your prince whom you are bound to obey and serve and for no worldly cause to withstand?' Perhaps this was the passage that Moigne thought it discreet to omit.

could muster sufficient force they should fight rather than advance, or that otherwise they should hold the cathedral close against the commons until the king's forces should rescue them. The next morning (Wednesday) the gentlemen in harness, with their supporters, met the commons in the fields, and refused to advance until they had the king's answers to the articles.

That evening Lancaster herald arrived in Lincoln, and on Thursday morning every man was commanded to be in the castle garth to hear the royal proclamation. It bade them submit and return to their homes. The effect was remarkable. Some of the rebels went home that day, and some the next.

Even before the arrival of the herald they had begun to dissolve. On Wednesday Richard Cromwell reported to his uncle Thomas from Stamford (where Suffolk had arrived) that the traitors about Lincoln were so dismayed at the assembly of noblemen against them that they knew not what to do. The Boston townsmen and others had already fled, and a messenger said there remained not 10,000 in Lincoln. The duke's intention then was to spoil Louth and Horncastle, as there were more traitors there than in any towns in England. Richard suggested hopefully that the whole shire should be sacked. By Friday he added that 'the traitors had dispersed and that the gentlemen had offered unconditionally to come in if the duke would receive them'.

The king was faced with a more formidable rising in Yorkshire, but the Lincolnshire collapse gave him confidence, and he countermanded a large number of orders sent out for the raising of further forces; and he issued a proclamation accepting the submission made to the herald. Suffolk was instructed that the rebels were to be shown mercy if they left their harness and weapons in the market place at Lincoln and went home. When he reached Lincoln he was to remain in the Close with an eye to the country round. The Lincolnshire towns were to be kept from pillage, but four captains of Louth, three of Horncastle and two of Caistor were to be detained. Suffolk and the lord admiral were to view the cathedral church and close and signify their opinion of the site, 'for we be yet in mind' in memory of the insurrection to establish a garrison there, to remind posterity that their forefathers were traitors.

The lord admiral arrived in Lincoln on Tuesday, 16 October. Richard Cromwell, who was with him, reported that 'we found as obstinate persons as ever I saw, who would scarce move their bonnets to my said lord, and probably would have withstood us if we had not stolen upon them'. Like other young campaigners Cromwell was no doubt exaggerating the perils of the service, and he probably did not allow for the Lincolnshire phlegm. The duke came in on Wednesday.

The king was concerned to teach the gentry a lesson. They were now pretending fidelity, but he bade Suffolk examine the ringleaders of the multitude to discover how they had really behaved. Though he was not to be overhasty in executing such of the mean sort as could give evidence against them, he had leave to execute as many of the commons in Lincoln, Horncastle and Louth as should seem requisite 'for the terrible example of like offenders'. Any of the gentlemen who had notably offended were to be sent to the king or kept in ward. Suffolk had offered to move against the Yorkshire rebels, but Henry wished him to stay at Lincoln or thereabouts for the pacifying of those parts.[1]

Suffolk remained in Lincoln. It was no doubt at his bidding that the common council resolved on 8 November that every man who had a horse or could afford a horse should keep it in readiness to serve the king's grace at any time when he should be called upon. Moigne having forfeited his office as recorder by taking part with the rebels, the council resolved on the same day that Suffolk should have the nomination of Moigne's successor 'with our service next under the king's grace'.

The nominee was Anthony Mussenden, who last appeared as Rutland's servant.[2] He was elected recorder and sworn a freeman and counsel of the city at a common congregation held on 14 December. Although there were already seven justices including the mayor, two additional ones were elected.[3] Bartholomew Willeford was chosen common clerk 'after the departure of John Dyon'. These words seem to imply that Dyon was involved in the rising, which is likely enough, for the relations of recorder and common clerk must have been close.

The duke of Norfolk, who commanded against the Yorkshire rebels, was in Lincoln in January, and Suffolk was there in February, probably to await the trial of the rebels. On 6 March Sir William Parr, with a special commission, sat there to try the abbot of Kirkstead, Moigne and about thirty others. The Lincoln jury was disposed to be favourable. Moigne

---

[1] The rebels had been visited in Lincoln by the Yorkshire leader Aske. One witness saw Aske and Moigne ride together talking beside the rebels in front of 300 footmen. Aske himself stated in examination that on hearing that the king's pleasure touching the Lincolnshire petitions was known by Mr Heneage, he repaired to Lincoln. There he was told that either the gentlemen or the commons would slay him for deserting them; and he left his lodging at the sign of the 'Angel' in Lincoln, and lodged with a priest, his host's brother, departing homeward the next day. He invoked the good man of the 'Angel', which stood at the north corner of Bailgate and Eastgate, to corroborate his statement.

[2] See above, p. 28. For the Mussendens of Healing see A. R. Maddison, *Lincolnshire Pedigrees* (Harleian Society, 1903), II, 697. He is there described as a serjeant at law.

[3] Robert Sutton continued in office as an alderman and a justice. If he was 'brought in' by the rebels he was evidently not implicated.

spoke in his own defence for three hours, and so skilfully, according to Parr, that but for the diligence of the king's serjeant the prisoners would all have been acquitted. The Crown, however, secured the verdict, and the abbot, Moigne and others were executed at Lincoln the following day. Others were convicted and pardoned, though a few were executed at Horncastle and Louth. The abbot of Barlings and others were tried and executed in London.

There remained the craven Hussey, whose shifty look and beady eyes are preserved in the portrait at Doddington. He had been a knight of the shire and a royal servant. He was appointed to attend the king at his reception of Charles V, and at his meeting with Francis I of France at the Field of Cloth of Gold. He became a peer in 1529, and in the following year he was one of the lords who signed an address to Pope Clement VII praying him to consent to the king's wish in the matter of his divorce. He was steward of the lands of many religious houses. Whether he was guilty of any overt act during the rising may be doubted, but he certainly showed no zeal against the rebels, and he was indicted and condemned. When the news of his sentence reached Lincoln is unknown, but it is notable that on 8 June Parr wrote to Cromwell that he had just heard that there had been riots and unlawful assemblies at Lincoln. On 28 June Hussey was sent to Lincoln, and the king wrote to Suffolk that he was sending him 'whom you shall cause to be beheaded at our city of Lincoln at such time soon after his arrival as you shall appoint taking order that you, with a suitable number of gentlemen, shall be at his execution, which we desire may be done notably with a declaration that of our clemency we have pardoned all the rest of his judgment'.

A few days later he was beheaded.[1] There may have been another riot on that occasion, for on 14 July Parr reported to Cromwell asking what he was to do with the persons whom he committed to ward for the late riot at Lincoln. It is clear that although the city was not involved in the rising as deeply as Louth and Horncastle, there was a body of citizens who sympathised with it. The occupation of Lincoln by a great undisciplined host even for a few days must have wrought great damage, but there is no evidence of its extent.[2]

[1] Leland mentioned 'the house or manor place, lately almost new buildid of stone and timbre by the Lorde Husey, standith southeward withoute the town' (*Itinerary*, ed. L. Toulmin Smith (1907), I, 27). Stukely, a much later and less reliable authority, wrote of a building over against the house said to be John of Gaunt's palace, and added that the bow window out of which Hussey went to execution had been taken down in the preceding year (*Itinerarium Curiosum* (1724), p. 85).

[2] This narrative of the rising is compiled from the evidence contained in *L. & P. Henry VIII*, XI and XII (and see Dodds, op. cit.). For Hussey, see R. E. G. Cole, *History of Doddington* (1897), pp. 73–9; and see also A. R. Maddison, 'Lincolnshire gentry during the sixteenth century' in *A.A.S.R.* XXII (1894), pp. 205–6.

PLATE 3

JOHN, LORD HUSSEY

By permission of Colonel C. F. C. Jarvis

After the collapse of the rising the dissolution of the religious houses went on, and the citizens, putting aside any dislike of public policy, were still seeking a share of the spoil. On 9 August 1537 Parr wrote to Cromwell that he had been commanded by the king to accompany the royal surveyor, Pollard, in surveying the lands of Lord Hussey and the abbeys of Barlings and Kirkstead. The Lincoln people had petitioned for the lands of the two abbeys in the city, but Pollard had surveyed them all to the king's use, to the impoverishment of the city and to the reproach of Parr, who had pleaded the city's cause, and who now asked for reconsideration. The plea failed.

The Gilbertine house of St Katharine was the first house in Lincoln to be surrendered, and little local regret can have been felt about its fate. Griffiths, the last prior, was a turbulent man. He was said to have been deprived for promoting the rebellion, and for dissipating the goods of his house. He had entered the priory by force, expelled the new prior, and maintained his position until the surrender of the house; and in spite of his conduct he received a pension of £40. The priory was surrendered to Dr Thomas Legh, one of Cromwell's agents, on 14 July 1538. The thirteen canons were pensioned, but the lay sisters received nothing.[1] The priory lands were granted to Suffolk.

There followed the four friaries in the city, which were surrendered to Richard, bishop of Dover, in February 1539. They were all poor houses, there being nothing left but stone and poor glass, though 'meetly leaded'. Whether the citizens regretted their loss there is little to show. The only hint of civic support for the friars was an annual payment by the common chamber of 2s. to a wax light at the Black Friars. The city's thoughts turned at once to the Grey Friars' water supply, which must be mentioned later.

The cell of St Mary Magdalene, the Black Monks' cell, which has left its mark in the modern city in the tiny ruin of 'Monks Abbey' and Monks Road, had come under the notice of the king and Cromwell at an earlier date. In 1531 Henry wrote to the abbot of St Mary of York, whose cell it was, to say that he considered the cell to be a 'mean to provoke liberty and conversation not decent and meet for religious persons'. The abbot replied that he was not bound to keep any monks there, and that he was willing to recall the prior and brethren, and to support three more students at the university from the revenues of the house. In 1533 the abbot wrote to Cromwell, admitting that the prior had managed his house so liberally that he had brought the abbey into expense and trouble; that it was not intended to depose him, but only to admonish him to look the better to it.

[1] *V.C.H. Lincs.* II, 188, and references there cited; R.E.G. Cole, 'Priory of St Katharine without Lincoln', in *A.A.S.R.* XXVII (1904), 316.

Two years later the abbot wrote first to the king complaining of the conduct of the brethren at Lincoln, and asking that they might be called home to York for ever, and later to Cromwell saying that the brethren at York were much divided as to the suppression of the cell. Sir Thomas Audley reported in 1536 that there were no longer any monks in St Mary Magdalene's priory.

As danger increased the abbot began to defend the cell more strenuously. On 1 March 1539 he wrote to Cromwell in reply to a letter complaining that there were but one or two monks at Lincoln, and sometimes none, and that there was 'no hospitality kept, nor God Almighty served, nor any religious order'. He protested that from time out of memory there had been a prior and two monks, and 'at this day God well served, religion kept, and poor folk relieved' after the ability of the brethren, as all the country could testify, and especially at the last commotion. He asked that the cell might be spared. It was too late. Other letters during the same year imply that the brethren were withdrawn, and the cell leased to a dependant of Cromwell.[1]

The religious houses of the city having gone, it was not to be expected that the tempting treasures of the Minster should be spared. On 6 June 1540 a royal order was issued for the removal of 'a certain shrine and divers feigned relics and jewels, with which all simple people be much deceived and brought into great superstition and idolatry'; and also of superfluous jewels, plate and copes. Under this order there were removed from the cathedral church 2621 ounces of gold, 4285 ounces of silver and a great number of pearls and precious stones. The golden shrine of St Hugh and the silver shrine of John Dalderby are apparently included in these totals. Some of the vestments and a large part of the plate evidently escaped on this occasion, for there was a further raid a few years later.[2]

In 1541 Henry VIII visited York to confer with his nephew the king of Scots, and had an opportunity of seeing for himself conditions in the districts which had so lately defied him. He reached Lincoln on 9 August,

[1] *V.C.H. Lincs.* II, 129–30. *L. & P. Henry VIII*, VI, no. 746; VIII, no. 944; XIV (i), nos. 591, 963; XIV (ii), no. 522.

[2] *L. & P. Henry VIII*, XV, no. 772; Sir William Dugdale, *Monasticon Anglicanum* (1830 ed.), VI, 1278–80, 1286–7; Canon Wordsworth's letter in *Lincoln Diocesan Magazine*, V (1889), 92; *V.C.H. Lincs.* II, 51. More than a generation later, in 1586–7, a commission was issued to inquire about a gold or silver gilt image of Our Lady set upon the altar on festival days before which tapers were burnt; to know who paid for the tapers; and whether they were lit at times of day when darkness did not make them necessary. The oldest inhabitants remembered the image well. Thomas Lambe, clerk, aged 89, had known the Minster for 72 years at the least and as a boy had served Dean Constable (1514–28) there (*P.R.O. Lists and Indexes*, XXXVII; List of Special Commissions and Returns in Exchequer, no. 1312).

and was in York in the middle of September. News of his impending visit caused a flutter of anxiety in Lincoln. The common council resolved on a huge propitiatory gift of twenty fat oxen and one hundred fat muttons, to the value of £50, towards which all the people had to pay. The aldermen who had passed the chair were ordered to provide themselves gowns of scarlet, the other aldermen gowns of crimson, and the rest of the inhabitants gowns of London russet or other such colour. The king's arms were set on the Bargate and the south side of the Stonebow. Two boon days were appointed during which all must turn to clear away dunghills and filth from the streets and sand them.

The king and queen were met at the farthest part of the liberties by the mayor, recorder and his brethren. There they knelt before the king, and the recorder made a 'proposition', and the mayor kissed the mace and delivered it to the king, who immediately returned it to him; then the mayor on horseback alone bore it before the king and before Lord Hastings with the sword and others with the king's maces, until such time as the king entered the bishop's palace. The *naïveté* of the citizens must have given Henry some pleasure, for the address mentioned the value of the gift of sheep and cattle; and an address to the queen offering pike, bream and tench declared their value at £7. So far as the city was concerned the visit passed without any untoward event.[1]

In Henry's closing years Lincoln lay under the shadow of the rising. Suffolk had built a house unpleasantly near at Grimsthorpe, and he was not to be withstood when he directed the common council to appoint his henchman George St Paul recorder; they had already retained him as their standing counsel. St Paul represented the city in parliament in 1542 at the death of Mussenden, and later remitted the burgess money due to him for expenses. The duke of Norfolk visited Lincoln about October 1542, and to him the town clerk, William Hynde, turned when he was in fear of dismissal. The duke wrote that he knew him to be an honest man in danger from some of his 'backfriends'. The request was supported locally by Sir Robert Tyrwhitt, and the council compliantly resolved that Hynde should continue in office, and that the duke should be so assured.

It was perhaps the hope that the king might be able to spare some of the spoils of the monasteries that prompted the city to petition for relief. At Candlemas 1542 two aldermen presented a petition 'for the weal and profit of the city'. It declared that Lincoln was decaying daily, and without aid would be desolate in a few years. There was a sum of 20 marks yearly payable to Lord Rutland, and a further £80 to the dean and chapter,

[1] The queen was Katharine Howard, and later some of the charges against her were based on incidents said to have taken place in the bishop's palace.

besides other charges. On the income side there was common land worth not more than £20 a year, but there was no such trading or crafts as would sustain the charges. The staple and the cloth trade had gone, and even the tax exemption which the city had often enjoyed had been omitted in 1541 when—and here was the point—the city was charged to pay in four years four fifteenths and tenths, to wit £400. The result would be to drive the citizens away. They asked for exemption, and the appropriation to the dean and chapter of the benefice of Cottingham in Yorkshire in release of their part of the fee-farm rent. The petition was not wholly in vain. Half of the £400 was remitted, and the other half to be paid at the rate of £50 a year.[1]

The next year the burgesses in parliament, the recorder and alderman William Alanson, were to sue for a discharge. Alanson was paid £40 on condition of success, and the two were promised another £80 if they succeeded. The duke of Suffolk was invoked, and he wrote to 'our loving friends the mayor and the residue of his brethren', saying that he would be a suitor to the king when convenient opportunity offered; meanwhile he did not a little marvel that they would say him nay in a request that John Dyon should be one of their justices of peace, who was a man of good learning, judgement and right mete for the same. He therefore required them eftsoons to proceed to his election, or give in writing the reasons for their denial. To this the council replied at once. The purport of the reply is not given, but there is no entry of Dyon's election, and Suffolk did not mention the matter in his next letter. Probably the council were able to give good reason for refusal: a John Dyon was presently in disgrace with the county authorities.[2]

The duke's second letter promised the king's aid in granting benefices to be impropriate for discharge of the £80 due to the chantry at the Minster. It was to be assured to them as soon as the king returned from France. After much coming and going letters patent were sealed granting to the city the advowsons and patronages of Hanslope in the county of Buckingham, and Hemswell, Surfleet and Belton (in Axholme) in the county of Lincoln, with authority on the death of the then rectors, to take possession of the estates and revenues, endowing thereout perpetual vicarages.[3]

---

[1] *L. & P. Henry VIII*, xvii, no. 362.

[2] *H.M.C. Rutland*, i, 56; *H.M.C. Salisbury*, i, 80, for a complaint by the vicar of Tathwell near Louth to Cecil against Dyon, 'a busy naughty man'. He was a justice of the peace for the county. This can hardly be the John Dyon who was common clerk before the rebellion. It is said that there was a Joe Dun who was such an efficient bailiff of Lincoln that his name gave a new verb to the language. See *Oxford English Dictionary*, sub 'dun'.

[3] Birch, p. 165. The grant was confirmed by statute in 1593, presumably because the citizens thought their title in danger (35 Eliz. I, c. 12; *C.S.P.D. 1591–94*, p. 333).

The grant was obtained just in time. Within a month Henry VIII was dead. At the election of the first parliament of Edward VI the result of the poll was for the first time recorded in the council minutes. St Paul, the recorder, received twenty-nine votes and Thomas Grantham thirty-six, they being elected; alderman John Broxholme received fifteen and alderman William Yates four votes. It would seem that only the common council voted.

In pursuance of their policy of buying goodwill the council presented lord protector Somerset, returned from his defeat of the Scots at Pinkie, with four fat oxen. The bishop received fish, the duchess of Suffolk, now a widow and become a great dame, and her son, two cranes and four swans, the earl of Rutland three cygnets, six bittern and sixteen knotts; and the protector Northumberland in 1552 received four cranes, four cygnets, six bittern, twelve godwits, two dozen knotts, two great pike, two great bream and two great tench. The gifts recall how great a part fishing and fowling played in the life of a city on the edge of the fens. The policy had results. Exemption was obtained from two fifteenths and tenths; and the city kept in touch with the recorder on legislation which might affect it.

There had been a lull in negotiations with Rutland about the fee-farm rent. In 1542 he was feeble, and beseeching Norfolk to be kind to him.[1] He died in 1543. His son Henry, the second earl, came of age in 1547, and two years later was appointed Lord Warden of the East and Middle Marches on the Scottish border, 'as meet for nobility of blood, courage and good cultivation', but being young was given advisers;[2] he was lieutenant of the royal army in Scotland, and he sacked Haddington. He was for a time joint lieutenant of Lincolnshire and Nottinghamshire (1551), and took the latter county when Lord Clinton took the former. In 1558 he went to Calais, and he became Lord President of the Council of the North in 1561.

His men of business soon began to look into the matter of the fee-farm rent, and to use it for purposes of securing patronage. Rutland's servant Robert Farrar[3] was admitted and sworn a freeman of the city on 3 November 1552. The earl asked for the nomination of one of the burgesses in parliament, which was granted, with the gift of a tun of claret; there can be little doubt that Farrar was the nominee. Burgess pence had to be found for the recorder, the other burgess, but not for the nominee, which was a powerful argument for accepting the earl's patronage. Farrar was certainly returned in 1553. The common council were not, however, pre-

---

[1] *L. & P. Henry VIII*, xvii, no. 1045.
[2] *C.S.P.D. 1601–3 (& Add.)*, p. 396.
[3] *H.M.C. Salisbury*, i, 140; iv, 355; *H.M.C. Rutland*, iv, 362.

pared to admit in principle what they had conceded in practice, for a note was made in the minute book of the 'remembrance' that no person should at any time thereafter be elected to represent that city unless he had held office as mayor or alderman, except the recorder.

Rutland's claim went further. He claimed a horseman for service under the queen. This was too much. 'You are misinformed', wrote the mayor and others with spirit, 'in saying that we are your fermors. Although the queen's progenitors granted to your ancestors a part of the fee farm of the city, more than it has been able to pay for a long time by reason of its decay, we are not tenants to you, the said rent having ever been a rent seck'. Nevertheless, they sent £6. 13s. 4d. by way of gift towards Rutland's charges in the queen's affairs, adding that they would have sent more if they could have afforded it.[1] Farrar was returned to parliament again in November 1554 and 1555.

In December 1557 Farrar and the recorder St Paul were duly returned in open county court. After the election a letter arrived from Rutland requesting the election of 'one Francis Kemp, macebearer to the lord archbishop of York his grace and lord chancellor of England'; whereupon Kemp was appointed citizen for the said parliament in the stead of Farrar 'by the assent of the aldermen upon divers good considerations'. Arrangements were made for him to be sworn a freeman under letters of attorney from the mayor. The earl's altered nomination was clearly prompted by the government of Philip and Mary, which was engaged in packing the new house with catholics.

In 1553 the recorder and several aldermen had been sent to confer with Rutland about the rent and its arrears, in the hope of settling upon an annual payment of 20 marks as in Sir Thomas Lovell's time.[2] The mayor and others waited upon him by appointment at Eagle, the former commandery of the Knights Hospitallers given to his father by Henry VIII, and terms were reached for redemption of the rent. The devices for raising money illustrate the city's lack of it. It was decided to sell or pawn three chalices, sell the lead of the late Trinity church at 11d. a stone, the Great Gild's brass pot at 33s. 4d. a hundredweight, and reversionary leases were granted for fines paid in hand. Something was then said about the parsonages granted to the city; perhaps Rutland was more interested in them than in cash. At every stage there was delay. First it was proposed to assign Belton parsonage; then it was agreed to settle for Surfleet parsonage and £300 cash; then the deeds were sealed by the city and

---

[1] *H.M.C. Rutland*, I, 60. A rent seck was a rent without the power of distraint for non-payment; it did not create the relation of landlord and tenant.

[2] *M.L.* p. 285.

acknowledged before Mr Justice Dyer; then Rutland thought this not enough, and it was agreed to execute a deed in another form and have it enrolled in the Exchequer. Yet Rutland made no move, and the mayor and others were sent to persuade him, if necessary invoking Dyer and stimulating his good will by the gift of a gelding. There was still no settlement in 1559, and Rutland was offered a great horse and sent a couple of fat oxen. At last the assurance came for enrolment. But there were still three years' arrears outstanding, as well as a claim for repairs to Surfleet parsonage. Rutland received another gift on visiting Lincoln in 1561, perhaps for the last time, for he died in 1563. Dealing with magnates was hard work.

By the time that the struggle with the second earl had begun the city was involved in the legislation of the Edwardian government for the suppression of chantries and gilds, at least in their religious aspect. The number of such foundations had declined in the years between the suppression of the monasteries and the death of Henry VIII by surrender of a number of them, voluntarily or otherwise, to the Crown. Coming events were casting their shadows before.

There were two gilds over which the common council exercised a special measure of control. One was the gild of St Anne, attached to the church of St Andrew in Wigford, whose special function has already been described.[1] The other gild directly controlled was the Great Gild of St Mary, whose gildhall still stands. In 1538, no doubt thinking of the fate of the religious houses, the council ordered that all the gild plate should be given to the commons of the city. Perhaps this order was not acted upon, for in 1541 it was resolved to use the plate to meet temporary needs, but to pay it back in plate or like value. Then to meet the expenses of the effort to dispose of the fee-farm rent the council decided to take over all plate and money of the gild. Alderman Yates, the graceman, refused to yield it up, and he was detained in ward in the gildhall until he gave way. Honour being satisfied the plate was sold for £24. 13s. 4d. and the money handed to Yates in another capacity; he was conducting the suit for redemption of the fee-farm rent.

There was ample warning of the fate of the chantries and religious gilds. They were dissolved by an act of 1545, but action was checked by the death of Henry VIII. Another act of December 1547 was aimed at all foundations which involved masses for the dead or the religious commemoration of benefactors. It was anticipated by the common council. In November they ordered the jewels, plate and ornaments of St Anne's procession to be sold and the proceeds paid to the common chamber.

[1] See above, p. 33.

A few days earlier they had enrolled a deed whereby Yates, still graceman, with the wardens and fraternity of the Great Gild, granted to the city all the lands of the gild, and auditors were appointed to get all the assets in quickly, obviously to avoid the effect of the impending statute.[1]

It appears that the council for a time thought that the craft gilds were involved. The shoemakers admitted to having 28s. in hand—it was shared among ten members who must account to the king when called on—and it was resolved that their hall be let and their deeds and papers brought in. The keepers of the clerks' gild promised to bring in their profits and all plate, jewels, implements and papers. The mistake was soon discovered. The clothiers, who had been promised the shoemakers' hall, were told that they could not have it, and shortly afterwards the tailors were promised a new charter. Yet the sense of crisis, coupled with high prices and bad times, and the injury done to the gilds by the lopping of their religious functions and incomes, ensured that it was to be some time before they resumed their normal craft life again. The cordwainers, whose register survives, made only two brief entries in it between the suspension of their activities in 1545 and full resumption in 1562.

Liquidation was the order of the day, and the council were busy on their own account in dealing with the fabrics of disused parish churches. In 1541 the central church of St Peter at Pleas was ordered to be taken down, and the lead, ornaments and bells sold to the use of the common chamber. It was roundly declared that all other churches in the city which should decay, or whose parishioners should be assigned to another parish, should be taken down and sold. The church of St John in Newport followed; a first thought to give tile, timber and vestments to St Nicholas was abandoned, and only the books were handed over. The sheriffs were granted St Stephen in Newland in lieu of money in relief of their office. The bells of Holy Rood and St Edward and the chapel on the High Bridge were taken into care, and the chapel ordered to be converted into a dwellinghouse and let.

This piecemeal process with its assignment of parishioners to other parishes, all carried out by authority of the common council, led to a scheme for reorganising the whole of the parishes of the city. A petition was presented to parliament which was embodied in the preamble to a statute passed on 13 May 1549 to give effect to it.[2] It recalled that the many parishes were once well peopled, and provided good and honest

---

[1] A similar situation arose on the nationalisation of the gas and electricity undertakings of local authorities without compensation in 1947–8; and where possible assets were put out of the reach of the statutes.

[2] 2 & 3 Edward VI, no. 9. The act is printed by Birch, p. 186.

livings for learned incumbents and parsons, because of the privy tithes of
rich merchants, clothiers and artificers and the offerings of a great multitude of people. The ruin of the city and of the trade of clothmaking and
merchandise had reduced the livings to not above 30s. a year, which was
not a competent and honest living for a good curate, and nobody would
take them but for reasons of poverty and necessity. The result was that
some late religious persons with pensions had taken the said benefices,
'which for the most part are unlearned and very ignorant persons not able
to do any part of their duties, by reason whereof the said city is not only
replenished with blind guides and pastors, but also the people very much
kept in ignorance and blindness as well of their duties towards Almighty
God as also the king's majesty their sovereign lord and the commonwealth
of this realm and to the great danger of their souls'.

The argument for the union of the parishes that the income of some of
them was not enough for a decent living was clearly justified, and the continuing rise of prices soon made even the united incomes poor; and it may
be that the charges against dispossessed monks and friars supplementing
their pensions were also justified. Naturally, however, the draftsman of the
petition would be anxious to make its argument as attractive as possible to
parliament, and the supremacy of protestantism under Edward VI no
doubt influenced the terms of his draft.

The statute authorised the ordinary or his deputy, the mayor and
recorder, and the justices of the peace for the city, or any four of them of
whom the ordinary or his deputy and the mayor must be two, to carry out
a union of parishes, provided that the clear yearly value of any one benefice
to its incumbent did not exceed £14. Superfluous churches were to be
demolished and bestowed to repair and enlargement of the other churches,
or the bridges of the city or the relief of the poor. Patronage was to be
equitably distributed and existing rights of prebendaries and pensioners
preserved. The act was to be in force for six years only.

The constitution of the commission shows that the city's claim to substantial control was not disputed.[1] The council appointed four aldermen,
who were to be attended by four of the discreetest of every parish and the
aldermen of the wards, to record the rental value of all property and the
endowments of each church. It was resolved that for every 12d. rent
2d. should be paid as an honest stipend for a curate. The bishop, Holbeach,
had some suggestions to make upon the manner and form of future payment of tithe. Its nature does not appear, but it was unanimously rejected;
and he was pressed to let matters proceed.

By the middle of 1550 the scheme of union was complete. The city,

[1] See above, p. 20.

excluding Bail, Close, Newport and Eastgate, was organised in nine parishes. In Wigford, St Margaret and part of Holy Cross were added to St Botolph; Holy Trinity, St Edward, St Andrew and the remainder of Holy Cross to St Peter at Gowts; the site of the White Friars was added to St Mark; part of St John went to St Mary le Wigford and part to St Benedict. North of the river, St Peter at Pleas was united to St Peter at Arches; the Black Monks and the former Grey Friars and Black Friars to St Swithin; St Lawrence and St Mary Crackpole to St Martin; and St Cuthbert to St Michael. The property of the former parish churches was also dealt with, together with tithe from various closes on the fringes of the city, taken in from the commons. The formal award was signed in the minute book of the council in 1553. It was signed by John Taylor, who had become bishop in 1552, William Hutchinson, mayor, and George Stamp and John Fawkener, two of the justices of the peace.

Without waiting for signature the common council proceeded to deal with the disused churches. Lead and bells, jewels, plate and ornaments were held to be at their disposal. St Margaret and St Andrew were ordered to be taken down, and Holy Trinity was offered to the mayor, whom failing, it was sold to a syndicate of thirty people for 40 marks. It was thought first to convert St John's church into a house, but it was later ordered to be taken down. St Lawrence was let at 21s. a year, and stone from St Augustine was devoted to the repair of Bishopbridge, and from Holy Trinity and St Edward to paving. A claim by the Sutton family to own St Andrew in Wigford was rejected.[1]

In December 1552 the king's commissioners of church goods were making inventories of church plate, jewels and furniture; and their activities brought to the notice of the council a startling omission from the act of union of parishes. It did not state that bells, jewels and ornaments of disused churches should belong to the city. The commissioners were demanding inventories of them; and the mayor and aldermen in secret council agreed to offer William Dalison, a serjeant at law who was a commissioner for church goods, a present of 40s. to set his hand and seal to a suitable certificate of church goods within the city. The gift was not in vain, and no more was heard of the legal difficulty.

The reform movement wrought the well-known changes in doctrine and church order: services in English, marriage of the clergy, removal of church altars and ornaments and whitewashing of church walls. The vast diocese of Lincoln was partitioned and endowments stripped from it. The dean and chapter too lost lands under their control, and it was long before they could be sure about the lands and houses left to them. All these rapid

[1] *M.L.* p. 166.

changes had far outstripped the movement of opinion, and it is perhaps significant that in 1554, soon after the accession of Mary, the common council resolved that St Anne's gild should produce the Corpus Christi play. The old custom of pageants was revived, and the companies—the old gilds—ordered to contribute according to their assessments.

The Edwardian bishop Taylor was deprived, according to Strype, because he was married; but the order depriving him refers to his irregular appointment by letters patent instead of by right of election and his subsequent teaching of erroneous doctrine as the grounds of deprivation.[1] Some of the clergy were deprived, mostly on account of marriage, and among them Matthew Parker, dean of Lincoln, and future archbishop.[2] John Aylmer, archdeacon of Stow, was deprived because he opposed the doctrine of transubstantiation in convocation. He fled to the continent, and during his exile helped John Foxe the martyrologist. The incumbent of St Mary le Wigford was also deprived, his successor being appointed in 1554.[3]

The chance survival of an account book of St Martin's parish[4] gives glimpses of the return to the old order. The church fabric had suffered by either abuse or neglect, and had to be repaired, and a rate of $4d.$ was levied on the head of every house, and $2d.$ on each clothier, towards the cost. A rood loft was erected. A parishioner, Edward Smith, gave a cross of copper and gilt, with staff and cross cloth thereto belonging; a double gilt 'pyxet' for the sacrament; and a little silver 'mazard'. He also gave towards the building of the steeple. In an inventory of ornaments and vestments he showed himself a cautious benefactor, for he gave a banner cloth on condition that it should not be lent to 'foreigners' without his consent, and he kept in his own custody a cross cloth of silk given by old Mr Smith. The entries in the inventory have been struck out; the life of Smith's gifts was short and their end probably violent. St Martin's was soon to witness a different scene.

The zeal of the Marian bishops, John White, who visited his diocese 'roundly' before being translated to Winchester, and Thomas Watson happily did not extend to burnings, of which, it appears, there was only one in the diocese, and none in the county.[5] Two women, however, who were associated with Lincolnshire, were deemed worthy by Foxe of a place

---

[1] Thomas Rymer, *Foedera* (1728), xv, 371; *V.C.H. Lincs.* ii, 52.

[2] In 1558 Parker told Sir Nicholas Bacon that he had rather have Bene't College, Cambridge, and 20 nobles a year than dwell in the deanery of Lincoln, which was 200 at the least (John Strype, *Life of Parker* (1821 ed.), i, 73).

[3] *Lincs. N. & Q.* v (1896–98), 179.

[4] It is in the Lincoln Corporation Muniment Room.

[5] Thomas Fuller, *Church History of Britain* (1842 ed.), ii, 395.

in his *Book of Martyrs*. Only one of them was burnt, and she under Henry VIII. Anne Askew, or Ayscough, the daughter of Sir William Ayscough, who took part in the Lincolnshire rebellion, and sister of Sir Francis, a well known and trusted figure in Lincoln, became the wife of Thomas Kyme, a local squire, and took to preaching in different parts of the county. She expounded the New Testament in Lincoln Minster until she was ejected by the dean and chapter. When she went to London she was arrested; in examination the privy council found her very obstinate and heady in reasoning in religious matters,[1] and after being tortured she was burnt at Smithfield. Her constancy and her barbarous fate won for her a respect and repute which she had probably not enjoyed in her life; ordinary folk were more likely to sympathise with her husband, who turned her out of his house because she was constantly 'gadding to gospel and gossip it at court' as the Jesuit Parsons said, instead of looking after her children.[2] The name of Anne was cherished in the Ayscough family, and it may have been partly her memory which brought so many of her collateral descendants out on the parliamentary side in the Civil War.[3]

The other woman was a very different person. She was the duchess of Suffolk, born Katharine, only child of William Lord Willoughby de Eresby, and her mother a near relative of Queen Katharine of Aragon. She became first the ward and then the wife of Charles Brandon, duke of Suffolk, who died in 1545, leaving her a widow at the age of 26. She at once emerged as a great lady, living mostly at Grimsthorpe near Bourne. Gossip had it that she might have married the king of Poland, and she was even suggested as a possible seventh wife of Henry VIII; perhaps happily for her the vacancy did not arise. She was friendly with William Cecil, whose maternal grandfather lived at Bourne; the tutor to her two sons was Thomas Wilson, to become M.P. for Lincoln, and she was friendly with Martin Bucer, a continental reformer brought to England by Archbishop Cranmer.

According to Fuller she was a lady of a sharp wit, and sure hand to drive her wit home and make it pierce when she pleased.[4] The position she assumed in Lincolnshire is shown by a letter to Lord Rutland, apparently written in 1545:

In Leicestershire Lord —— and the Earl of Huntingdon have the rule; in Lincolnshire Lady Suffolk. If —— have all the shire, there is but Nottinghamshire for you.[5]

[1] *A.P.C. 1542–47*, p. 462.
[2] Fuller, op. cit. II, 114; John Foxe, *Acts and Monuments* (4th ed. n.d.), v, 537–50. It is said that her brother Sir Francis betrayed her and that until her death he saw ever before him a bright light, which he himself compared to that reflected from a great fire upon a glass window (Edward Trollope, 'Anne Askew', in *A.A.S.R.* VI (1862), 124).
[3] See the table at p. 127.   [4] Fuller, op. cit. II, 423.   [5] *H.M.C. Rutland*, I, 32.

PLATE 4

KATHARINE, DUCHESS OF SUFFOLK

From a miniature by Holbein, by permission of the Earl of Ancaster

Among her friends was Hugh Latimer, who preached at Stamford in 1550, doubtless at her instance: he seems to have regarded himself as breaking new ground there:

> I never preached in Lincolnshire afore, nor came here afore, save once when I went to take orders at Lincoln, which was a good while ago; and therefore I cannot say much of Lincolnshire, for I know it not.

It was in this sermon that he said he always began and ended with the Lord's Prayer, as he found that people did not know it.[1] The first edition of his sermons preached before Edward VI bore the duchess's arms, and he paid a long visit to Grimsthorpe in the winter of 1552, preaching a series of sermons there.[2]

On the accession of Mary the duchess made no attempt to hide her opinions, and she sent aid to Bishop Ridley when he was in prison.[3] Richard Bertie, whom she had lately married, was ordered to London for examination by Stephen Gardiner, bishop of London, whom the duchess had offended by jests at his expense; and presently she and Bertie thought it wise to leave the country. They certainly did not flee, for their five-weeks' progress from London to Gravesend was so leisurely that it looks like a deliberate defiance of the queen and a challenge to her to do her worst.[4] The privy council appointed commissioners in Lincolnshire to schedule her property, she 'being contemptuously without licence departed the realm'; the next year they caught one of her messengers, and intercepted leases she was trying to grant; and they asked the bishop of Lincoln to search for 'naughty books' at Grimsthorpe.[5] She and Bertie remained in

---

[1] *Latimer's Sermons*, ed. Canon Beeching (Everyman ed. n.d.), p. 245.

[2] 'Certayn Godly Sermons, made uppon the Lord's Prayer, preached by the right reverende Father, and constant martyr of Christ, Master Hughe Latymer, before the right honorable and vertuous Lady Katherine, Duches of Suffolke, in the yeare of our Lorde, 1553. Whereunto are annexed certaine other sermons preached by the said reverende Father, in Lincolnshire, which were gathered, and collected by Augustine Bernher, a servaunt of his, though not so perfectly as they were uttered: yet faithfully and truly, to the singular commoditie and profyt of the christē reader, faythfully perused and alowed according to thorder appointed in the Queenes Majesties Iniunctions. 1562.'

[3] *Ridley's Letters*, ed. H. Christmas (Parker Society, 1843), p. 382.

[4] 'It is not easy to believe in the desperate plight of the duchess of Suffolk, who found it possible to flee for her life with a major-domo, a 'gentlewoman' and six servants—a joiner, a brewer, a kitchen-maid, a laundress, a Greek rider of horses, and a fool. This unique flying-squadron took five weeks to get from London to Gravesend (1 Jan.–8 Feb. 1554-5), resting awhile in Kent, and all this, we are asked to believe, was accomplished without Gardiner's knowledge, though 'the fame of her departure reached to Leigh, a town at the land's end, before her approaching thither' (C. H. Garrett, *Marian Exiles* (1938), p. 11. Foxe, op. cit. VIII, 569-76).

[5] *A.P.C. 1554-56*, pp. 180, 277, 283-4, 294.

exile in Brabant, Germany and Poland, sometimes in sore straits, until Mary's death.[1]

In the twenty years preceding that event many momentous things had happened: the breach with Rome, successive changes in doctrine and church order, savage persecution, clerical deprivation, the dissolution of religious houses, and perhaps coming closer to the citizens, the dissolution of the chantries and religious gilds with its marked effect on those bodies which were half religious, half secular. Furthermore, there was the change in ownership of a high proportion of the land in the city and neighbourhood. It was seldom in any grant of land in Lincoln in the later Middle Ages that one of the boundaries was not a boundary of land belonging to a religious foundation; sometimes two of them were, and as one boundary was usually upon a highway, it may be guessed that perhaps a third of the land in the city and suburbs was affected. In 1291 fifty-five ecclesiastical foundations had land in the deanery (that is, the city) of Lincoln. The Minster total was the highest; Bardney, the Black Monks (the Lincoln cell) and St Mary of York came next. Kirkstead, Revesby, Kyme, Barlings, Worksop and Stainfield formed a second class; St Katharine came relatively low, but its demesne lands were important.

All these things coming together would have a great effect upon the modern mind. It is not so clear, however, how much the plain folk of the time understood, or indeed how much they knew. The changes in ownership only worked themselves out slowly, and there is no sign that there was a sudden orgy of land speculation. In the course of several generations the great holdings broke up, and separate properties came into the hands of the citizens. There can be little doubt that in the long run the break-up of great estates held in mortmain must have been a healthy thing; it made for enterprise.[2]

Nevertheless, the process was probably unpleasant. The enormous grants of monastic lands procured by Suffolk made him the leading landowner in the county, and with his grants of lands of St Katharines, Barlings, Louth Park, Kirkstead and Nocton he became also a great Lincoln landlord. After his death his duchess was at least twice in Lincoln, no doubt in part

---

[1] Writing to Cecil from her exile, she warned him of the evils of halting between two opinions in matters of religion. Sir Richard Morison, our ambassador at Augsburg, complained of 'Lady Suffolk's heats', which have 'oft cumbered him'. 'It is a great pity', he adds, 'that so goodly a wit waiteth upon so froward a will' (*C.S.P. For. 1547–53*, p. 101; Garrett, op. cit. p. 89.) There is a modern biography by Lady Cecilie Goff, *A Woman of the Tudor Age* (1930).

[2] Cf. White's *Gazetteer* for Lincoln (1856), p. 62: 'If the ecclesiastical property, which abounds in Lincoln, could be rendered freehold, or granted on long leases at fixed rentals, many of the unsightly old buildings which disfigure the principal streets would soon be supplanted by handsome new erections.'

engaged on estate management. Already in his lifetime he had begun to sell lands to pay his debts. In 1540 he obtained licence to sell St Katharine's priory to Vincent Grantham and his son Thomas,[1] who at once became busy in land in that area, and the great interest which Vincent took in the lead of the disused churches suggests that he was building or repairing his new property. The Kirkstead Abbey grange of Sheepwash at Canwick, which Suffolk was inclosing in 1543, presently appears as the property of Thomas Wilson's family. The Barlings grange, now known as Grange de Lings, he sold to his servant George St Paul in 1544; when George bought Suffolk's grange of Westlaby he borrowed the money from his father.[2] What remained of Suffolk's estates when his sons died was widely dispersed among his heirs general. Some of the Nocton and Louth Park lands in Lincoln came into the hands of the earl of Derby, who in 1583 sold them to Robert Smith of the Black Monks.[3]

The Black Monks lands, first leased to a dependant of Thomas Cromwell, came into the hands of the Sapcote family by 1548, and later of Robert Smith,[4] with both of whom the citizens had much bickering about rights of common until they were settled by Smith's surrender of land which became the Monks Leys Common, and is now the Arboretum.[5]

The lands of three of the friaries were not very important. The Austin Friars, four acres, was let to Robert Dighton,[6] a member of a Lincoln family who bought Stixwould and Haverholme priories; the Black Friars, ten acres, were let to alderman Thomas Burton, and sold, after an unsuccessful bid by alderman Rotherham, to John Broxholme of Owersby and John Bellow of Grimsby, speculators who dealt largely in monastic lands. The bells and lead of the White Friars were taken to the king's use, and Henry Sapcote tenanted the land until it was sold to Broxholme.

The fourth friary met with a better fate. The site of the Grey Friars, with about four acres of land, was let in 1540 to William Monson, then of Ingleby, for 21 years.[7] It was included in particulars for a grant to Bellow and another, but it had become Robert Monson's property by 1568, and he put it to a worthy use.[8] The friars' water supply was secured for the city.

---

[1] L. & P. Henry VIII, xv, no. 831. Vincent's younger brother, Hugh Grantham of Dunholme, was the duke's auditor (ibid. XVI, no. 714).

[2] L. & P. Henry VIII, XIX (i), no. 812 (p. 507); A. R. Maddison, Lincolnshire Wills 1500–1600 (1888), p. 139.

[3] The deed is in my possession.

[4] L. & P. Henry VIII, XIV (i), nos. 591, 963; XIV (ii), no. 522. In 1579 Henry Sapcote sold the Black Monks to Robert Smith of South Ingleby and Richard Smith of Lincoln for £1015, and Richard in 1580 released his interest to Robert (Lindsey County Council, B.R.A. deposit 57/11).

[5] M.L. pp. 341–3.

[6] A.A.S.R. XXII (1894), 192.

[7] L. & P. Henry VIII, xv, no. 561.

[8] See below, p. 102.

In 1535 the common council had given the warden of the friars leave to lay his conduit in the city's common land. After the dissolution the city bought two conduits. One was ordered to be brought to the city and set up in such a place as the workmen should choose; the other was to be taken up and kept. Any lead not needed was to be sold to pay the workmen, and the balance to go towards the purchase of the conduits from the king. In 1540 the inhabitants of the south ward were given a supply of water to a conduit to be set up where they should think best. It was erected, and still stands, in front of St Mary's church: Leland called it the 'new castelle of the conduite'.[1]

In the decade after the break-up of the religious houses came the end of the chantries. The traffic in their lands was in the control of the Court of Augmentations, which made large claims against the city for arrears of rent due to the chantries. The greatest buyers of chantry lands in the city were Sir John Thynne, steward to the protector Somerset, and Thomas Throckmorton. They bought the lands of Tattershall and Fitzmartin chantries, a house of Dalderby chantry, lands of Cantilupe, Benson, Cancia and Lacy chantries in the Minster, and the rent of seven marks payable for religious purposes to the Great Gild.[2] William Cecil bought Burton St Lazarus in Leicestershire, which gave him the Malandry in Lincoln, and the Blyton and Burghersh chantries were sold to speculators from the south.[3]

The mayor and his brethren viewed the whole of the chantry lands in the city, and resolved to buy in the 7 marks of rent charged on the great gild lands, employing Broxholme as their agent for the purpose. Matters of account remained outstanding for many years; in 1593 the common council were still faced with demands for arrears of rent for their gild lands. The city was also concerned with the Burghersh chantry, to which had been granted part of the fee-farm of the city, and they inquired whether their payment was entered in the books of the Court as a fee-farm rent or an annuity.

It seems also that the dean and chapter were confronted by a claim that some of the chantry endowments had not been surrendered as they should have been, the non-disclosure having been brought to light by a commission of concealed lands. In 1590 the dean and chapter employed agents to buy them in, allowing the agents to reimburse themselves by leases for 80 years, and being content themselves with the reversion.[4] They had to

---

[1] *Itinerary*, ed. Toulmin Smith, I, 31. Fragments dug up on the site of the White Friars in 1832 included canopies and other ornamental details similar to those on the conduit (Willson Collection (Society of Antiquaries), v, 59).

[2] *C.P.R. Ed. VI*, II, p. 332.

[3] *C.P.R. Ed. VI*, v, p. 182; I, p. 409; III, p. 46.   [4] L.A.O., D. & C. A/I/8–9.

PLATE 5

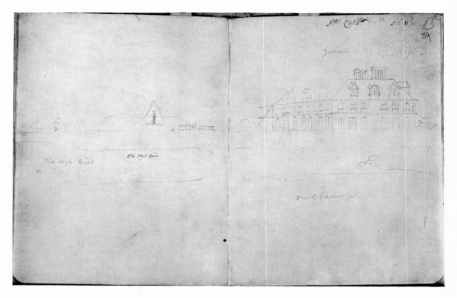

THE GRANTHAM FAMILY MANSION,
formerly on the site of St Katharine's Priory
From Buck's sketch book in the Bodleian Library

wait until 1604 for a grant of all manors, etc., formerly granted to superstitious users, with confirmation of ancient liberties.[1]

All this upheaval and uncertainty must have caused dislocation and distress, and contributed to the great influx of beggars into the towns which was one of the most serious problems of the century. There was, however, another cause, which came much more closely into the lives of all. It was the general rise in prices. This was due to reasons beyond the understanding of plain folk. Silver was pouring into Europe from the mines of Mexico and Peru, and so reducing the purchasing power of money. Henry VIII's debasement of the currency had aggravated the problem, and even its restoration by Elizabeth was not to arrest the price rise. In times of inflation some classes can maintain or restore their real incomes; wages gradually follow prices, as do rents as leases fall in. But the poor, the aged, and those on fixed incomes are powerless, and charity is not so elastic as wages and rents. And even those living on wages and rents must suffer in the short run, for there is a time lag in the adjustment of levels, and in a slow-moving age the process of adjustment might well occupy a generation or more.

A clear indication of the significance of the price rise is given by the verdicts of one of the juries at the annual Michaelmas court leet. The average price of the best corn during six recorded years in the decade 1520–30 was 7s. 4d. per quarter; for the eight years 1543–50 it had risen to 12s. 4d.; for nine years in the period 1551–60 it was 15s. 2d. At first it was only wheat prices which were thus recorded, in spite of various difficulties with the bakers,[2] and the inference that the common people generally ate white bread seems to be justified. During the period 1533–9 the price was not recorded. When it was recorded again in 1539 wheat showed no increase, but beans and peas and oats for the first time appear in the returns of the jury. Beans and peas were 4s., oats 3s. For the eight years 1543–50 beans and peas averaged 6s. 1½d., and in 1551–60, 8s. 10½d. In 1544–50 oats averaged 3s. 9d.; in 1551–60, 5s. 5d. Barley was still not returned.

Some years were especially bad. At Michaelmas 1549 best wheat was 12s.; by November it was 13s., and search was made for grain withheld from the market; in December it was 14s. 6d., and the bakers gave up their assize because wheat was in fact over 20s. By Easter it was 15s., and after harvest it was 21s. Oats had not exceeded 3s. until Michaelmas 1549, when they were 4s.; at Easter 6s.; and at Michaelmas 1550, 8s. Beans and peas

---

[1] *C.S.P.D. 1603–10*, p. 129.
[2] See above, p. 30. All average prices are based on Michaelmas figures, and where there is more than one price the highest has been taken.

were, Michaelmas 1549, 5s. 4d.; Easter 1550, 8s.; Michaelmas 1550, 14s. In November 1551 a secret council decided, wheat being at a high price, 23s. or 24s. or more, and other grain also very high, to fix the assize at 22s. 6d.; ale was not to exceed 3d. a gallon. Soon afterwards there was a period of five weeks in which there was no wind, the mills stood still, and horse mills and querns were brought into use; even horsebread gave out. An assize was fixed at 24s., and bakers were ordered to send their grain to be ground at country water-mills.

In twenty years the cost of cereals had doubled, and whether or not their prices are a reliable index of the cost of living it is clear that so rapid a rise must have caused intense hardship to a community living close to the starvation level, at the mercy of each harvest, and with the difficulty and cost of transport too great for a stricken area to receive relief from other areas. A comparison of decennial averages for Lincoln with Thorold Rogers's figures for the country generally[1] shows no wide differences. London prices were sometimes higher and sometimes lower than Lincoln prices; markets cannot much have influenced each other. In trying to compute hardship it must, moreover, be remembered that great fluctuations are more disturbing than a gradual rise. A famine year like 1550 would ruin many and throw others out of work, and a partial fall in prices in following years would not avail to rehabilitate them if they had joined the army of unemployed and perhaps taken to the road.

The able-bodied unemployed were the sturdy beggars of the period. Perhaps it was to discourage them that a pillory was set up in St Benedict's parish. In 1541 the constables were ordered to search for vagabonds and unauthorised beggars and bring them before the mayor; and when the order was repeated in 1544 it was added that the names of authorised beggars should be recorded and that ensigns should be given to them to wear. A new poor law measure led to a definition of the four wards of the city, the 'four towns' ranking as a fifth, several aldermen being assigned to each for the reformation and punishment of vagabonds and for the putting to work of young people. Nine aldermen were given areas in 1547. They were to see the streets kept clear, and all valiant vagabonds, strong beggars and idle suspicious persons punished and expelled from the city. The impotent poor might be given beggar badges if they had been in the city for three years past or born and brought up in the city; unlawful games must be prevented and offenders put in the stocks. These orders were proclaimed by the bellman throughout the city, and every curate read them in church.

The orders were not easy to enforce; they were repeated in February

[1] *History of Agriculture and Prices*, IV (1882), 292.

1548, and the mayor was asked to parade all the poor in St Hugh Croft; the able-bodied must be put to work, and the prisons and the stocks repaired.

Plague made matters worse. To avoid risk of infection and keep the sick in their houses a fund was opened for their relief in 1550, every alderman paying 4*d*. weekly, and every sheriff's peer 2*d*.; constables and church-wardens collected in the parishes and accounted to the mayor. If any refused to pay he was assessed by the mayor. Compulsion was creeping in. When plague broke out again in 1557 the masters of the Close and gentle-men of worship and others of ability living uphill were invited to subscribe. The plague still raged in the following spring, when aldermen were appointed to parishes to see good order kept and risk of infection reduced.

There was a more constructive effort to cope with the problem of unemployment in 1551, when four aldermen, William Alanson, George Stamp, William Hutchinson and William Rotherham, with John Hutchin-son, proposed to establish the cloth trade, and asked the council for land and premises. The proposals were welcome. The promoters, with the mayor, were voted a piece of ground for a walk mill at 4*d*. a year, and the disused church of Holy Rood for a dyehouse, with a condition that if twenty broadcloths were not produced yearly—save in time of plague—they must pay a rent of £10. Tenters could be set and cloths dried on the close at the west end of the church, and they could have the churchyard if they could get it. They were also given a piece of the commons beyond Bishopbridge to inclose, so that spinners and weavers might have fodder for kine in winter and pasture in summer. They were promised the clerks' hall and the shoemakers' hall at 2*s*. a year.

The cloth workers designed to take all idle people, young and otherwise, and have them for eight or nine years, finding them meat, drink, cloth and other sufficient necessaries. Idle persons who refused work were to be given a month's warning to leave the city. If any stole wool or yarn delivered to them they would for the first offence be punished as vagabonds, and for the second whipped out of the city and forbidden to return. Freemen might join the fellowship on payment of an entry fee. By way of encouragement buyers of cloth or sellers of raw material were to be free of toll for seven years.

There were difficulties at once. The shoemakers resisted the grant of their hall, and a house was found instead. The relation of the new craft to the old gild of weavers had to be defined. Clothiers were directed to pay to the weavers for their upset in being sworn brethren 3*s*. 4*d*. with a yearly payment of 1*s*. for the farm of their looms; with a proviso that they should not work any cloths other than their own or those of other clothiers, on pain of the penalties in the weavers' charter. A statute having been passed in 1551 for the protection of craftsmen, the Lincoln clothiers were helped by the common council to apply for royal licence to buy and sell wool throughout the county, to be shipped at Boston haven, and for the inclusion of towns and hamlets within four or five miles of the city within the city's liberties.

The enterprise did not prosper. In 1558 the council asked whether the twenty broadcloths a year had been made which would release them from payment of rent for Holy Rood. It appears that for several years few or none had been made; rent was demanded, and no more is heard of the clothiers for some time.

In the general shortage of ready money young craftsmen had difficulty in finding money to set themselves up, and in order to increase the funds available for loans to them, it was resolved in 1557 that the mayor should abate £10 of his official salary, and the sheriffs have only £20 and the rent corn of the White House at Canwick (which was barley) and the weavers' £6, and during the rest of their year they were allowed to take reasonable tolls. This proviso seems to refer to a short-lived experiment tried in 1554, when Lincoln was declared a free city and tolls abolished for inhabitants and strangers, kendall men and through wavering men, alike. It was fair rather than free trade; if any towns took toll of Lincoln then toll was to be taken of their men. The setting up of the young craftsmen with tools and perhaps stock was of vital importance; without them the companies would die out and the whole city become unemployed.

CHAPTER IV

THE REIGN OF ELIZABETH I

WHEN writs were issued for a new parliament on the accession of Elizabeth I the common council accepted Rutland's nomination of Farrar for one seat,[1] and resolved that a calendar be made of three or four townsmen from whom the other should be chosen; there was no intention of surrendering the second seat also.[2] The recorder St Paul was dying, and in his place they elected Robert Monson, who was to prove a good friend to the city. He was a younger son of William Monson of South Carlton, and was educated at Cambridge and Lincoln's Inn. He sat in the last parliament of Edward VI and several of Mary's for Dunheved or other Cornish borough, and his father's death having put him in possession of property near Lincoln he no doubt welcomed a seat nearer home. He took a lease of a house in the Close of the dean and chapter; it stood on the east side of Pottergate.[3]

In parliament he became one of the Puritan leaders,[4] and sat on several important committees, notably on one set up in 1566 which petitioned the queen to marry. He made some strong remarks on the evasive nature of her reply, and 'grated hard on her royal prerogative'.[5] In 1574 he became a judge of the common bench, but two years later displeased the queen by expressing doubts as to the force of a statute of Mary under which a prisoner's hand was cut off;[6] in 1579 he was a prisoner in the Fleet, being later allowed to go home.[7]

The city needed all the support it could get against Rutland, for when a few days after the election St Paul died, the common council with significant haste elected Anthony Thorold as recorder in his stead.[8] There

[1] See above, p. 53.
[2] The writ had not arrived, and when it came the sheriffs were alarmed lest they should get into trouble if the election were deferred to the next county day, and they wrote to the privy council with an explanation, which was accepted (*A.P.C. 1558–70*, p. 41).
[3] Ex inf. Mr C. L. Exley; and see *St Margaret's Parish Registers 1538–1837*, ed. C. W. Foster (L.R.S. 1915), pp. 33–4, 36, 52–3.
[4] J. E. Neale, *Elizabeth I and her Parliaments, 1559–1581* (1953), index.
[5] *Parliamentary History* (1806), I, 709, 715, 779.
[6] It was the case of John Stubbs, the author of a Puritan tract.
[7] *C.S.P.D. 1547–80*, p. 530; *A.P.C. 1578–80*, p. 350; E. Foss, *The Judges of England* (1870), *sub nom.*
[8] St Paul made his will 30 December 1558; it was proved 22 February 1559. A. R. Maddison, *Lincolnshire Pedigrees* (Harleian Society, III, 845). Thorold was appointed on 16 January, and sworn a freeman and in office on the 19th.

can be little doubt that Thorold was Rutland's nominee, elected under pressure instead of Monson, whom the council probably had in mind.

Thorold's family seat was at Marston near Grantham; he was M.P. for that borough in 1557, probably nominated by Rutland. Later he was deputy lieutenant to the fourth earl, and was one of the chief mourners at his funeral in 1588. His stately tomb, with Sir Anthony, as he had become, in full armour, survives at Marston.[1]

The city's representatives were asked to sue for anything which they thought would be for the weal of the city; and if it should be decided to set up the staple within the realm (Calais having been lost), to petition that Lincoln should be the staple town for the east midlands as it had once been. Failing this, they might ask that the city should have the portsail and shipping of wool in the county either for ever or for a term of years on payment of the queen's customs, with the right for the whole corporation to buy and sell wool to merchants or clothiers within the realm. The extension of the county of the city to a radius of three or four miles was mooted again, with a note that York had towns twelve miles away within the liberties. Finally, it was desired to seek the usual remission of tenths and fifteenths. The sole result of this ambitious programme was that Mr Secretary Cecil promised the city's burgesses exemption from the tax. This was granted, and was soon being sought again.

It is significant of the city's attitude to Thorold that it retained for its legal business Monson and Christopher Wray, first voting them 26s. 8d. each yearly, and then promising Monson 40s. yearly for life. Wray was later to become speaker of the House of Commons and chief justice of the queen's bench, and one of the judges at the trial of Mary Queen of Scots. He had already been in parliament; in 1563 he became Member for Grimsby, and by 1576 he had bought an estate in Lincolnshire and founded his family at Glentworth. But even so he had not established the position in the county that Monson enjoyed, for in that year he complained to Rutland that Justice Monson had been packing the commission of gaol delivery with his friends, and leaving out those of best worship.[2]

The retainer of Monson and Wray evidently vexed Thorold, for within a few weeks the common council resolved that he, who was after all their recorder, in consideration that he should be diligent, should hold office for

[1] He seems to have been a dull man, though not too dull to quarrel with Arthur Hall, the irascible M.P. for Grantham. About this quarrel Roger Manners wrote in 1582 to the third earl of Rutland that 'I am glad to hear that Mr Thorold in his old age is become so lively that he is charged with making a riot or an unlawful assembly' (*H.M.C. Rutland*, i, 145, 244, 248; H. G. Wright, *Life and Works of Arthur Hall of Grantham* (1919), pp. 98–102).

[2] *H.M.C. Rutland*, i, 110.

PLATE 6

MEMORIAL BRASS OF ROBERT MONSON
formerly in Lincoln Cathedral

By permission of the Winchelsea Settled Trustees

life at a fee of £4. But they relied on Monson, and in 1564 laid it down that it should be lawful for the mayor to have him at any meeting of the council or secret council, and use his aid and counsel for the weal and profit of the city and the administration of justice within it; though it looks as if Thorold countered again in a resolution that dinner at quarter sessions should be at the mayor's house, so that the mayor and his brethren could debate secret matters with the recorder. When the city became involved in disputes it was to these lawyers that they turned, with the addition of John Aylmer the strong-minded archdeacon of Lincoln,[1] and local notables like Lord Willoughby of Parham, who had married a Heneage and settled at Knaith, and Sir Francis Ayscough.

Presently Thorold and Monson drew together, and in 1570 Thorold asked to be displaced from the recordership in favour of Monson, he taking the lesser retainer of 40s. and Monson the larger of £4. Monson and Farrar were returned to parliament by the city again in 1562, but in 1571 there came in with Monson Thomas Wilson, 'elected for divers good considerations and for the weal of the city'.

Wilson was one of a distinguished group of Lincolnshire men of whom Fuller remarked that as the county equalled other shires in all ages, so it went beyond itself in one generation in the reign of Elizabeth.[2] He was born at Strubby near Alford, and in his book *The Arte of Rhetorique* draws for his examples on his memories of the Lincolnshire rising, Partney fair, and the like.[3] At Cambridge he came under the influence of the great Greek scholars Sir John Cheke, Sir Thomas Smith and Roger Ascham. He acquired 'all the Elizabethan's impatience of rusticity and dulness';[4] and yet he owed much to his Lincolnshire friends. It was at the house of Sir Edward Dymoke that he wrote his book on rhetoric. He enjoyed the friendship of the formidable duchess of Suffolk, and was tutor to her two sons, and he was helped to high office by Cecil.

He was a zealous protestant, and under Mary he went into exile at Padua with Sir John Cheke. In December 1557 'he became implicated in an intrigue at the papal court against Cardinal Pole. In January he was summoned by Philip and Mary to return to England and appear before the privy council. There can be no doubt what was the fate they had in

---

[1] See below, p. 96.

[2] *History of the Worthies of England* (1840 ed.), II, 265. For Wilson see John Strype, *Annals of the Reformation* (1824), I (i), 345–8; I (ii), 285–8, 367–9; II (i), 45–48, 340; II (ii), 152. Among the other worthies were Clinton (Lord Admiral), William Cecil (Lord Treasurer), Chief Justice Anderson, Archbishop Whitgift, and Peregrine Bertie (Lord General in France).

[3] *The Arte of Rhetorique*, edited by G. H. Mair, was reprinted in facsimile in 1909; see pp. 140, 210.   [4] Ibid. p. vi.

store for him; Wilson apparently recognised the meaning of the summons; he paid no heed, and was arrested in Rome by the Inquisition on a charge of heresy. His position was one of the greatest danger, and only the fortunate accident of an insurrection in the city prevented his death; apparently he had been already put to the torture.'[1] On the accession of Elizabeth he returned to England and found work, and in 1561 became Master of St Katharine's Hospital in the Tower and Master of Requests. He served as ambassador to Spain and Portugal and the Netherlands. In 1572 he was sent to 'expostulate by way of accusation' with Mary Queen of Scots, and in 1576 conducted negotiations for the proposed marriage of the queen with the duke of Anjou. He became secretary of state in 1577 and held office until his death in 1581.[2]

When Wilson was proposed as a burgess, probably by Monson, the council were at once agreeable. They resolved to make him a freeman without fee, and Monson, then recorder, was empowered to administer the oath to him. At the election of 1572 Monson was returned for Totnes (as his father had been in 1547), and Lincoln returned Wilson with alderman Welcome. When the council directed the collection of burgess money for Welcome from all the parishes they added hopefully that it should be levied also for 'Mr Dr Wilson the other citizen of the parliament if he will have it'. The following year Welcome was in disgrace. Among the charges against him was one that he had disclosed to Wilson a secret letter sent to Monson, 'by discovery whereof he did what in him might be in that matter to have procured the displeasure of Dr Wylson to this city who have ever been a very good and dear friend to the same'. Welcome was disaldered; but there is no hint of the subject-matter of the letter to Monson, still the city's closest confidant.

Meanwhile Edward Manners, third earl of Rutland, had come of age. He had been the queen's ward and under the supervision of Cecil, who drew up strict rules for his behaviour when he went to France. He served in the army during the rebellion of the northern earls in 1569, and was warmly commended by Sir Ralph Sadler.[3] Later he could be described as 'that magnificent Earl who kept an house like a Prince's Court'.[4] Very soon after he had taken charge of his own affairs he or his men of business reopened the old matter of the fee-farm rent. He demanded payment in

[1] *The Arte of Rhetorique* (ed. G. H. Mair), p. xi.

[2] For his will see *H.M.C. Salisbury*, ii, 391. The Wilson family acquired Sheepwash Grange, formerly parcel of the abbey of Kirkstead, through the Suffolk connection. Thomas's elder brother Humphrey became involved in a dispute with the city about rights of common.

[3] *C.S.P.D. 1566–79*, p. 180.

[4] *Memorials of the Holles Family*, ed. A. C. Wood (Camden Series, 1937), p. 215.

1573, and a perturbed common council sent to confer with the recorder and other counsel. Power was given to the mayor and others to deal with the earl at Newark, with an offer to abide by the award of Mr Justice Wray and Mr Justice Monson; there was nothing like having arbitrators who were friends. As before, the claim was being used as a means to secure patronage; this time Rutland was demanding the office of steward of the city. The request was firmly refused, but the council were so unwilling to fight that they were prepared to pay up to £300 in settlement, failing which they would defend any claim in the courts. Rutland pushed them to their limit, and they resolved in 1574 that as they would very shortly need great sums of money for the behoof of the common chamber 'as well for the payment of £300 to the earl of Rutland for the clear redemption and release of the fee farm of this city and also for other special causes as shall be more plainly declared and set forth hereafter in this book but not now to be spoken of', it was agreed to grant Monson a longer reversionary lease of Hanslope parsonage, to wit, 99 years at a rent of £80 to the city and £16 to the vicar or curate, Monson paying a total fine of £200; Hemswell and a farm at Canwick were also to be let. The promise to set out the secret reasons in the common council book was not redeemed; perhaps they referred to the customary stimulation of the goodwill of the arbitrators. The Rutland claim at last was laid.

Influence, however, continued. Monson ceased to be recorder in 1572, when Stephen Thimbleby was elected in a contest with Gregory Ion, it being declared that a promise had been made to the former before letters were received on Ion's behalf. Thimbleby was made recorder for life in 1573. At the parliamentary election of 1584 John Joyce, a stranger, sat with Thimbleby; and in 1586 John Savile, who bought Doddington in that year, and who was Thimbleby's half-brother, sat with Thomas Fairfax junior. Joyce and Fairfax were probably Rutland nominees.[1] Whether Thimbleby and Savile owed anything to the earl is not clear. Rutland's position was acknowledged in 1581 by John Monson when he wrote to the earl proposing his kinsman and friend Robert Dymoke of Lincoln, servant to the lord chamberlain, as burgess in Wilson's room.[2] The third earl died in 1586, and when soon afterwards Thimbleby died, Anthony Thorold wrote to the fourth earl (brother of the third) asking him to intervene on behalf of Mr Broxholme, and he did so. The common council had, however, already chosen George Anton as recorder and so forestalled them.[3] Broxholme was retained as counsel; the usual consola-

---

[1] J. E. Neale, *The Elizabethan House of Commons* (1949), p. 204. For Savile, Thimbleby and Anton see R. E. G. Cole, *History of Doddington* (1897), index.

[2] *H.M.C. Rutland*, I, 126.   [3] Ibid. p. 225.

tion prize. Within a few months the fourth earl was dead, and the Rutland family influence fell into abeyance during a long minority.

Anton had bought part of Doddington, and he married Jane, the daughter of Thomas Tailor, also of Doddington. He was returned to parliament for the city in 1588–9 with Peter Evers, who probably belonged to the family of that name at Belton in Axholme and Washingborough. Anton was returned again in 1592–3, this time with Charles Dymoke of Howell, who was made a freeman at the request of his nephew Sir Edward Dymoke, with a view to his election, he having always shown himself very courteous to the citizens, and promising to attempt in parliament anything that might be beneficial to the corporation and further that he would not claim burgess money.[1] Their successors in the parliament of 1597 were Thomas Monson and William Pelham, and in 1601 Anton sat again, this time with Francis Bullingham, son of the bishop, who was or was soon to become bishop's registrar; he asked for the seat.

The practice of returning citizens to Parliament had ceased. The council preferred the gentry; the lawyers they chose generally belonged to this class. Gentry had several advantages: they would not ask for burgess pence, they had to buy the freedom of the city, and their support was useful without being dangerous.

The nobility and gentry had some rights of entry to the city which the charters did nothing to prevent. They could not come in as justices of the peace; but when privy seals were issued by the queen for what were virtually forced loans they were sent to the county justices. In 1590 Sir John Monson was appointed commissioner under privy seal for Lincoln.[2] They could also enter as commissioners of the musters, and in troublous times, when danger threatened in turn from France, Spain, Scotland and Ireland, military preparations loomed large in the life of the time.

The rebellion of the northern earls in 1569 involved elaborate measures. Dudley earl of Warwick and Lord Clinton were joint lords lieutenant; of the county forces Robert Carre of Sleaford was treasurer, and among the officers were Heneage, Dymoke, Nevile and St Paul.[3] Treasure was sent to Carre at Newark in readiness for Warwick, who was urged to press north to Doncaster, and to draw on the manpower of Lincoln, Nottingham and south Yorkshire, and was assured that the rebels were common vulgar people and unarmed.[4] At Lincoln there was a great parade of all persons

[1] In this parliament was obtained exemption from six fifteenths granted to the queen.
[2] A.P.C. 1590–91, p. 186.
[3] M. P. Moore, The Family of Carre of Sleaford (1863), p. 16.
[4] H.M.C. Salisbury, I, 447–9.

chargeable with armour at the long butts in St Botolph's or in St Hugh Croft, in order that their long bows, arrows and quivers might be inspected; general watch was kept during the days of danger. When Clinton visited Lincolnshire he found the county apathetic. It had not yet been converted to protestantism; and an address, largely signed by the knights and gentlemen of the county, to Philip II of Spain, greeted him as the prince with the chief right to the crown.[1]

Preparation was intensified when the threat from Spain became sharper. In 1580 the city musters were committed to Lord Treasurer Burghley, Lord Lincoln (as Clinton had become), Rutland, Willoughby, the lord chief justice (Wray), the mayor, Robert Monson, Richard Bertie, Thimbleby, some gentry and six aldermen.[2] In 1583 the mayor and citizens protested that they could not furnish a lance and a light horse, and urged that at least a light horse might be substituted for the lance.[3] The next year the privy council sent notice to the sheriff and commissioners of musters that a gentleman was being sent down to see and report.[4] They in turn reported that they were having decayed armour made good, and asked that 200 pikes and burgonetts might be remitted.[5] Rutland, who was lord lieutenant, ordered the city to have in store £40 worth of gunpowder and match, and the common chamber was charged with this amount.

Thorold and Dymoke, who were deputy lieutenants, ordered the mayors of Lincoln and Boston to send money to a London merchant to buy the powder and match they were required to have in store. Both towns pleaded that the other corporate towns should be made to contribute, because Boston was charged with the haven, the sea dykes, and for the defence of Holland, and both towns were greatly charged with poor. The citizens of Lincoln, 'being no merchant venturers', would not commit their money to the sea with its perils of storm and piracy, and were sending it in carts early in the summer.[6]

By the time that the Spanish invasion was expected, Rutland was dead, and Lord Treasurer Burghley had taken over the lieutenancy of his native county. He was of course unusually dependent on his deputies, appointing Lord Willoughby of Parham, his son Sir Thomas Cecil, Dymoke and Thorold.[7] Orders already made were put into operation; they have a

[1] J. A. Froude, *History of England*, IX, 159.
[2] *A.P.C. 1580–81*, pp. 55–6.   [3] *C.S.P.D. 1581–90*, p. 125.
[4] *H.M.C. Rutland*, I, 163.   [5] *C.S.P.D. 1581–90*, p. 156.
[6] *H.M.C. Rutland*, I, 193. In 1588 the deputy lieutenants reported that the towns of Lincoln, Boston and Grimsby had fallen into great decay and poverty by God's long visitation (*H.M.C. Cowper*, I, 10).
[7] *H.M.C. Savile Foljambe*, p. 25, and see p. 37.

familiar sound to the present generation. Petronels were provided, carriers of news repressed, and a look-out kept for landings, in this case of Jesuits.

Like arrangements were made when danger of invasion recurred in 1595, when Willoughby of Parham reported to Burghley that he had viewed the horse and foot bands in Lindsey and Lincoln, and supplied their wants with sufficient and able men. Many of the foot had bows and bills, but by the advice of Captain Buck he had changed the bows into swords, muskets and calivers, which made the bands much fairer and stronger than before.[1] That year the mayor was allowed payments to the muster master in his accounts, and gunpowder was bought for twenty nobles. The gunpowder in store had either deteriorated or had a mishap, for in 1597 some of it was 'repaired', and the rest changed or made new or new bought; an extraordinary watch and ward was instituted.

The expedition to Ireland in 1599 brought on the county an assessment of twenty-seven lances and thirty-nine light horse; among the contributory gentry were Thomas Grantham, assessed at one lance and two light horse, Sir Thomas Monson, two lances and three light horse, and Charles Hussey, two of each.[2] Sir Edward Dymoke asked for employment; seeing that he was her majesty's 'sworn and born champion' he wanted either the charge of the Lincolnshire lances or the vacant charge of Sir John Bolles, then in Ireland.[3] By 1599, 300 men from the county were under arms for the Irish expedition.[4] It was commanded by Lord Essex. In the rising that he attempted on his return the young earl of Rutland and two others of the Manners family were implicated. Rutland was sent to the Tower, but presently allowed to go to the house of Roger Manners at Uffington.[5]

The authority of the gentry in military matters, coupled with their great influence rooted in ownership of land, social position and money power, made it difficult for the citizens to withstand interference by them.

[1] C.S.P.D. 1595–97, p. 109. In 1596 the county was ordered to provide 3000 men against a Spanish invasion. A.P.C. 1596–97, p. 290. For Buck, see H.M.C. Ancaster, passim.
[2] H.M.C. Savile Foljambe, p. 80. When 150 were ordered to Plymouth for Ireland, Burghley as lord lieutenant objected, and in deference to him they were sent to Chester (A.P.C. 1597–98, p. 600).
[3] H.M.C. Salisbury, IX, 299; XII, 517; XIV, 148. Some of the horses were inspected at Chester and found defective. Three men ran away.
[4] A.P.C. 1598–99, pp. 96, 490, 543, 678. New levies were made in 1601 to meet the Spanish invasion of Ireland (A.P.C. 1601–4, pp. 225, 242, 476); money was required from the county to equip the London levies (ibid. p. 77); eighteen of the gentry were summoned to furnish each a man and horse with equipment (ibid. p. 280).
[5] In the last years of the reign Thomas Cecil, now become Lord Burghley, became President of the North, and was nominally engaged in 1603 in readiness to withstand the Scots, until his brother Robert, now Secretary, was ready to acknowledge James VI of Scotland, with whom he had been in touch, as king. Clinton, earl of Lincoln, was also found to have been in touch with James (C.S.P.D. 1601–3, pp. 225, 230).

A government concerned with emergency measures, armed with arbitrary powers and impatient of any chartered rights which stood in the way, made the danger to the boroughs all the greater. The executive would no doubt have liked to assimilate the boroughs to the counties. It would have made for administrative ease, but it could only be done at the expense of the rights and privileges of the corporations. An example of this tendency occurs in 1596. The privy council wrote to the mayor, aldermen and other officers of the city, recalling that they had lately written to the county justices requiring them to take good order for the reformation of many abuses in markets whereby the dearth of corn was grievously increased. The justices had returned that the city of Lincoln, being a special county of itself, did not admit the commissioners of the shire:

> You are to consider that in a time of such necessity as this it is unfit to stand curiously and precisely upon advantages of privileges, when it is much more fit for every man to put his helping hand to supply the common want and to relieve the extremity of the poor people, and therefore we do pray and require you, all such curiosity set apart, to join with the commissioners and justices of that shire, and in all such orders as they shall go about to execute according to our directions to proceed jointly with them for the said reformation, that the same being followed by common consent of you and them, may take place both within your city and without and everywhere in the county, wherein you shall do us very good service unto your country, and yet without any impeachment of your liberties.[1]

The privy council had in the first instance either forgotten or ignored the county of the city of Lincoln, and then sought to blame the city. Within the velvet glove of co-operation was the iron hand of absolutism, which was bound to clash with the common law and the chartered rights of the towns.

After the violent changes of the Reformation period, the policy of Elizabeth and her ministers was to seek stability and order in ecclesiastical and social affairs. They held that, so far as possible, men should remain not only in the station to which God had called them, but preferably also in the craft and even the parish to which they belonged. A general review of all questions of employment and unemployment was therefore

---

[1] *A.P.C. 1596–97*, p. 188. Coventry was charged with standing on overmuch nice and curious construction of liberties, and ordered to send up its charter to be considered (*A.P.C. 1597*, p. 175; *A.P.C. 1597–98*, p. 178). For Bristol's dispute with the lord lieutenant of Gloucester about musters, see A. L. Rowse, *The England of Elizabeth* (1950), p. 170. In 1596 Lord Cobham and Sir Robert Cecil wrote to Lincoln claiming that the mayor and citizens had promised the office of sheriffs' clerk to Edward Wadeson. The mayor denied the promise, and referred the claim to the sheriffs, who said they had already made a promise to another. The place 'is not worth half the suit that is made for it'. The reply was signed by the mayor and eight aldermen; the other four made their marks (*H.M.C. Salisbury*, VI, 422).

needed. A programme of legislation, framed no doubt by the queen's Secretary of State, William Cecil, in 1559, planned to abolish the maximum wage of earlier Statutes of Labourers, and to substitute the fixing of wages by justices at sessions. He proposed to add the rule that no man should employ a servant without a testimonial from his last master, sealed with a parish seal kept by constable or churchwarden, witnessing that he left with the free licence of his master; and 'so, by the heed of the masters, servants may be reduced to obedience, which shall reduce obedience to the Prince and to God also; by the looseness of the times no other remedy is left but by awe of law to acquaint men with virtue again, whereby the reformation of religion may be brought in credit, with the amendment of manners, the want whereof hath been imputed as a thing grown by the liberty of the Gospel etc.'[1]

In pursuance of this policy there was passed the Statute of Artificers in 1563.[2] It left its mark on the life of the country for several centuries, lasting longest perhaps in the provision that contracts for service in many of the crafts must not be for a period of less than a year. Servant men and women out of a place attended the 'statutes'—or the stattice—where they could hire themselves for a year and accept the hiring penny. In Lincoln one of the retiring sheriffs became high constable for the next year, as the one retiring sheriff still does; and it was his duty to fix and proclaim the date of the hiring statutes. The annual notice, to which less and less attention was paid with the passing of the years, continued to be posted, directing unemployed workers to attend at the Stonebow, until 1925.[3] The justices early made the rule that unemployed workmen and labourers must repair to the Stonebow every morning and stand there with their tools for one hour at least, on pain of imprisonment without bail during the mayor's or the justices' pleasure.

The statute required the justices to fix the wages of artificers, husbandmen and labourers, and certify them to the Court of Chancery; whereupon the rates should be proclaimed and all persons commanded in her highness's name straitly to observe and keep the same. The mayor and justices duly certified on 12 June 1563 that they had not only conferred with other

[1] *H.M.C. Salisbury*, I, 162–5, quoted in R. H. Tawney and E. Power, *Tudor Economic Documents* (1924), I, 325.

[2] 5 Eliz. I, c. 4.

[3] By that time only agricultural workers still hired themselves by the year. By the High Constable's Office Abolition Act 1869 (32 & 33 Vic. c. 47) the office of high constable was abolished save where that officer was a returning officer, was charged with the supervision of the register of electors, or was vested by virtue of his office with any real property. He seems not to have performed any such duties in Lincoln, but the retiring sheriff continued to assume the title, as he still does, in lofty disregard of the Act (see *Notes and Queries*, 10th ser. XII (1909), 309).

discreet persons of the city and suburbs and county of the city, 'but also having understanding and respect to the scarcity and dearth of all kinds of grain and victuals there at this time, that is to say, the quarter of wheat sold for 40s., the quarter of rye sold for 36s. 8d., the quarter of malt sold for 22s., the quarter of beans, peasen and barley sold for 26s. 8d., the quarter of mutton and veal sold for 20d., the quarter of beef sold for 16d., and white meat after 5 eggs a penny, the buttercake weighing one lb. and three quarters 5d., and the stone of cheese after 20d., and other necessary victuals very dear', they fixed the wage scales accordingly. The proclamation with the justices' certificate was duly printed and set up in public places. Perhaps it was the first time that printing had been used for municipal purposes in Lincoln, for the whole was solemnly written in the minute book, including not only 'God save the Queen' but also the printers' imprint: 'imprinted at london in Powles Churchyard by Richard Jugge and John Cawood prynters to the Queen's Matie. Cum privilegiis regie maiestatis.'[1]

The statute further prescribed a minimum apprenticeship of seven years for the crafts, and made necessary a review of the charters of the gilds or companies. The need for such a review was obvious enough. The loss of religious functions and endowments, and the income from 'honorary' members, or outbrothers, who had shared in the spiritual benefits of the gilds, cannot fail to have had a great effect on their affairs. There was also a decline in the number of craftsmen which made it necessary to combine some of the smaller trades in companies for effectiveness. If the cordwainers can be taken as typical of the crafts, it would seem that they had not resumed their craft functions after the legislation of Edward VI. When the cordwainers resumed their entries in their register in March 1562 they not only elected officers but compounded for the admission of journeymen and ex-apprentices, which suggests that there had been no regular business done for some time. Quarterly payments by the brethren were not begun again until 1563.

Municipal control over the trades was resumed with the enforcement of the old rules of apprenticeship and craft monopoly without waiting for the passing of the statute. The common council then turned to the overhaul of the gild charters, beginning with the tailors. Their charter was examined and corrected; the council approved 'provisoes' and left it to the mayor and aldermen to put them in and seal the charter. It was sealed in 1562. It recited that the occupation was not great in substance, and that the statutes long time theretofore granted by the mayor and citizens had, to the hurt of the city, not been observed. It confirmed a monopoly of the

---

[1] For the wage rates see App. II.

trade in the city and suburbs to the company—the old name of 'gild' had gone. A seven years' apprentice or a journeyman after four years' service was admitted a member for a fee of 3s. 4d., but a foreign trader only on payment of an 'upset' fee of 40s. and a fine of £3. 6s. 8d. if he had not had four years' service. The fine for infringement of the monopoly was 46s. 8d., of which 10s. went to the common chamber, 6s. 8d. to the sheriffs, and the rest to the master of the company. 'Foreign' tailors were forbidden to work in private houses, and even a member of the company must not do so save for one day at the customer's pleasure; if a citizen employed a tailor in his house who was not a master man and a brother he too was fined. Refusal to pay penalties meant trial according to the laws and customs of the city, with committal to ward without bail for guilt or obstinacy.

Standards of work were enforced by rules for manufacture and the appointment of searchers for faults. Every brother must attend the quarterly mornspeech day, and serve in office when required. For a brother in need there was 6d. a week for life, with provision for burial. A tight hand was kept on the journeyman. If he worked with a master for 15 days he must pay for his knowledge 4d. to the company; if for a year, 12d. Any hired servant must pay 12d. If a master hired a servant engaged by another master without the latter's licence he was fined. Disputes were referred to the arbitration of the mayor, an ex-mayor, the master of the company and four brethren.

The cordwainers followed the tailors. Their charter declared that they had in time past laudable ordinances, as appeared by a charter of 1389, ratified in 1516. The mayor and citizens 'remembering how mete a thing it is for a craftsman to judge of a craft...have thought it good to grant... these articles'. They were like those of the tailors. There were to be no markets on Sundays, or wares sold at church doors, except at fairtime, or to any gentleman, or in case of need. No cordwainer might have two shops, or sell at St Hugh's Fair or Midsummer Fair. All must keep open shop where they dwelt according to custom. That inferior being the cobbler must keep his place; he must not use new leather, horseskin, or unlawful leather in deceit of the common people. Searchers for leather were appointed yearly by the common council.

When the council came to the painters, gilders, stainers and alabastermen they adopted the pre-Reformation charter, written for better understanding in English. Soon afterwards there was made the interesting declaration that the dyers and listers were then of a wealthy and commodious occupation, and need not use any other trade; and they were therefore forbidden to trade as shearmen or fullers.

PLATE 7

THOMAS WILSON

By permission of the Trustees of the National Portrait Gallery

It was repeated in 1563 that all occupations should have charters, and a new one was granted to the artificers, smiths, ironmongers, armourers, spurriers, cutlers, horse-marshals and wire-drawers. This was not a new amalgamation, for they had of ancient time been of one company 'to the maintenance of cunning workmanship and the extirpation of uncunning deceivers'. Rules of a familiar kind were made. Only a smith or an iron-monger might be graceman of the company. 'Foreigners' might only sell in gross to a brother, and no 'foreign' horse-marshal might trade for more than three days without an agreement with the mayor.

Next came the artificers, glovers, girdlers, skinners, pinners, pointers, scriveners and parchment-makers, also of ancient time one company. For their protection tanners were forbidden to buy sheepskins which were their stock in trade. The artificers, tilers, masons, bricklayers, plasterers, pavers, tile-makers, glaziers, lime-makers, millers and thackers were put together in one company; the wrights were promised a charter; the tanners and butchers were combined and promised a lease of the chapel on the High Bridge, and the carpenters and their associates were promised a house.

As became their vital importance to the citizens the victualling trades were subject to special control. Every year the mayor fixed the assize of bread per quarter of corn, and ale per gallon, and there was a formula relating the size of the loaf to the price per quarter.[1] Bread was in future to be weighed oftener, and the bakers were set to watch the millers, and the millers the bakers and the weighing of their wheat. In 1558 the bakers were told that they could have a new charter on condition that they served the city with all kinds of bread henceforth according to the intent and meaning thereof. Having promised to conform, they were granted their charter, and warned that they must answer for not having bread. They were again allotted bakers' marks to be pricked on their bread, and their defaults were presented monthly by the coroners to the mayor and aldermen.

But being severely controlled they must be protected from unauthorised competition. The difficulty was that the inhabitants could take their own corn to the millers to be ground, and when they made bread for themselves it was difficult to prevent them from supplying their friends, or selling bread and cakes in their houses. In 1571 there was a secret conference between the mayor and the graceman and others, at which it was agreed that four named persons—one of them Ellen Rotherham, a widow,

---

[1] In 1568 there was entered in the minutes the order of the city of London concerning the assize of bread when wheat is sold after 15s. the quarter; the halfpenny loaf must weigh 13 oz. 6½ dwt.; the penny loaf of all grains 53 oz.; the pennyworth in horsebread 1½ dwt. of wheaten bread.

perhaps of an alderman—should be allowed thereafter weekly to bake, utter and sell within their houses on market days one peck each in spite of the charter. Apart from this measure of poor relief the bakers' monopoly was enforced, and the graceman was empowered to take a constable and search the houses of persons suspected of selling bread whenever he thought necessary. The charter was considered again in 1578 and 1581.

Meat had to be dealt with on different lines, and 'foreign' butchers were welcome, especially in bad times, though they had to submit to regulation for the benefit of Lincoln butchers. If they brought in mutton or beef they were required also to bring in the skins and tallow of the same beasts and sheep. Forestalling was forbidden; that is to say, there must be no selling before the market bell was rung. Fishmongers had their prices fixed; in Lent 1562, for example, six herrings or three browet eels were sold for 1d. Fish once brought in must not be taken away again without leave, and there were fines for selling corrupt fish or charging too much.

The control of brewers was like that of bakers. The vessels in which they might tun their ale to their tipplers were prescribed, and they must tun 14 to the dozen, of stale ale 13, and of small ale according to custom. Delivery of ale to tipplers at Christmas was forbidden. The price was controlled. In 1562 beer was 2d. a gallon, single beer 1d. There was an ale-taster in each ward, and the authorities did 'straitly charge and command in the Queen's Majesty's name and behalf' that brewers should not sell until the aletaster had taken his sample. He forfeited any beer not wholesome for the people or not worth the price fixed by Mr Mayor, and gave it to the poor. Prices were specially proclaimed in 1572. A barrel of double beer was to sell at 6s., a kilderkin at 3s., a firkin at 18d., and every beer-brewer was to serve the city with ordinary beer at 1d. a gallon, and every alebrewer at 2½d. as well within the house as without, and to make only 'goodness' of ale thereafter. By 1587 ale was 3d.[1]

The tipplers raised the additional problem of disorderly houses. In 1553 it was declared that because there were so many tipplers in the city and suburbs there was not only much idleness and evil rule in the tippling houses, but also much bribery and petty larceny used and thereby maintained, as well to the displeasure of Almighty God as also to the hurt of the public wealth of the city. For the reformation of these evils it was ordered that the number of tipplers should be limited to thirty, and that they should be admitted by the mayor and justices and the aldermen for each parish. The orders were renewed in 1558 and 1561. Every tippler must keep good order and rule, and allow no unlawful games. There must not be more than

[1] In 1624 the Lincoln brewers obtained a grant of incorporation with control over the trade within 4 miles (C.S.P.D. 1623–25, p. 314).

three in each parish, the two largest parishes—St Martin and St Swithin—alone excepted.

In the increasing strictness and perhaps rising standards of the Elizabethan age fresh measures were found necessary. A secret council declared in 1566 that many great hurts, hindrances and enormities had of late crept into the city, as well by evil rule in alehouses, as also by the continual and daily resort, long continuing, of divers and many workmen, craftsmen and labourers, in the same houses there, loitering and drinking of overstrong and mighty ale, to the increase of idleness and drunkenness. It was determined that only the best and most honest inhabitants should be common brewers and tipplers. Common brewers must sell their ale and beer by dozens and half-dozens to the tipplers, and not sell in their own houses. Tipplers in turn must sell ale and beer by pennyworth and halfpennyworth, or by pots out of the house, and not otherwise. Prices were fixed and licences controlled.

In order to prevent abuse of authority, no justice of the peace or alderman might be a common victualler or tippler, or take money or gain for ale, beer, meat or other victuals to be spent in their houses, except in times of assizes and fairs. Haunting alehouses and sitting there drinking in working hours was an offence; but the rule did not apply to members of the council if they were of the degree of chamberlain. If a thirsty inhabitant thought to evade the law by drinking in Bail or Close he incurred a double penalty. Nor must any inhabitant give aid to alehouse-keepers in Bail or Close by lending them featherbeds or other bedding, to the hindrance of licensees in the city. Public policy dictated an exception to the rules about drinking out of hours at matches for shooting with the long bow; national defence must be encouraged.

Candles were of common concern. In 1562 cotton candles were 3*d*. a pound and wick candles 2½*d*. As prices were controlled, there was a danger that tallowchandlers would seek better markets outside the city, and they were forbidden to do this without licence from the mayor and justices. By 1575 cotton candles were 3½*d*. and wick candles 3*d*. when sold to inhabitants, but the chandlers were allowed to sell to strangers as they could agree.

Building materials were also controlled. For a time the common lime-kiln had a monopoly; no temporal inhabitant was to buy from any other kiln, and none might sell limestone save to the common kiln. The monopoly broke down, though private lime-burners were only allowed subject to regulation. They were forbidden to break any stones for the kiln, and the price of lime was fixed at 8*d*. a quarter. By 1550 the price was 14*d*.; the following spring it was 16*d*. and by autumn 20*d*. In 1552 a scale of prices was settled for the building trade. Tile of the largest mould, and sufficiently burned, was put at 16s. a thousand. Brick was 10s. a thousand after the rate of six score bricks to the hundred; this was the long hundred which had persisted since Domesday Book.[1] Lime was still 20s. By 1562 an attempt was being made to get prices down.

The poor were especially interested in the price of fuel. In the winter of 1566–7 the mayor and his brethren took control of prices of thatch, turf and wood brought to the city and sold at the waterside. In March 1571 blame was placed on the greedy persons who had secured monastic lands and felled and taken away timber which would have come to Lincoln for building and fuel, and providing work for the poor. But as there was still timber in other counties—Nottingham, Derby and York—whence it might be brought by water, it was resolved to seek an Act or special commission to gentry living to the west of the city, and to some citizens, to assess persons of ability in towns and places within a radius of seven miles, and to find ways and means of dyking, cleansing and scouring the Fossdyke, 'so that yearly sufficient water might be brought out from the Trent to the city' to bring the timber to Lincoln by boat. It is significant that this time coal also is mentioned. A year later appointments were made to provide and buy wood, coal, thatch, turf and other fuel. It was sought to renew the commission of sewers in 1586, and the following year the whole of the inhabitants were called on to scour the river or eau from Brayford head to Stamp End for three days.

The Fossdyke must have been used, when its condition permitted, for the carriage of wool to the clothing towns of the West Riding. In 1569 the York authorities were trying to cope with unemployment, and they sent men into Lincolnshire to buy wool to set the poor on work. The Yorkshire woollen trade records are full of complaints of the way in which south country clothiers bought up the best Cotswold, Lincolnshire and Norfolk wool.[2] It was noted about 1580 that Halifax men used fine wool mostly out of Lincolnshire, and that they sold their coarse wool to Rochdale men. In 1594 Lincoln citizens trading in Bradford complained that they had long been made to pay toll there contrary to the city charter. When the Suffolk clothiers complained of brokers making a corner in wool and driving up prices, the privy council ordered that brokers and forestallers be called before quarter sessions in Lincolnshire and the eastern counties and the law enforced.[3]

---

[1] Little evidence remains of the use of brick for building in Lincoln at this period: perhaps tile was the chief product of the brick kiln. But Doddington Hall was built of brick at the end of the century: according to tradition the brick was burnt in a field near the hall (R. E. G. Cole, *History of Doddington* (1897), p. 59).   [2] *V.C.H. Yorks.* II, 415.

[3] H. Heaton, *Yorkshire Woollen and Worsted Industries* (1920), p. 64; *H.M.C. Kenyon*, p. 573; *V.C.H. Yorks.* III, 460, 466, 468. In his account of the drapery industry of York,

Poverty and unemployment, combined with the inherited memory of what wool had once meant to Lincoln, and the knowledge that brokers were travelling from farm to farm buying for despatch to Yorkshire and the eastern counties wool that might serve the city, constantly prompted the idea of re-establishing a cloth industry in Lincoln. In 1567 the recorder suggested that the city should apply to the privy council for twenty households of strangers, good artificers, lately come into the realm—Huguenots from France—to be brought to practise their crafts, provided they did not enter the retail trade, but sold their wares by gross. Certainly there were clothiers in 1581 as there had been earlier.[1] In that year the council entered into an agreement with them, and the freemen were assessed towards the clothiers' charges, those who had not paid by July 1582 being threatened with disfranchisement.

Meanwhile the Company of Merchant Staplers, having lost its staple town of Calais, was turning over to the home trade in wool. In 1584 they procured a renewal of a monopoly of export for seven years, and applied themselves to driving other people out of the wool trade altogether. It was to be expected therefore that they would oppose the city's efforts. In 1588 the city presented a petition in Parliament reciting the impoverishment, ruin and decay to which Lincoln had come through the failure of the trade in wool and cloth, and asking for leave to buy and sell wool. The Staplers petitioned Burghley in reply, recalling their own grant, and urging that if Lincoln were to have relief the citizens should only be allowed to sell wool within the liberties of the city, for if they were allowed to sell Lincolnshire wool they would under colour of the grant buy and sell anywhere. This privileged trade by 'broggers' or brokers would overthrow a statute of 1552 forbidding the purchase of wool, save for manufacture within the realm, or for export by Staplers to Calais, and Staplers would prefer free trade to such a state of things.[2]

The Lincoln petition was sent to a committee of the Commons on 11 March 1589. Then other members, including Peter Evers, one of the city's burgesses, were added, and the bill was committed to Sir Edward Dymoke.[3] After amendment in both Houses it became law. It empowered freemen of the city residing there for two years, or their servants dwelling there, to buy wool and yarn grown, spun or wrought in the county of Lincoln or the county of the city up to a limit of 10,000 tods yearly for seven years, and

c. 1595, Thomas Caesar mentions that the chief buyers included Nicholas Baste of Lincoln (*V.C.H. Yorks.* ii, 413).
[1] See above, p. 67.   [2] B.M. Lansdowne MS. 58, no. 74.
[3] Sir Simonds D'Ewes, *Journal* (1682 ed.), pp. 444–6, 448–9, 451. In the Lords the bishop of Lincoln, Burghley, Lord Lincoln and the two lords Willoughby were on the committee (*L.J.* ii, 164–6).

to sell it anywhere in the kingdom, provided that a quarter of all such wool and yarn should be made into cloth within the city.[1]

There is no evidence to show how much use was made of the grant, or any sign of an attempt to renew it after the seven years. The growing demand for wool from Yorkshire and the eastern counties must, however, have prompted a general inclination to breed more sheep and to increase the area of pasture. A comparison of successive glebe terriers shows that there was going on a gradual process of enclosure by agreement.[2] William Broxholme had by 1607 turned his land over to pasture; Robert Smith of the Black Monks converted 12 acres; alderman Robert Rishworth turned a house of husbandry—a farmhouse—into a barn, and Thomas Halman abandoned the barns, stables and outhouses of another farmhouse. Alderman Morcroft had taken land from a farmhouse and either turned the house into cottages or let it stand empty.[3] But though the balance between arable and pasture was changing, both were liable to bad years as well as good; farming was subject to violent fluctuations, and in a farm review each year has to stand by itself. In 1586, a bad year, Hamlet Marshall, the vicar of Legsby and Stainton by Langworth, father of the precentor of the same name, was writing to the diocesan registrar Francis Bullingham at Buckden. He reported a general rot among sheep in the county; he had lost most of his own. There had been great storms, and many cattle were either drowned or had died from lack of fodder. Even in June the water was still high in the Till valley, and sheep had to be carried by water to Lincoln. Prices were high at Louth and Caistor markets, but higher still at Lincoln.[4] The chief value of such facts is to bring a touch of realism to the discussion of agrarian topics, upon which it is so tempting to generalise.

Corn was of more immediate and vital interest to the citizens than wool; and in 1563, in order to give the citizens a fair chance to buy, maltsters, bakers and brewers were forbidden to buy wheat, corn, malt or other grain on market day before the second bell at 2 o'clock. In 1577 this time was altered to 1 o'clock, and maltsters were forbidden to buy barley unless they brought in for sale an equivalent quantity of malt. Corn brokers had to be licensed by the justices; a Waddington corn carrier was licensed for one

[1] 31 Eliz. I, no. 21. The limit of 10,000 tods is interlined in the engrossment on the statute roll. The text of the statute is entered in the common council minute book among the entries for 1581, but there is no trace of such a statute of that date in the Journals of the House of Lords. A later town clerk has inferred that the act of 1589 was a renewal; a marginal note says 'renovat 31 Eliz.' *H.M.C. Lincoln*, p. 68, has been misled on this point.

[2] This has been shown by Mrs Varley for Kesteven.

[3] B.M. Add. MS. 11574, ff. 70, 71, 72, 73. As to this see below, p. 140. Rishworth held of the Granthams a farm at Waddington (L.A.O. Andr. 1, f. 137b).

[4] L.A.O., Cor.R. 1/16–24.

year in 1564 to buy barley or oats in any city market, to convert it into malt or oatmeal, and sell it in the market or to any victualler. The Bardney men were overbuying in 1566 and were stopped. In bad times steps were taken to ensure that corn was not withheld from the market; and in 1594 no grain was allowed to be set up in any house for sale until it had been three hours in the market after bell ringing.

As the population of the country grew, especially in London and the industrial areas, there was an increasing call on the corn-producing counties. Corn was sent regularly to London and Newcastle; in 1565 the county justices were ordered to help in the victualling of Berwick with wheat, malt, beans and barley.[1] There can have been little surplus in the famine years at the close of the century, which wrought great hardship. The export of grain was forbidden in 1590. In 1591 Arthur Hall, M.P. for Grantham, wrote to Burghley that corn was very dear, though he was writing against his own interest, for the better third of his living consisted of grain of his own growth.[2] Archbishop Whitgift wrote to Bishop Chaderton saying that in that hour of scarcity preachers should exhort the wealthier sort to contribute to the relief of the poor, and hoarders of corn should be admonished and made to realise how great an offence they committed in the sight of God.[3] Commissioners at work in the county dealing with the dearth of corn and the abuse of markets complained that the privileges of the city were a great hindrance.[4]

Prices, which had been rising for some years, rose more sharply at the end of the reign. The prices recorded at the Michaelmas leet, which for 1543–50 had averaged 12s. 4d. per quarter for wheat and 6s. 1½d. for peas and beans, had averaged as follows:

	Wheat		Peas and beans	
	s.	d.	s.	d.
1551–60	15	2	10	0
1561–70	15	10	9	7
1571–80	18	6	8	11
1581–90	21	1½	11	3
1591–1600	28	0	13	8½

As the value of money fell, other charges rose in sympathy.[5] The price to be paid on the purchase of the freedom of the city rose gradually from

---

[1] *A.P.C. 1542–47*, p. 123; *A.P.C. 1550–52*, p. 80; *A.P.C. 1558–70*, p. 274; *A.P.C. 1571–75*, p. 135; *A.P.C. 1581–82*, p. 405; *H.M.C. Salisbury*, II, 501; N. S .B. Gras, *The Evolution of the English Corn Market* (1915), p. 297.   [2] Wright, *Arthur Hall of Grantham* p. 203.

[3] Francis Peck, *Desiderata Curiosa* (1779 ed.), I, 168, 172.

[4] *A.P.C. 1596–97*, p. 188.

[5] In May 1586 the county justices reported to the privy council that they had appointed some of their number to every market. The price of boots and shoes had grown without cause, considering the low price of hides. (P.R.O. State Papers, Domestic, Eliz. I, CLXXXIX, no. 35.)

20s. to £5, payable in cash; though this latter proviso was evaded by a loan back to the new freeman, to be repaid over a period.

The figures of admissions to the freedom and enrolment of apprentices give some hint of the progress or decline of the community. In the period 1541–58, 182 freemen were enrolled, an average of ten per year. Of this number twenty-seven claimed by patrimony, forty-one by apprenticeship, seventy-three by gift and forty-one by purchase. These two latter figures ought perhaps to be combined, for the gifts include a number of grants in the gift of the mayor and sheriffs for each year, and they probably made their own terms with the would-be citizens. A considerable part of the entry therefore consisted of purchasers. Of apprentices enrolled the average was between five and six. There were probably others bound but not enrolled who later had to buy the freedom. In the period 1560–70 the number of freemen enrolled averaged fifteen and the number of apprentices twelve; there was stricter control of enrolment and admission. In the three following decades admissions to the freedom averaged fourteen, twelve and seventeen respectively, and apprentices averaged fourteen, thirteen and fourteen. Admission to the freedom by apprenticeship was practically constant, but admission by patrimony and purchase had both grown. Perhaps it may be inferred that more men were coming to Lincoln to trade in the crafts and to pursue other occupations, and that the non-craftsman element was growing also.

In 1562–7 Archdeacon Aylmer made a return to the bishop of the number of families in parishes. In ten Lincoln parishes—not including St Mary Magdalene, St Margaret and St Nicholas—459 families were returned, or, on the usual assumption of five to a family, about 2300 people, to which total perhaps 100 could be added for the missing parishes.[1] Two parish registers survive to give a little help. At St Peter at Gowts Mr Dudding has calculated that for the period 1542–56 the yearly average of baptisms was 7·7 and that of burials 8·12. For the period 1566–1615 the position was reversed: baptisms 10·24, burials 9·14. The figures are more interesting, however, if they are broken down further:

	Baptisms	Burials
1541–50	53	75 (1551, 18; 1552, 16)
1551–60	63 (to May 1559)	64 (to 1556)
1566–70	41	28
1571–80	110	85
1581–90	100	128 (1586, 25; 1590, 25)
1590–1600	98	86
1601–10	131	93

Apart from plague years the population was growing. A somewhat similar impression is given by the figures for St Margaret:

[1] Lincs. N. & Q. IV (1894–5), 247, quoting B.M. Harl. MS. 618.

PLATE 8

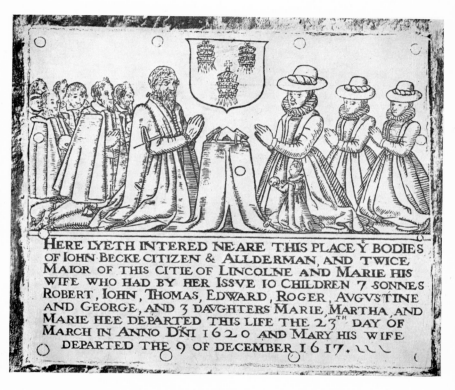

MEMORIAL BRASS OF JOHN BECKE AND MARY HIS WIFE,
in St Benedict's Church

	Baptisms	Burials	Marriages
1541–50	40	27	11
1551–60	20	58	7
1561–70	56	27	18
1571–80	97	68	32
1581–90	83	97	46
1591–1600	65	90	76
1601–10	58	62	—

There seems to have been a notable increase of population in the middle of the period, followed by a fall in the plague decades; the marriage figures may be misleading, as St Margaret was to become, and perhaps was already, a fashionable church for marriages.[1]

There is some evidence therefore that the city was growing slightly, and there were in various ways rising standards of comfort, as in the civic sphere, and as is suggested by the study of wills and inventories. At the end of the reign, however, it is almost concealed from view by the undoubted distress which is indicated by the poor-law measures.

Poor-law legislation moved by stages from voluntary giving to compulsion. A statute of 1551–2 ordered mayors in towns to call householders together, and nominate two collectors to gather alms from each parish. If any refused to give, he was to be exhorted by the parson, and if the parson failed the bishop was to try his hand.[2] Another statute of 1563 added that if he was obstinate he might be bound by recognisance in £10 to appear before the mayor in a town, and on refusal to give could be assessed to a weekly payment, with imprisonment for default.[3] In Lincoln an officer to oversee the poor and idle—the beadle of the beggars—appears in 1560. In 1569 Aylmer, the archdeacon of Lincoln, by the queen's command, directed his curates to exhort their parishioners to give their common alms at their churches according to statute for relief of the poor; and to procure remedy against wealthy folk who would not give.[4] Systematic parish collection began about that time; there are signs of it in the surviving accounts of St Mark and St Martin.[5] By 1592, certainly, there were collectors in every parish, and defaulters were presented to the mayor.

Occasional measures of charity are recorded. At Christmas six poor men were given gowns with badges bearing the city arms, one of them becoming the master of the poor people. A coat was given to a blind boy. One winter 20 chalder of coal were sent for from Newcastle to be sold to the

---

[1] The parish registers of St Margaret and St Peter at Gowts have been printed by the Lincoln Record Society (Parish Register Section).

[2] 5 & 6 Edward VI, c. 2. [3] 5 Eliz. I, c. 3.

[4] Lincs. N. & Q. VI (1900–1), 115.

[5] The churchwardens of St Martin prayed to be allowed in their accounts moneys remaining in the hands of the poor which they could not get in; which points to loans, perhaps for the purpose of setting up.

poor. Freemen were authorised to buy wood, coal, thatch or turf for relief of the poor, to be sold in winter at controlled prices. Volunteers could give in their names and say what quantities they had bought, but thereafter they defaulted at their peril. Alderman John Wilson left £40, the income whereof was laid out in fuel for the poor, and a charitable benevolence was sometimes voted by the common chamber. To enable young men to set up in their trades Sir Thomas White, a lord mayor of London and founder of St John's College, Oxford, had founded his charity in which twenty-four towns, including Lincoln, were to benefit by turns. In 1588 the council were able to make from it sixteen loans of £25 for ten years, free of interest; local benefactors followed suit, and the city occasionally made like grants.

The duties of the master of the poor were defined as keeping, shutting and sparring of the Bargates, for which he was paid 20s. yearly, and the ordering of the poor, punishing and expelling vagabonds and strange beggars, for which there was another 20s. All persons without a living who had not been born in the city or lived in it three years were searched for monthly, and presented to the alderman of the ward to be dealt with according to statute. Here was the law of settlement; the city would maintain its own poor, but must guard itself against the burden of maintaining others' poor. A new project, a house of industry for relief, is mooted in 1578 in accordance with a new statute,[1] and a committee was directed to confer with Mr Justice Monson and the recorder. A stock of hemp and wool was provided for each parish for employment of its poor.

In the later part of the reign the problem of poverty was aggravated by plague. It raged in the summer of 1586, a fearful year when the crops failed and the floods were out, and although contributions were coming in from the country they were both inadequate and slackly collected. The common council therefore resolved that various pieces of land should be sold or leased. By December the poor had so swarmed into the city for cover that the council forbade any freeman or inhabitant to receive into his house more than one couple; all others must be gone by Mayday unless they had been there more than three years. No new arrivals would be permitted without leave of the mayor and his brethren; freemen offending would be disfranchised and non-freemen fined £4. Aldermen and chief constables of wards must order petty constables fortnightly to certify to a justice what strangers were living in their wards. Churchwardens were charged to seek out the sick in their parishes, and to certify their numbers and their diseases. So it was hoped to stem the influx of 'foreign' beggars and the onset of disease.

[1] 18 Eliz. I, c. 3.

Father Willyman appears in the following spring. Who he was, and the nature of his service, is not clear, but he was concerned with the poor. He was given the freedom, and a fishing and a reed bush and a house were let to him; he was to be paid 46s. 8d. yearly so long as he dwelt in the city. He must not travel to infected towns without leave.[1] Two months later he was made a grant for the repair of his house, and the mayor was authorised to give him money to give to the needy poor and those whom he ordered to keep to their houses. By 1588 it was resolved to let his fishing subject to his consent; thereafter he is not heard of again.

After the ordeal of 1586–7[2] the common council recorded that in view of the plague and the great impoverishment of the city, and because 'there be now great and manifest presumptions of some dregs and offscourings thereof yet remaining unavoided', the dean (Mr Griffin), the archdeacon (Dr Barefoot) and the chancellor (Dr Robinson)[3] came in to advise; and sitting in the inner chamber of the Gildhall, 'it was gravely and wisely considered of and a most convenient necessary course concluded of and determined absolutely to be put in practice' by the authorities, 'as well for the safeguard and preserving of the good estate of this city, which God defend and keep, as for the benefit of the excessive number of poor people within the same', to divide the wards for the better discovery of plague or other sickness. Justices and aldermen were left to effect the subdivisions.

The devastation wrought by the plague is confirmed by the deputy lieutenants of the county, writing to Burghley; they reported that Lincoln had fallen into great decay and poverty by God's long visitation.[4] It was all the more urgent therefore to avoid the burden of foreign poor. A blacksmith who put up a mud building to house many beggars under one roof was ordered to pull it down. Freemen having unfree tenants who had not lived in the city three years were ordered to be rid of them, and to take no more strange poor in. Presently it was realised that this rule meant that good workmen wanting to come to the city would be excluded, and the mayor and justices were given a discretion to admit suitable people.

Plague came and went, and in 1590 or thereabouts its results were so dramatic that they were recorded in a ballad. After deaths of judges and lesser men at Oxford and Exeter assizes there followed deaths at Lincoln assize of the judge (Robert Skeete), one Hollice, a justice of the peace,

---

[1] The plague had abated. In June 1587 the mayor and others wrote to Rutland denying rumours of the plague at Lincoln (*H.M.C. Rutland*, I, 216).

[2] There were five mayors in office in that year. See below, p. 231.

[3] *Rectius* precentor.   [4] See above, p. 75 n.

master Tyrwhite the foreman of the jury, the clerk of the peace (Welby) and others:

> How sore for sinne the Lord offended was,
> How sore for sinne his wrath from him did pas,
> And for sinne the prudent of our land,
> Hath felt the force of his most heavie hand.[1]

In this plague period the project of a house of industry was revived. Mr Grene of Boston offered to set 400 poor on work for five years if the city would find him a house and lend him £300 free of interest for that time. The council decided to negotiate. It seems that he came, for in 1596 dealings were going on with one Cheeseman for a like project.[2] By the end of the year an arrangement had been made with William Marett for setting and keeping the poor at work with knitting and spinning, with a room in the lower floor of the Grey Friars. All chamberlains' peers and those of higher rank were to pay a bustage for relief of the poor while they were learning, in order to keep them from begging, other inhabitants giving according to the mayor's assessment. Marett was given the freedom of the city, and a lease of the rooms at the Grey Friars so long as he kept at work (making no midden in the garden), and also the sheep-market ground subject to its use for markets and St Hugh's fair. His work is described as the spinning and knitting of 'gersey' and his school was the Jersey School; he bore a Jersey name. It seems probable that he came from Jersey with the new knitting industry, that island having captured a large share of the trade of supplying the new fashionable demand for stockings.[3]

There was plague again in the spring of 1599, when pest houses and furniture were being taken by constables by the mayor's order on a warrant 'from above', and they were promised indemnity by the common council. So the century drew to a close in a distressed and impoverished city.

But the gains of the earlier and middle years of the reign were not all lost. The economic position of the gentry was improving, and they brought their money to market and to the shops of the Lincoln tradesmen. A large volume of business, both ecclesiastical and secular, had brought modest prosperity to notaries like Peter Effard and Henry Sapcote earlier on; lawyers like Christopher Wray and Robert Monson were linking the gentry

---

[1] *A mournfull Dittie on the death of certaine Judges and Justices of the Peace, and divers the Gentlemen, who died immediately after the Assizes, holden at Lincolne last past. To the tune of Fortune.* Imprinted at London by John Wolfe for William Wright, 1590 (B.M. Huth, 50 (62)).

[2] The fragment relating to Cheeseman printed in *H.M.C. Lincoln,* p. 17, relates not to Lincoln but to York. Presumably Cheeseman had been engaged there.

[3] G. R. Balleine, *History of the Island of Jersey* (1950), pp. 129–30.

with the citizens; and attorneys were buying land. Thomas Tailor, the diocesan registrar, who had married a daughter of Martin Hollingworth, alderman and draper, bought Doddington and built the hall; John Becke, alderman and draper, founded a notable citizen family, and left behind him a memorial brass in St Benedict's Church which happily has survived.[1] Robert Smith had acquired the Black Monks, and Richard Smith earned the gratitude of the council for looking after the city's interests.[2] Their kinsman, Dr Richard Smith, having made money in physic in London, was soon to found Christ's Hospital in Lincoln.

It was taken for granted that the more substantial tradesmen should be of the common council, and the richer of them held office as alderman and mayor.[3] When assessments were made on the freemen it was assumed that aldermen should pay the most, followed by the sheriff's peers. Accordingly they were required to keep their position. The wearing of liveries was already forbidden, but the council were especially concerned to prevent office-bearers, past or present, from doing so. The mayor promised to speak to the bishop and ask him not to insist on livery for one of his servants Justinian Crome, who was a sheriff's peer. As the century wore on, all freemen were compelled to take the oath of liveries, and for breach of it they were disfranchised.

A new emphasis on civic circumstance points in the direction of rising standards. Only freemen and such as the mayor and his officers thought well of were allowed to come to the mayor's breakfasts, and freemen must come orderly in their gowns. They must attend the mayor to the gildhall and to church. The swordbearer and the macebearer were given new hats and coats, the new mace was to be made greater and fairer than the old, and the greatest and least swords repaired.

In 1572 the sheriffs and some of the freemen had the temerity to contend against the mayor and aldermen about the election of common council-men. For the removal of doubts it was laid down that the mayor by assent of a majority of aldermen who had been mayor should nominate to the twelve aldermen twenty-four of the most discreet and able men who had been sheriffs and chamberlains to be of the common council. The mayor should then rehearse the same openly in hall to the freemen. If any man were objected to, he should not be of the council, and the mayor and his brethren should nominate another in his stead. It was in theory the

---

[1] Becke left behind him goods and debts to the value of over £2000. In his corn chamber were malt, rye and other corn. (L.A.O. Lincoln Inventories, 124/45.)

[2] It was noted in 1621 that when Richard Smith was first an attorney in Lincolnshire there were but three others in the county, but the number had grown to ten or twelve score (*H.M.C. Rutland*, IV, 216).

[3] Study of the Subsidy Roll of 1551 clearly illustrates this point.

function of the common council to make do and ordain everything for the weal and preservation of the city; but in practice it had nothing but a power of veto, and the initiative lay in the Inner House.

The council dealt with a wide range of matters, and whether they were clearly within their power or not could generally ensure compliance by freemen on threat of disfranchisement. The rural side of city life is recalled by rules about the removal of dunghills from the streets and foul water from the river, the killing of moles and the muzzling of dogs. The conduits were maintained for water supply; buckets, ladders and clamps of iron as fire precautions; church bells were rung at 5 a.m., 8 a.m. and 9 p.m.; weights and measures were tested; some roads and marketplaces paved— coggles were coming in. Most roads were the liability of frontagers, but some main roads where there were few or no buildings fell on either the council or the parish.

There was appearing about this time the vested interest of individual freemen in leases of corporate property, which by 1835 were regarded almost as customary freehold. It had been the practice for chamberlains to let waste lands in their wards under their own seals. In 1565 all such leases were called in, and the lands let under the common seal, sitting tenants having the first refusal at a rent others would pay. Freemen were allowed reversionary leases for 90 years without covenants; twenty-five such leases were at once made. On reflection they were revoked, and forty-one year leases substituted, small plots being sold. The new leases were mostly to aldermen or their sons and heirs. It was the accepted view that individuals had the right to individual benefit from the common property.

The exclusive right of the freemen to carry on their trades in the city was soon to be challenged. In 1621 the common council expressly declared, perhaps for the first time, the ancient custom that no woollen or linen draper, mercer, merchant, haberdasher, miller, pewterer, clothier, ironmonger, smith, shoemaker, broker, tanner, glover, tinker, dyer, walker, carpenter, joiner, pedlar or tradesman (other than victuallers) might set up a stall or sell by retail—except in fairtime—save such as be free. Some sheriffs had taken bribes from unfree men. It was noted in 1633 that the act of the council had not worked well. The difficulty continued to grow until the monopoly broke down a century later. Furthermore, the poor law came into some conflict with it, at least so far as common victuallers were concerned. When it was ruled that only freemen might be common victuallers, some poor unfree people who had so made their living were deprived of it, though they could not be driven out of the city because of their long abode. Faced with a choice between licensing them as victuallers or tipplers and keeping them on the poor rate, the council resolved in effect to leave them alone.[1] It was evidently because the freemen's monopoly had thus been abandoned that the custom grew up of requiring alehouse keepers and victuallers who were not freemen or the widows of freemen, on their first taking an inn or alehouse within the jurisdiction of the city justices, to pay £5 to the mayor to be spent in placing out the sons of poor freemen as apprentices to trades.

[1] For this licensing money see *Report of Charity Commissioners, 1839*, 'Lincolnshire', p. 362.

CHAPTER V

ELIZABETHAN CHURCH AFFAIRS

I T was the policy of Elizabeth I to return to the religious order established by the royal injunctions of 1549 and the Prayer Book, and a summary form of subscription to the settlement was required of the clergy. The vast majority of them subscribed; in the diocese of Lincoln in 1561 there were only thirty-eight vacant benefices. Among those who were deprived were Bishop Watson, several archdeacons including those of Lincoln and Stow, a few prebendaries and the master of Lincoln grammar school. Visitors were appointed to act as spiritual judges to deal with moral offences and to enforce the settlement. Those for Lincolnshire included proven friends of the city like William Lord Willoughby of Parham and Sir Francis Ayscough.[1]

The see of Lincoln remained vacant until 1560, when Nicholas Bullingham was appointed. He had become archdeacon of Lincoln in 1549, but being a married man was deprived on the accession of Mary, and apparently he fled to Emden.[2] On Mary's death Sir Francis Ayscough petitioned Cecil that his former preferments might be restored.[3] He was a good theologian and a moderate man. When in 1571 he was transferred to Worcester he was succeeded by Thomas Cooper, who was zealous in the suppression of popish recusants but inclined to sympathise with puritan zeal. His attitude is illustrated by a letter he wrote soon after his accession to Lincoln, apparently to the dean and chapter, pointing out that although in almost all cathedral churches there was a divinity lecturer for the instruction of the people, there had not been one in their church for some years, that this had been a matter of reproach to him, and asking them to to look to it.[4]

The city of Lincoln was more closely concerned with the new archdeacon of Lincoln, John Aylmer, who was appointed in 1562. He was a Cambridge scholar and a learned man, who after being tutor to Lady Jane Grey became archdeacon of Stow in 1553. On the accession of Mary he boldly offered in Convocation to dispute with all the learned papists in England. He was deprived, and according to Strype fled first to Strasbourg and then to Zürich. Whilst in exile he helped John Foxe in the preparation of his

---

[1] Henry Gee, *Elizabethan Clergy and the Settlement of Religion, 1558–64* (1898), pp. 97, 124, 154, 241.

[2] C. H. Garrett, *Marian Exiles* (1938), p. 99.

[3] *C.S.P.D. 1547–80*, p. 118.   [4] L.A.O. Cor. B (1), no. 6.

PLATE 9

JOHN AYLMER

By permission of the Bishop of London

Book of Martyrs, and himself published from Strasbourg in 1559 *An Harborough for Faithful and True Subjects* in reply to John Knox's *First Blast of the Trumpet against the Monstrous Regiment of Women*. In several passages he advocated puritan principles, though Knox commented to Cecil that Aylmer rather sought the favour of the world than the glory of God.[1] In *An Harborough* he attacked bishops in terms so general that they applied equally to popish and protestant bishops, and presently to himself: it was too much to expect his enemies to refrain from quoting against the lord bishop of London, as he became, passages such as this:

Come off, ye Bishops; away with your superfluities: yield up your thousands, be content with hundreds, as they be in other reformed churches, where be as great learned men as you are....Let the queen have the rest of your temporalities...and...build and found schools throughout the realm; that every parish church may have his preacher, every city his superintendent, to live honestly and not pompously.[2]

Further preferment was slow, for his book was remembered against him, but at last in 1576, through the influence of Sir Christopher Hatton he was appointed bishop of London. There he acquired the name of a harsh and arbitrary prelate, dealing severely with puritans and catholics. By the puritans he was especially detested, because they regarded him as a renegade, and he was savagely attacked in the *Marprelate Tracts*.[3]

After a visit to Court in 1565 Aylmer wrote to Sir Nicholas Throckmorton saying that it was no small comfort to him to find his old friends continuing their friendship while he studied to be forgotten and buried in the country—a phrase that hardly rings true. He added that Mr Secretary Cecil had taken a note of a commission to the bishop of Lincoln and others for reforming the church and diocese of Lincoln, whereof he had also written to Lord Leicester; Lincolnshire had as much need of it as any place in England.[4] At Lincoln, says Strype, he dwelt much, living in good reputation, being a justice of the peace for the county and an ecclesiastical commissioner, and an active and bold man, as well as wise and learned. Strype attributes to him the credit of carrying the church settlement into effect in his own area. 'He first purged the cathedral church of Lincoln,

---

[1] *Works of John Knox*, ed. D. Laing (1864), VI, 45.

[2] *An Harborough*, p. 148; see John Strype, *Annals of the Reformation* (1824 ed.), I (i), 181.

[3] It is thought that Edmund Spenser referred to him in his *Shepheard's Calendar* when he described Morrell (by syllabic transposition from Elmer) as 'the proud and ambitious pastor' (see *D.N.B.*). He acquired lands at Revesby, which he gave by will to his son John, who, it appears, married and lived there (John Strype, *Life of Aylmer* (1821 ed.), p. 114). His leasing of ecclesiastical lands for his own benefit brought him a sharp rebuke (*A.P.C. 1578–80*, p. 411; A. Peel, *Seconde Parte of a Register* (1915), I, 248).

[4] *C.S.P.D. 1601–3 & Add.* p. 563.

being at that time a nest of unclean birds: and next in the county, by preaching and executing the commission, he so prevailed, that not one recusant was left in the country at his coming away; and many years after it remained a diocese well settled in religion as he mentioned himself in one of his letters to the Lord Treasurer.'[1] There is much exaggeration here, but he no doubt achieved a large measure of conformity.

In 1564 the privy council asked the bishops to consult leading men in their dioceses who were favourable to the royal policy, about the justices and others, who were to be classified according to their religious convictions. For the county of the city of Lincoln bishop Bullingham consulted Aylmer, his registrar Thomas Tailor, and Thomas St Paul. They returned that the mayor and one alderman (John Hutchinson and Nicholas Fawkener) were earnest in religion; seven aldermen (Wright, Stamp, Goodknap, Kent, Porter, Fulbeck, Ellis) were indifferent; three of them (Carter, Scolfield and Halleley) were hinderers. A former alderman, Martin Hollingworth, was described as very earnest in religion, honest and politique. Of the gentry with whom Lincoln was concerned, Anthony Thorold, Richard Bertie, Thomas St Paul and Robert Monson were earnest; Sir Edward Dymoke and Christopher Wray were indifferent.[2]

Reliable laymen like Robert Monson, Thomas St Paul and Martin Hollingworth sat frequently with Aylmer to receive reports from churchwardens of the destruction of the 'monuments of superstition' in churches.[3] Only one return from a city parish seems to have survived, that for St Paul's. There the rood with St Mary and St John was said to have been burnt in the first year of Elizabeth, the mass book had been taken away by the parson, and other things destroyed, but a 'crosse crismatorie' had gone they knew not how or when, and they denied knowledge whether they had had any cruets in Queen Mary's time, which could not have been true.[4] It is likely enough that the missing articles had been hidden against a return to catholicism.

The old gild plays vanished from city life, but a desire for pageantry led the common council in 1564 to order that a standing play of some Bible story should be played for two days during the summer. Collectors of money were appointed. The play chosen and performed was the story of Tobit. Evidently it was appreciated, for two years later and two years after that there were repeat performances. Thereafter the plays disappeared altogether.

---

[1] *Life*, pp. 13–14, and see p. 59.
[2] *Camden Miscellany*, IX, 'Letters from the Bishops to the Privy Council, 1564', pp. 26, 33.
[3] E. Peacock, *English Church Furniture* (1866), passim.
[4] *Lincs. N. & Q.* XIV (1916–17), 149.

Perhaps their disappearance and the energy with which the law as to church attendance was enforced were the results of the new church settlement and the growth of puritan feeling. Compulsory church going was not new. Attendance on the mayor to the Minster had been ordered in 1525. A few weeks before Mary's death all past and present office-holders were ordered to attend the mayor to sermons at the Minster or elsewhere. The penalties ranged from 8d. for an alderman to 2d. for a chamberlain or his peer. They were all to wear gowns. These rules were framed partly to uphold the dignity of the mayor, but they became wider in their scope until they embraced the citizens generally. Victuallers were ordered to shut their shops on Sundays and other holy days, when the second peal should ring for service, and thereafter none should keep servants or others in his house at play or in idleness during the time of divine service, and no bread or ale was to be carried on Sundays or during such time on festival days save by the mayor's licence.

The Act of Uniformity of 1559 required church attendance, but it was not until 1572 that machinery for enforcement of these rules was provided by the common council. In November of that year it was resolved that the mayor and aldermen should appoint one or more persons, being constables or churchwardens, in every parish, who should search every Sunday to see in what households the majority of persons were not at sermons at the Minster; offenders were to be presented to the alderman of the ward, who could in his discretion impose a fine of 2d. on every offender for each default, the fines being given to the poor.

An increase in the fines indicates the difficulty of enforcement. In 1584 one-half of the people of every house (save those excused by the mayor and justices) must be at the beginning of every sermon on Sundays in the forenoon; and one of each household at the beginning of every sermon in the afternoon of every Sunday or festival day, and every Wednesday. The penalty imposed on every householder for every one of his household improperly absent on a Sunday was 20d. and on a Wednesday 12d. Searchers were appointed. One limitation was set to the householder's vicarious liability; if he appointed a servant to repair to sermon and the servant went not, the servant was to be punished and not the master. It is difficult to believe that fines of this size were imposed and collected, or that they were intended to do more than intimidate the would-be malingerer.

Sunday closing of shops was rigidly enforced. Shop doors and windows of drapers, mercers, butchers and other handicraftsmen must not be opened, though those who could only get into their houses through their shops were allowed to open their doors for passage in and out. A few exceptions were allowed. Tradesmen having wares come home from

London, Stourbridge, Stamford and other fairs were allowed to open their shop doors and windows for the purpose of taking in their wares. Butchers on any Sunday out of Lent, and fishmongers on any Sunday in Lent, might open from 5 in the morning until the market bell, and from 1 to 3 in the afternoon if in that time there were no sermons, but at no other time except to an innholder on the sudden coming of a stranger to an inn. Strangers passing through the city might, however, be served by any mercer, draper or other artificer on any Sunday without offence. The city was not responsible for the soul of the stranger, and it would be a pity not to take his money.

Emphasis is constantly laid on attendance at sermons rather than at divine service, and it is the Minster that is mentioned rather than any parish church. Indeed, if a sermon were wanted there was little choice, for most of the beneficed clergy in the city were not licensed to preach by the bishop, and none might preach without a licence. There has survived a survey, made by the puritans in 1585, for the purpose of 'ascertaining the number of preaching ministers and of those who were insufficient in learning or of scandalous lives'.[1] The return for the city mentions fourteen parishes in charge of eleven clergy. Ten of them are described as 'no preacher' (four of them being double beneficed), two as readers, laymen who were not licensed, but 'tolerated' to read prayers.[2] Fortunately this puritan return can be compared with the official record of the bishop, compiled a few months later. In this list John Sylvester, curate of St Benedict, is described as a preacher; whether the puritans would have so described him is not clear, for St Benedict is not mentioned in their survey. But Robert Sergeant, of St Swithin and St Nicholas, whom the puritans call 'no preacher', is given as a licensed preacher in the official list; the latter mentions that the curate of St Peter at Gowts is 'literate'. Canon Foster has remarked on the fairness and moderation of the puritan survey of Lincolnshire, which are in contrast with the returns from some other dioceses.[3]

Bishop Cooper's *Liber Cleri* of 1576 mentions three of the city clergy. The vicar of St Martin, a survivor from pre-reformation days, ordained 49 years before, was aged 78 and unmarried. He knew but little Latin, and was little versed in sacred learning. His living was worth £3. 13s. 4d. per year. The rector of St Peter at Arches, worth £5. 2s. 8½d. a year, was 40; he knew but little Latin, and was moderately versed in sacred learning. The vicar of St Mary le Wigford (worth £5. 3s. 9d. a year) was 40; he knew

---

[1] Peel, *Seconde Parte of a Register*, II, 88 et seq. For the date see C. W. Foster, *State of the Church* (L.R.S. 1926), I, xxxiv.

[2] Peel, op. cit. p. 124.   [3] Foster, op. cit. pp. xxxvii, 63.

Latin moderately, and was to the same extent versed in sacred learning. He said the public prayers, administered the sacraments, and used the ceremonies according to the manner and form prescribed by parliament. To the credit of all three it should be added that they resided upon their benefices.[1]

All the city livings were poor, and it is not surprising therefore that the clergy were not of high quality. On the accession of James I the parson of Bassingham was brought in to preach at St Benedict's; in 1601-2 a list of the 'better sort' of ministers who were required to contribute for the provision of light horse in Ireland did not include any city incumbents, though in 1590 the rector of St Mary Magdalene provided a petronel—a large pistol used especially by horsemen—and the vicar of St Mary a bow.[2]

Clearly therefore the parish churches could do nothing to satisfy any desire beyond that satisfied by the formal services prescribed by the Prayer Book. For 'the preaching of the Word', in the phrase so much used by the puritans, there was no provision. Whether the common council were spontaneous in their original desire for regular sermons may be doubted. They could only have taken their early measures in concert with the church authorities, and it is probable that they were prompted. In 1571 they resolved that Nicholas Catskyn, clerk, should have an annuity of £5 so long as he should be beneficed in the city or suburbs for being mayor's chaplain and for preaching as well at the parsonages belonging to the city as within the city itself. They went further in 1578, when they decided to pay out of the common chamber £6. 13s. 4d. to a learned man to be appointed and chosen by the advice and consent of Mr Dean of the cathedral church (William Wickham), to be reader in the Minster and to preach on Wednesdays in some parish church within the city.

The council resolutions become less coldly official and import more warmth as time goes on. By 1583 the council were calling for a preacher who should be virtuous and learned, who should teach the inhabitants the word of God, and who should visit and give good counsel to the sick as need should arise. The stipend had risen to £20. Mr Jermyne became the preacher, though it was agreed that on a change part of the stipend should abate. There was more behind this decision than meets the eye.

In the next few years there raged a violent and furious struggle in the common council, the noise of which engaged the attention of the privy

[1] C. W. Foster, *Lincoln Episcopal Records, Bishop Cooper, 1571–84* (L.R.S. 1912), pp. 158–9. It must not be assumed that the incumbents' incomes were limited to the official figures (Foster, *State of the Church*, i, lx). The vicar of St Martin received an annuity from the churchwardens of 26s.

[2] Foster, *State of the Church*, i, xcvii, 145, 465.

council in London. One party manifested zeal for Sabbath observance and the preaching of the Word; clearly it acted under ecclesiastical patronage. It stood for order and good government. On the other side were those who resisted the tightening up process; they preferred old easy-going ways, and so they were hostile to the church authorities. All who leaned to the old faith therefore sympathised with them, and some may even have prompted them. Some secular-minded laymen saw in the controversy nothing but a faction fight, but others saw a great deal more. They saw the hand of Rome, and in days when the threat from the catholic powers of France and Spain was ever present there was no disposition to take unnecessary risks.

The division of parties manifested itself in several issues of policy. There were then two grammar schools in Lincoln, one in the city and one in the Close. The former was under the joint supervision of the dean and chancellor and the common council; the latter was the chapter's school. The affairs of the school in the city came under discussion early in the reign. In 1560 the council resolved to allow the usher £10 for one year out of the revenues of their parsonages, provided the school was kept in the old schoolhouse in the city, and the masters of the Close made it an able schoolhouse and kept it in repair; a proposal which only becomes intelligible when it is realised that it was being proposed to unite the schools, and to lay the stipend of the master on the chapter and that of the usher on the city. Two years later the proposals were hanging fire, and in 1563 the recorder and Robert Monson were appointed to deal with the chapter about making the schoolhouse fit to teach in, and who was to do it and pay the usher. In default of agreement the city resolved to make its own appointment. In 1567 John Drope, who was 'allowed and sent' by the archdeacon of Lincoln, was appointed, and when he left the next year Aylmer's own servant John Staynton was appointed. It is clear that Aylmer was the motive force behind the new interest in the school, and that he was using the common council to put pressure on his less energetic brethren in the chapter.

In 1568 Robert Monson announced his intention of providing a free school in the Grey Friars (which had become his property) at his own expense, and the council gladly contributed the glass from the old school. This handsome provision aroused new enthusiasm for the school, and in following years there is mention of occasional grants to students at Oxford and Cambridge. A salary of £10 for the usher was found burdensome by the common council, and voluntary payments were invited towards it, with poor results; it was agreed in 1575 to assess the inhabitants for the amendment of the living of the schoolmaster.

The council acquired the property from Monson in 1574. They agreed to give him a reversionary lease of Hanslope parsonage for 40 years for a fine of £100 and a rent of £80; he was to have a lease of the Friars land other than the school premises at a nominal rent until his Hanslope reversion fell in. The deed of covenant referred to 'the good affection that the said Robert Mounson hath towards the maintenance of a free grammar school or school house within the said city in perpetuity hereafter': and it declared also his intention that the citizens should enjoy a conduit or watercourse lately in question without interruption. So with livery of seisin was completed the city's title to property which continued to provide a home for the grammar school for 300 years.

The conversations with the dean and chapter had aimed at removing the overlapping of the two schools in Lincoln, and getting better teachers without assuming an impossible financial burden, and at last terms of union were agreed:

Whereas there has been heretofore two grammar schools kept at Lincoln whereof the one of them was kept in the close of the said cathedral church of Lincoln and the schoolmaster that taught there was maintained by the dean and chapter of the said cathedral church and had his wages and stipend paid by them, and the other was kept within the city of Lincoln and the schoolmaster that taught there was maintained by the mayor sheriffs citizens and commonalty of the said city and had his wages and stipend paid by them.

And Whereas the scholars that were taught in the said two several schools did not (as by experience it is found) so much profit and proceed in learning as it was looked for and wished by their parents and kinsfolk to their no little grief, whereby divers did withdraw their children from the said schools, and others being thereby discouraged did forbear to put their children to school to the hindrance of good knowledge and learning And the greatest cause thereof thought to be in this, that the said several stipends were not sufficient to find and maintain able and sufficient schoolmasters to teach in the said several schools.

By 1582 articles of agreement were in draft, and openly read in the council 'touching the election of a learned schoolmaster and also for the election of an usher, that better order of teaching may be had for the profit of youth and scholars in the free school'. Without waiting for the formalities to be completed the council agreed to lend 20 marks to the schoolmaster Mr Temple for three years if he continued there so long.

The deed of union was dated 18 January 1584. The dean and chapter were to appoint the schoolmaster, who must be a Master of Arts, able to teach both the Greek and Latin tongues learnedly and skilfully; and the mayor, recorder and five of the most ancient aldermen were to appoint the usher, 'who must have commendable knowledge in the Greek and Latin tongues and be also able to versify and teach the Greek grammar at the least'. The master was to receive £20 yearly from the chapter and £6. 13s. 4d. from the city, and the usher £13. 6s. 8d. from the city. The city must maintain the building; and the bishop covenanted that he and his successors 'shall not at any time hereafter licence neither willingly or wittingly permit and suffer any other grammar school to be kept and taught within the said city' or within three miles of it.

Only such children as were able to enter into grammar were to be admitted. The children of freemen and inhabitants of the city and county thereof, Close and Bail, were on admission to pay only 6d. to the usher, and when placed under the master—in the upper school—only 1s. to him. No other payments might be demanded, but parents and kinsfolk of the boys might of their own goodwill bestow 'a more better reward' on usher or schoolmaster. Both the chapter and the council were to appoint visitors, the chapter visitor redressing any default on the part of the master, the city visitor any on the part of the usher.

The schoolmaster William Temple was to rise to some eminence. He had been at King's College, Cambridge, of which Bishop Wickham had been a fellow; and the bishop may have nominated him. He cannot have held the office long, for by November 1585 he had accompanied Sir Philip Sidney to the Low Countries as his secretary, and was with him when he fell at Zutphen. Temple went with Essex to Ireland, and later became provost of Trinity College, Dublin.[1]

The union of the schools was one of the measures for which the orthodox party in the common council, led by alderman Robert Rishworth, took the credit. After the party had lost control of the council they set out these measures, showing how their opponents had acted after coming into power. There was first the provision of a city preacher, who, the orthodox complained, was obstructed and slandered by their opponents, some saying that they desired as much a tale of Robin Hood as to hear him preach, others that he and his sermons had made all the contentions in Lincoln, and yet others that he had done more harm than ever he would do good. Secondly, there were the steps taken to enforce observance of the Sabbath day, with church attendance and the closing of shops; the opposition refused to enforce the rules, and had encouraged the setting up of maypoles and may games. Thirdly, there was the union of the schools, the opposition having endangered the union and kept an unfit man as usher. Fourthly, there were steps to bridle the able poor from begging and stealing, and to

---

[1] There is a letter from Sidney to Temple, dated 23 May 1584, before they had met, in Sidney's *Defence of Poesie etc.* p. 145. Temple was grandfather of the more famous Sir William Temple, statesman and essayist.

teach and keep them at such work as would enable them to get a living. The opposition would have discharged the clothiers who had been brought to the city for this purpose but for Rishworth's party, who encouraged them to go forward. In Rishworth's mayoralty there were nine score in the trade, and other poor people kept at work, which earned out of that house six and seven pounds weekly; since when the place had been so neglected that earnings had fallen to 10s., and the poor suffered to loiter and go begging. Fifthly, there was the better control of alehouses, and the putting down of unfit persons for the same; there had been in Lincoln seven or eight score alehouses, of which divers were discharged, both because of their number and of the vile abuses as well on the Sabbath and in sermon time as in the weekday daily used and practised. Control had since been relaxed, the full number allowed, and as much swearing, dicing, carding and drunkenness used as before. And sixthly, the assize of bread, ale and beer had been overseen so that the poor were not robbed. There had been times when, wheat being at 20s., bread was sold after 40s., and the assize not observed.[1]

This is an *ex parte* statement, but it is not difficult to divine the attitude of the conservative party; they thought it better to have Lincoln free than Lincoln (relatively) sober and strictly regimented. The story of the great controversy, lasting four years, throws interesting light on local affairs and manners, constitutional practice, and the supervision over local affairs by the privy council.[2] One of the most noticeable features of the story is the part taken by the bishop. He was the agent of the government in the maintenance of order in church and state, secular and ecclesiastical policy being only aspects of the same thing. Further, the bishop was especially concerned because he saw in the struggle the hidden hand of the papacy. The opposition, whatever their motive, keenly resented the idea that they should be kept in ecclesiastical leading strings. One freeman, Thomas Kendall, was reported to the common council to have said:

that it was never a good world since that the spirituality must have the choosing of our mayor, and that they would have chosen him in the Palace, and that my Lord Bishop hath nothing to do with choosing of the mayor, and that if either the Lord Bishop or Mr Dean did come into the hall to choose any mayor there, they were as good not; and further that if they were cast out of the hall windows, that they knew the worst of it, and if they were hanged for it, that was the worst of it, And further said, it was shame for Mr Dean to deal as he did, for at his first coming he was all on the other side, but now he is contrary; and then he preached upon goodwill and for nothing, and now he selleth his sermons;

'and whether', said a witness, 'Kendall said that Mr Dean had 20 marks or 40 marks in the year, I am not sure, but sure I am he named either the

---

[1] P.R.O. State Papers Domestic, Eliz. i, cxcii, no. 67.   [2] See App. IV.

one or both, but very earnest he was'. For his lewd (and incoherent) speeches Kendall was disfranchised, but the council no doubt recorded his lewdness with zest.

It is impossible to believe that when Rishworth's party was thrown out of power a large majority of the council had suddenly become papist in sympathy. It is much more likely that they had become exasperated by the dictation of churchmen, and were easily led into hostility to those whom they thought mere tools of the clergy. Perhaps the bishop was right in thinking that Rome was somewhere behind the opposition, and in praying that the Lord should preserve and bless the Queen and defend her Church from the paw of the Lion. Some responsible laymen thought otherwise, but they may have been of catholic leanings themselves, and the best informed men, Burghley and his colleagues, agreed with the bishop. The interference of the privy council, however necessary it might be for reasons of state, was clearly an infringement of the privileges of the city, and the opposition could virtuously claim to have constitutional right on their side.

The dean involved in the battle was Griffin. He seems first to have been in favour with the common council, but perhaps under pressure from his superiors changed sides. Later a sermon preached by him in the Minster was complained of by the canons to Whitgift. The archbishop called the dean before him, and tried to damp down the controversy, writing that the dean renounced his errors in doctrine, though Whitgift misliked his words and manner of teaching: they came from Luther and Calvin.[1] The battle was followed by a period of peace and submission to the bishop. The curacy of Belton in Axholme, in the gift of the city, being vacant, the council not only appointed the episcopal nominee, but added that his lordship could better judge of the sufficiency of the man than that house could. There were several appointments of city preachers in the last decade of the century, including Mr Booth, the parson of Wickenby, and Mr Bourne, perhaps the rector of Washingborough of that name. The calm was not to last for long.[2]

In order to understand the view of the privy council and the bishop of the faction fight in Lincoln it is necessary to recall the mounting danger

---

[1] John Strype, *Life of Whitgift* (1822), II, 62; H. Nicholas, *Memoirs of Hatton* (1847), p. 486.

[2] A different procedure was followed in 1593. Mr Melton, a candidate for the curacy of Belton, preached twice before the mayor and corporation, and the masters of the Close 'a good auditory, to his good commendation'; whereafter Thomas Randes sent him to the bishop to apply for licence to preach, asking pardon for his (Randes's) boldness in licensing him to preach before the mayor (L.A.O. Cor./B/1/no. 13, f. 26). It was a procedure of which Laud would strongly have disapproved.

abroad: in France the Guises were gaining on the Huguenots; in Spain Philip II preparing his armada; in the Netherlands William of Orange assassinated; in Scotland the French party in power; and in Ireland rebellion. Furthermore, militant catholicism had re-entered England with the Jesuit mission in 1580. In that year the privy council sent to the sheriff of the county and some specially chosen justices to say that not only were some people forbearing to attend their parish church, but were using popish services and 'by *Bulles*, *Agnus Dei* and other unlawful stuff brought from the parts of beyond the seas, have sought to allure and pervert her Majesty's good and well disposed subjects in those parts'. They were asked to make diligent inquiry and report to the justices of assize, and the sheriff was bidden to impanel a special jury of persons well affected in religion to be employed as needed.[1] The privy council had already moved, for two of the Tyrwhitt family were in the Tower. A challenge of the Jesuit Edmond Campion came to the hands of one Yaxley who sent it to one Skinner of Lincoln, and was then lost. The privy council ordered that Yaxley should be closely examined and then sent up to London with a report on his reputation in his own country.[2]

The centre of popish activity was Twigmore near Kirton Lindsey.[3] The place, wrote one of Cecil's agents,

is one of the worst in her Majesty's dominions, and is used like a popish college, for traitors that use the north parts are there harboured. It joins upon Humber, and great woods, caves, and vaults thereunto belonging. Their fraternity is great, their place strong with men, guns and weapons. Sometimes they are in Yorkshire, Derby or Bishopric, but their chief abode is at Twigmore, within twelve miles of Hull by water.

He asked that Hull men should be sent to search.[4] When Sir Thomas Cecil was Lord President of the North he wrote to his brother Robert that some of the most obstinate recusants had fled into Lincolnshire, which was more dangerous than most parts of Yorkshire. Some were hiring houses there, and offering treble rent, but no names had been discovered.[5] In 1600 Richard Thimbleby of Irnham was under arrest; evidence was given before the lord chief justice of things said against the queen's title, and of plans to bring troops into England. Thimbleby admitted having a letter from the Jesuit Parsons to take to Lord Douglas in Scotland.[6]

[1] *A.P.C. 1580–81*, pp. 70, 71, 285.   [2] Ibid. pp. 71, 285.
[3] *C.S.P.D. 1581–90*, p. 145.
[4] *H.M.C. Salisbury*, VII, 300.   [5] *C.S.P.D. 1598–1601*, pp. 333, 378.
[6] Ibid. pp. 423–5, 430, 434. Shortly before the Armada a Spanish agent was reporting that the county of Lincoln was full of all sorts of victuals, and well supplied with horses. 'I only know of five gentlemen able to raise 2000 men, but there are many well affected to the Catholic religion and of good repute. I have been unable to ascertain the ports for fear of discovery' (*Cal. S.P. Spanish 1580–86*, p. 609).

If the puritans did not similarly menace the state they caused trouble to the church authorities. In 1584 John Barefoot, archdeacon of Lincoln, wrote to Whitgift that a number of puritan ministers had been suspended, had appealed to London, and been allowed to return. Thereafter Barefoot had, as Whitgift directed, exhorted them to subscribe, and to 'leave off their fantasies, conceived without any great ground of learning, and listen to your Grace and other fatherly and learned counsel'; and telling them that though their suspension should continue their benefices should not be sequestered for a season, so that they might get conformable men to serve in their cures. They replied that they had been promised restoration, citing Bishop Cooper, then of Winchester, as saying he wished it were so for a season. Barefoot had replied by fixing a day by which they must conform, failing which he would report to Whitgift. They replied that they would return to London and renew their suit. 'But upon what heartening I know not', they at once began preaching and ministering in their charges as before. This upset some who had conformed, who began to wish they had joined the others in their recusancy, especially as they were reproached by their more strong-minded brethren. This movement had been strengthened by a letter from 'Mr Field of London' to the recusants, exhorting them to stand stoutly to the cause, affirming the same to be not theirs but the Lord's, saying that those who had subscribed had 'made a breach', were branded men and would never do good thereafter. Copies of the letter had been circulated and had caused grief to wounded consciences. Barefoot had not been able to procure a copy. One of the recusants, Mr Huddleston of Saxilby, was before the Court of High Commission, and might be made to produce the original letter. There was concern also among the laity, and those who were backward and more than half popish were commanders of the consciences of these men, and the wiser and godlier were wondering where it would all end.[1] Barefoot clearly had no understanding of the puritan position, and wiser men than he might have seen something of events yet half a century ahead.

---

[1] *H.M.C. Marquis of Bath*, II, 24; Strype, *Life of Whitgift*, I, 302. Field was the head of the London classis, and one of the compilers of the admonitions to Parliament in 1571 (R. G. Usher, *The Presbyterian Movement in the Reign of Elizabeth* (Camden Series, 1905), p. xi).

CHAPTER VI

THE EARLY STUARTS: RELIGION AND POLITICS

THE poverty of the city clergy in both quality and income has already been noticed.[1] The population of the parishes was so small that pluralism as distinct from non-residence in the city could hardly be condemned; and, these things considered, a report on the incumbents made in 1611 seems to be moderately satisfactory. All the parish clergy were then described as of good behaviour save the prebendary and curate of St Botolph, who was of indifferent behaviour, and as in addition he was parson of West Barkwith, he may also have been non-resident. Several others held more than one living. St Mary and Snelland were held together; St Mark and St Benedict; St Swithin was held by a vicar choral; St Paul and St Michael by another; St Nicholas by a third. The curate of St Peter at Gowts was usher at the grammar school. The rector of St Peter at Arches was non-resident; he was vicar of Haxey in the Isle of Axholme, and had no curate. Only five of the city clergy were preachers: the indifferent prebendary of St Botolph; the vicar of St Mary who held Snelland; the non-resident rector of St Peter at Arches; the vicar of St Martin; and the vicar choral who held St Nicholas.[2] There were 1912 communicants in city, Bail and Close;[3] and the fabrics of the churches were in good order and kept decently, with the exception of St Nicholas, where the dean and chapter had promised to repair the chancel.

Twenty years earlier the ecclesiastical authorities had been chiefly concerned to withstand papist influences, which they had discerned behind a faction fight in the common council.[4] The catholics were still to be reckoned with. Roman priests were moving about in concealment. There were several weighty families of gentry who were popish recusants. Mass was often said in the house of Anthony Monson of Carlton, where several prophesied just before the Gunpowder Plot that there would be a turn in favour of popery.[5] Some of the Thorolds, the Bolles and the Thimblebys were catholics, and the plot had its local associations. An anonymous letter which came to the hands of Robert Cecil told of a visit to a catholic gentleman's house in Lincolnshire.[6] John Wright, one of the conspirators, lived

[1] See above, pp. 100–101.
[2] L.A.O. Liber Cleri, 1611.
[3] C. W. Foster, State of the Church (L.R.S. 1926), I, 228, 319.
[4] See above, pp. 102, 106.
[5] C.S.P.D. 1611–18, p. 352. [6] H.M.C. Salisbury, XVII, 530.

at Twigmore, the 'popish college' for the northern parts.[1] Sir Edmund Bussy wrote to his cousin Sir William Armyne about searches for Jesuits and seminary priests: 'they have many obscure and secret rooms and corners in their houses, where they not only (as I suppose) hide their outward arms and weapons, not of defence but of offence, if there were power to perform the same, but also their inward incouragers, the firebrands to all sedition and rebellion, so it is very fitting that the same should be done presently and secretly, that they may have no time to convey the same out of the way.'[2] In 1612 the king, having learned that there were many Jesuits and arms in Lincolnshire, ordered his lieutenant to take precautions to prevent danger.[3]

But the coming battle of the Anglican church was not with the catholics but with the puritans, and as if to symbolise the change a feud broke out in the common council between the factions respectively championing authority and puritanism. The council had placed increasing emphasis on the duty of the city preacher 'to preach the Word'—the puritan phrase is used by the town clerk in his marginal note—every Sunday afternoon and Wednesday morning. First they resolved that their preacher must not hold a benefice outside the city, but must be continually among the citizens, which apparently disqualified the then holder of the office; and secondly, they were willing to pay an increased stipend of £43. 6s. 8d., a large sum, out of the inadequate city revenues. They found John Smith, a young Fellow of Christ's College, Cambridge, already known to be a puritan, and elected him preacher in 1600. During his stormy two years in Lincoln he buried a son, Jeruball, who must have been baptised in an earlier day of exaltation, and baptised a daughter Mara, whose name reflects a later mood of bitterness.[4] From Lincoln he went to Gainsborough, where he renounced his Anglican orders and formed a separatist congregation of Baptists; and whence he sought refuge in Amsterdam. From the incident of his having baptised himself he became known as the Se-Baptist.

His Lincoln ministry began inauspiciously when he was elected by a majority of eight votes to seven. His champions knew that they and he were insecure, and in 1602 he was given a life patent of office under the city seal. The next mayor in office, however, belonged to the opposite party, and he procured resolutions avoiding various measures lately taken, and declaring that Smith had approved himself a factious man by preaching

---

[1] See above, p. 107; *H.M.C. Rutland*, I, 400; *C.S.P.D. 1603–10*, pp. 240, 248–9; Sutton Nelthorpe, 'Twigmore and the Gunpowder Plot', in *Lincolnshire Magazine*, II (1934–6), 229.

[2] Dr Williams's Library, Morrice MSS. XI, p. 12.

[3] *C.S.P. Venetian 1610–13*, no. 610.

[4] R. C. Dudding, *Parish Register of St Peter at Gowts* (L.R.S. 1923), pp. 11, 40.

against men of good place in the city, that he was not licensed to preach and was even then inhibited by the bishop, and dismissing him from office.

The charge of personal preaching is proved by Smith's published work. In a series of lectures on Psalm xxii he dilated upon the bulls, the lions and the dogs that encompassed the Christian, and complained that persecutors of the Church took it in dudgeon if they were so called, adding:

Sometime it falleth out that the minister in his ministry is occasioned by the scripture to unfold the evil properties of wicked men in regard whereof they are compared to beasts, as the lion's properties are pride and cruelty, the fox's craft and subtlety, the hart's fearfulness etc., and it may fall out that some wicked man called lion hath the lion's pride and cruelty... now if these men take themselves either named or aimed at in the ministry... without doubt either gross folly, or an accusing conscience, or mere malice or brutish ignorance bring men into these surmises... the minister by God's providence, which to him perhaps is chance medley, sometimes shall wound him whom he never aimed at, or harden him whom he never thought of; for the word of God is both a savour of life and of death to several sorts of persons.[1]

It was hardly to be expected that alderman Leon Hollingworth, one of the opposite party, would regard this passage as impersonal, and the marvel is that Smith should maintain that it was. As a young man he must have been rash and hasty, though at the end of his life he retracted all his biting and bitter words.

Archbishop Whitgift had written to the bishop saying that he had licensed Smith to preach on the usual subscription to the articles, but had revoked the licence, it not being his intention to maintain any man in his contentious courses, adding—remembering his days as dean of Lincoln— 'especially in a place I wish so well as that'. Already before his dismissal Smith was charged in the archdeacon's court with preaching in St Peter at Arches and other Lincoln churches without lawful authority. On this Smith showed letters from the bishop allowing him to preach in Lincoln until he himself should come there. The archdeacon thought this not enough, but at the request of Smith himself, Dr Parker the precentor, and aldermen Robert Rishworth and Thomas Swift, he admonished him to procure a licence, and in the meantime inhibited him from preaching.[2]

John Becke, the mayor, and Hollingworth, with the consent of the council, exhibited articles to the bishop against Smith for erroneous doctrine and undue teaching of matters of religion and personal preaching. Smith threatened an action upon the deed granting him office for life, and either this action or an action by two displaced aldermen, or both (for they were

[1] *Works*, ed. W. T. Whitley (Baptist Historical Society, 1915), I, 44–5.
[2] L.A.O. Act Book 1580–1618, f. 179a.

tangled together), came before the judges of assize; they referred matters to Sir William Wray, Sir Philip Tyrwhitt, the dean, and Mr Edward King, who, failing to agree, referred them to Lord Sheffield. Sheffield awarded £50 to Smith for the surrender of his patent; the displaced aldermen should be re-elected on a vacancy, and if any should resign in favour of one of them he should receive £25 from the preacher. Failing this the displaced aldermen might pursue their own remedy.[1] The mayor and his brethren then wrote to the bishop that they were not proceeding further against Smith, and would make no claim for costs.[2] The faction fight in the council went on furiously, but Smith seems to have been content with Sheffield's award, as he later dedicated a book to him.

How Smith came to Lincoln does not appear, but he had weighty friends among the gentry. His exposition of Psalm xxii was dedicated 'to the Right Worshipful religious and courteous Knight, Sir William Wray, my approved good friend and benefactor',

because I have experienced yourself to be, under the King's Majesty, a principal professor and protector of religion in these quarters (for what a multitude of faithful ministers are debtors to you in the flessh), and for that I, among the rest, have rested under your shadow.[3]

Wray was the son of the Elizabethan lord chief justice. One of his sisters was wife successively of Godfrey Foljambe, Sir William Bowes (a kinsman of John Knox) and Lord Darcy of Aston. To her, as Lady Bowes, Thomas Helwys the Baptist dedicated one of his books, saying: 'I know there is none in the land that hath better means to procure a cause of religion to be handled according to the judgment of the best.' Her sister married first Sir George St Paul of Snarford, and afterwards the earl of Warwick. The two sisters sent to Cambridge Richard Bernard, the famous puritan vicar of Worksop, who after moving towards separatism drew back to conformity. He dedicated his *Christian Advertisements* to St Paul and his wife, hailing them as benefactors; other books he addressed to her as countess of Warwick; and his translation of Terence to Christopher and the other young gentlemen of Wray's family, whose tutor he had probably been. Even the royalist Gervase Holles noted that Wray's wife Lucy was a good

---

[1] L.A.O. Bp. Reg. Cor. Misc.

[2] L.A.O. Cor. B/2/4, f. 6.

[3] *The Bright Morning Starre, or the Resolution and Exposition of the 22nd Psalm, preached publickly in foure sermons at Lincolne by John Smith, Preacher of the Citie*. . . . The only known copy is in the library of Emmanuel College, Cambridge (*Works*, 1, 2). See also W. H. Burgess, *John Smith the Se-Baptist, Thomas Helwys and the First Baptist Church in England* (1911). Wray sleeps in effigy at Ashby cum Fenby, his sword by his side, but the Book clasped in his hands.

PLATE 10

SIR WILLIAM WRAY

From the tomb at Ashby cum Fenby

woman, adding that Wray himself was a simple and honest man, though without courage or clarity.[1]

Wray's brother-in-law Sir George St Paul of Snarford was a kindred spirit. Among his benefactions were the endowment of a free school at Market Rasen and the maintenance of a preacher at Welton, both of which foundations were at one time occupied by Edward Reyner, who was to become a famous puritan preacher at Lincoln. St Paul's virtues and good deeds were recited at length in the funeral oration of John Chadwick, the rector of Faldingworth, a one-time nonconformist, whom the church-wardens had failed to present for not wearing the surplice, but who, before a citation could be issued, subscribed.[2]

These two, Wray and St Paul, who both sat in different parliaments for the shire and for Grimsby, played an active part there, especially in religious matters. In 1604 St Paul promoted a bill against scandalous and unworthy ministers, and Wray joined him on the committee for the bill. In the next year St Paul was on the committee for the bill for a public thanksgiving on every fifth of November for the failure of the Gunpowder Plot, which was included in the Prayer Book and was to be such mighty anti-Roman propaganda for so long, and which must have turned against Charles I and Laud when they were suspected of Romanising schemes.[3]

Sir William Armyne of Osgodby belonged to the same circle. He was patron of Lavington (in which Osgodby was situate) and Silk Willoughby, where the rector was Hugh Tuke. Tuke was the father of Lincolnshire puritans; presented to his living in 1577, suspended for nonconformity in 1584, and frequently in trouble with the authorities.[4] He held the living until his death in 1626, leaning for support on Armyne—to one of whose sons he was tutor—and other friends, as is shown by his letter to Armyne in 1612:

although I know you be in trouble with many cares of your own and the country, so that I am loath to trouble you with mine, yet thinking you expect to know how it goes with me, and I desiring your worship's help and counsel for my stay in this place and calling, I pray you to lend a few thoughts hereunto. I told your worship the bishop [Barlow] threatened in a letter to proceed against me. Since that Dr Othill cited me to Grantham, whither I sent to be respited till

[1] *Holles' Church Notes*, ed. R. E. G. Cole (L.R.S. 1911), p. 64 and n. Lady Wray's tomb in the Minster perished in the Civil War, though a drawing of it survives in the Winchelsea Book of Monuments.

[2] John Wilford, *Memorials and Characters...of Eminent Persons* (1741), p. 179; Foster, *State of the Church*, I, cv; *A.A.S.R.* VI (1862), 164–5. The St Paul tombs at Snarford are sadly neglected and in danger of falling.

[3] *C.J.* I, 985, 990, 258, 426.

[4] Foster, op. cit. I, cxv.

they came to Sleaford, and long days and fairer weather.... The last Sunday as I was in the pulpit came into the church one John Stirrup...showed me a writing with a seal saying I must be at Bugden.... I pray your worship to set your hand to this letter or the like.

And he inclosed a draft letter to the bishop, asking him to forbear, and certifying that Tuke was an honest, godly and peaceable man; adding that he hoped to get Sir Edward Carr's and Sir Edmund Bussy's hands, and certain preachers thereabouts. Tuke's son Thomas had earlier written to Armyne referring to the book he had been bold to publish in Armyne's name in 1606, and acknowledging his duty to him for his constant goodwill to his father.[1] John Fisher, the nonconforming rector of Ingoldsby, was another friend of Armyne, and highly commends his family for virtue and religion; it is significant for the future that he speaks of the great hopefulness of William Armyne the son.[2]

Sir Thomas Grantham has more direct association with the city; he belonged to the same social, religious and political group. He sat in all the parliaments from 1604 until 1629, for either the city or the shire, and he frequently appears in action against popish recusants. He had been a ward of the second Lord Burghley, became a freeman of the city by purchase in 1597, and married a daughter of Lord Keeper Puckering. As the future Colonel Hutchinson lived with him when he and Sir Thomas's son attended the grammar school at Lincoln, Mrs Hutchinson described him in her biography of her husband. He 'was a gentleman of great repute in his country, and kept up all his life the old hospitality of England, having a great retinue and a noble table, and a resort for all the nobility and gentry in those parts'.[3] Sir John Eliot paid tribute to Grantham as 'a worthy gentleman of Lincolnshire who was never wanting to the service of his country'; and he adds elsewhere that Grantham disliked taxation in the form of fifteenths because it was likely to be burdensome to the poor.[4] Grantham's house at St Katharine's has perished, though Buck made a sketch of it in his notebook; of his house at Goltho there remain only a moat and (it is said) a few flowers from the garden that have seeded in the hedgerows; there is no known portrait, and his tomb effigy lies in

---

[1] Dr Williams's Library, Morrice MSS. XI, 8, 16. The court books for 1612 are missing. Dr Othowell Hill was vicar-general and official principal of the bishop.

[2] Ibid. p. 3; Foster, op. cit. I, cvii. No book published in Armyne's name can be traced, but Tuke published in 1607 *The True Trial and Turning of a Sinner*. ... Thomas was minister of St Giles in the Fields 1616, and vicar of St Olave Jewry 1617–57, whence he was ejected (Venn, *Alumni Cantabrigienses*, part I, iv, 271).

[3] *Memoirs of Colonel Hutchinson*, ed. Sir C. H. Firth (1906), p. 41. About 1618 he inherited the Black Monks, Lincoln, from his kinsman Robert Grantham of Dunholme (Lindsey County Council B.R.A. 7/11).

[4] J. Forster, *Sir John Eliot* (1872 ed.), I, 177, 307.

mutilated fragments after unseemly neglect and ill-usage, yet he deserves to be piously remembered in a book upon his own city.[1]

The puritan gentry of the county had a powerful friend in Theophilus Clinton, fourth earl of Lincoln. His brother-in-law Lord Saye and Sele was a leading opponent of the Court. Lincoln raised a troop of horse to aid the Elector Palatine in 1624. In the House of Lords he had brought in a bill against the haunting of alehouses, and was on the committee for the bill to prevent profane swearing and cursing.[2] Cotton Mather speaks of his family as being the best of any nobleman in England, and Roger Williams recalls riding with John Cotton, the puritan vicar of Boston, to Lincoln's house at Sempringham; Cotton's successor at Boston, Anthony Tuckney, had been Lincoln's chaplain. His father was a prime mover in the settlement of Massachusetts Bay, and his sister Arabella emigrated with her husband to New England in 1629.[3]

Between them these men held not fewer than twenty-seven advowsons, and no doubt could influence presentations to many others. The significance of the group of gentry for the history of the Civil War cannot be mistaken. In their households were growing up the men who would sit in the Long Parliament on the puritan side, and who would rule the county through the parliamentary committee. They early appear as a group on the accession of James I. The ministers of the diocese inclining to protestant nonconformity presented to the king an apology for refusing the subscrip-

---

[1] The north aisle of the chancel of old St Martin's church was the burial place of the Grantham family, who had formerly occupied the prebendal house in the parish (*A.A.S.R.* XIII (1876), 214). Holles describes the tomb, and says that the statues of Sir Thomas and his lady for proportion, visage, complexion, were 'effigiated so as to give a perfect representation of them as they were being alive, their hands elevated' (*Holles' Church Notes*, ed. Cole, p. 57). Willson visited the church in 1807, and found the canopy of Sir Thomas and Lady Grantham's tomb had fallen and broken the faces of the statues (Willson Collection (Society of Antiquaries), V, 54). When the tomb was injured by the fall of part of the church it was moved into the church tower, which remained standing. Thence, in 1889, it was removed by Mr Justice Grantham upon an unfounded claim of relationship and without a faculty. At the same time he removed an armorial glass panel of Thomas Grantham the son (dated 1657) from Goltho Church. Both were taken to Barcombe in Sussex. When challenged, the judge said that the tomb was doubtless once in the church; he had found it under a heap of rubbish near where the church used to stand. He did not mention that it was in the church tower. The challenge to his claim of relationship he met only by a vague phrase about 'knowing something more than your correspondent of the migration of my family more than two centuries ago'. It was said that he owned to an ancestor, one 'St Hugh Grantham, whom the Jews crucified at Lincoln'; which prompted the comment that presumably he did not claim more than collateral descent from the child of eight or thereabouts who is said to have been the victim of a ritual murder (*Notes and Queries*, 10th series, V (1906), 70, 231, 276, 338). The remaining fragments of the effigies are now in St Benedict's Church, Lincoln, but the Goltho glass is still in exile at Barcombe.

[2] *L.J.* III, 117, 118.　　　　[3] *Complete Peerage*, VII (1929), 696.

tion and conformity that were required, and stated in the published *Abridgement* thereof that thirty-three ministers in Lincolnshire shared their views.[1] Bishop Chaderton wrote to Robert Cecil that he understood that many of the knights of Lincolnshire had set their hands to a petition on behalf of some ministers not conformable; he could not get the petition, but he understood that Mr Atkinson of Glentworth was to deliver it. He urged strong measures.[2]

When therefore it is found that Atkinson is appointed city lecturer of Lincoln there is no mistaking the significance of the appointment. He had been vicar of Blyton, and transferred to the living of Glentworth—both in Wray's gift—and in 1604 was cited for not wearing a surplice and conforming to the ceremonies. He was excommunicated, but absolved on swearing to obey the law.[3] In 1614 he was on the rota for the lecture at Market Rasen.[4] The following year Robert Atkinson, preacher of God's word, was allowed £20 to preach and read lecture as the mayor should appoint, on Wednesdays. He was joined by Edward Reyner, a protégé of St Paul, who became Sunday lecturer in 1626, and the next year rector of St Peter at Arches and city preacher. According to Calamy, he was 'even then a nonconformist to the ceremonies, which created him adversaries, who would frequently complain of him, and threaten him, and yet his liberty of preaching was continued; and yet his moderation procured him favour with several that belonged to the minster, who would sometimes hear him in the afternoon. Sir Edward Lake himself, the chancellor (of the diocese) was often his auditor, and declared that he received benefit by his preaching, till he was reproved from above.' Bishop Williams (of whom much must be said later) appointed Reyner to preach at one of his visitations, but touched his tender conscience when he offered him a prebend: 'the importunity of friends prevailed with him to accept the bishop's present of a prebend, but when he came next morning seriously to reflect upon the necessary attendants and consequences of this his new preferment, he was much dissatisfied; for he found he could not keep it with a safe and quiet conscience'. He therefore prevailed with his relative Lady Armyne to go to the bishop to mollify the offence, and obtain release.[5]

But religion and politics were so inextricably mixed that it is necessary to turn to a more secular aspect of affairs in order to understand the local circumstances in which public dissension grew slowly into conflict. After

[1] P. 52.   [2] *H.M.C. Salisbury*, xvii, 34–5, and see p. 65.
[3] Foster, *State of the Church*, i, civ, 363, 365.
[4] 'Bishop Neile's Visitation Book', in *A.A.S.R.* xvi (1881), 14.
[5] Edmund Calamy, *Nonconformists Memorial* (1775), ii, 149–50.

the disgrace of Roger, the fifth earl of Rutland, for complicity in the Essex revolt, the family had recovered its leadership in the county. On the old queen's death Rutland was instantly urged by one of his men of business to proclaim King James in Nottingham, and perhaps also in Lincoln, and advised to send Sir George Manners to offer his service to the king.[1] Perhaps the advice was taken, for later in 1603 Rutland was appointed lord lieutenant of Lincolnshire, being followed on his death by his brother Francis the sixth earl.

At the parliamentary election that followed the accession young Thomas Grantham and Edward Tyrwhitt of Stainfield, who had both been knighted as the new king passed through Belvoir on his way to London, were returned, but in the parliament of 1614 Grantham was joined by Edward Bash, who was a Rutland nominee. Sir Robert Monson, like Bash, had bought the freedom in that year, no doubt with a view to election, but if so he failed. In that House of Commons Grantham argued that the redress of grievances about impositions ought to come before supply,[2] this being the majority view. Soon afterwards Bishop Neile of Lincoln, a strong supporter of the royal prerogative and the worst of episcopal time-servers, was severely criticised for saying that the Commons were striking at the Crown itself, standing upon the king's head, in attacking impositions, and that they were guilty of mutiny and sedition. In the Commons debate Grantham said that all of his country disavowed the bishop's action, and wished he might be punished. Others said that he discouraged ministers from preaching twice in the day, and was trying to put down lectures; he was alleged to have said that if he must go to the sermon he must sleep. The Commons resolved to forbear from all business until the matter was disposed of. In his place in the Lords Neile protested with tears in his eyes that his words were misconceived.[3]

Parliament was quickly dissolved, and letters were sent to sheriffs and mayors asking for gifts, with names of the givers, so that the king could take notice of their good affections.[4] At the same time a general view of the trained bands was ordered, especially on account of the danger to the protestants in the United Provinces.[5] This happened each summer for a number of years, horse and foot, arms and armour, powder and match and beacons, all being reviewed by the lord lieutenant and his deputies. The bishop was required to furnish a list of clergy who could provide arms.

In the parliament of 1621 Grantham was returned for the county with

---

[1] *H.M.C. Rutland*, I, 389.   [2] *C.J.* I, 474.
[3] Ibid. 496–7, 499; *L.J.* II, 709–13; S. R. Gardiner, *History of England* (1883 ed.), II, 243, 268 n. (Neile had been implicated in the burning alive of a heretic at Lichfield when he was bishop there).
[4] *A.P.C. 1613–14*, pp. 492–4.   [5] Ibid. pp. 552–5.

Sir George Manners, and the city returned Sir Edward Ayscough, a friend of Grantham, and Sir Lewis Watson of Rockingham Castle, who had just married into the Manners family. Subsidies having been granted to the king, the commissioners for their collection in Lincolnshire wrote to the privy council that, though they had done their best, the general decay of rents and estates made it impossible to bring the subsidy up to the previous one. Some justices could not bear to be assessed at £20, and so were willing to resign their offices.[1] This was partly because of the low price of corn, due both to excess of home supply and to importation of grain; neither corn nor wool sold as usual in 1620.[2]

Supply being insufficient, the king sent out a new appeal for money in 1622, referring in particular to the disaster which had befallen his daughter Elizabeth and her husband the Elector Palatine in the loss of the Palatinate. The knights and gentry and others were to be called—not too many at once—to see what they would give. When later the backwardness of some counties was complained of, Lincolnshire was not among them.[3] In the next year the musters were followed by a call for volunteers to fight in the United Provinces; the county was to find 500 men for Count Mansfeld's ill-fated expedition, half of them under the command of the young earl of Lincoln.[4] Another 400 men were called for in 1625, to be sent to Hull.[5] In the last parliament of James I, Grantham again sat for the county, ensuring that the city returned a kindred spirit in Thomas Hatcher of Careby along with Watson. When an order was made for presenting popish recusants Grantham presented Rutland among others.[6]

Charles I came to the throne in 1625, and the city returned Grantham and John Monson to parliament. On the very day that the duke of Buckingham addressed the Commons on the royal policy, Grantham, speaking in the debate on Supply, urged that they should postpone giving until later, and Sir John Eliot testifies that he spoke so promptly that the motion forthwith died.[7] As a result of the debate the House was quickly dissolved. In the second parliament of the reign (1626) Grantham sat with Sir Robert Monson, but it was soon dissolved in order to save Buckingham from impeachment. Privy seals were sent out for loans in default of supply. The collector for Lincolnshire was Sir William Armyne the younger, who had succeeded his father, and already sat in several parliaments. Some collectors refused to act, and some contributors were willing to pay but not to subscribe their names as required, and instructions were sent that they

---

[1] *C.S.P.D. 1619–23*, p. 305.
[2] Ibid. p. 130. Corn was short in 1623, p. 553.   [3] *A.P.C. 1621–23*, p. 176.
[4] *A.P.C. 1623–25*, pp. 8, 249, 351; *C.S.P.D. 1623–25*, p. 409.
[5] *A.P.C. 1625–26*, pp. 37, 42–5, 141, 321.   [6] *C.J.* I, 776.
[7] Ibid. 814; Forster, *Sir John Eliot*, I, 177.

need not do so. These were not sent to the county, but they were to the city, implying that scruples were felt there.[1]

But things in Lincolnshire were much worse than this suggests. The story told in London, and reported by the Venetian ambassador to the Doge and Senate, was that Rutland had returned hurriedly from Lincolnshire, reporting that only three persons had consented to the loan, 'all the rest having tumultuously joined in the refusal, giving signs of almost open rebellion, venting their rage on the house in which the royal commissioners were sitting'.[2] Lord Lincoln was summoned before the council, charged with evil speaking against this new form of raising money, and sent to the Tower.[3] Warrants were issued for his servants, no doubt to get evidence against him, for, wrote the Tuscan Resident, he was committed not so much for having refused to pay his share of the loan, as for having dissuaded others from doing so.[4] The leading gentry, all commissioners for the loan, were summoned to appear before the privy council and committed to prison: Armyne, the mayor of Boston and others to the Fleet; Sir John Wray, Sir Thomas Grantham and Sir Edward Ayscough to the Gatehouse; William Thorold, committed to the Marshalsea, was discharged on submission. In June Wray pleaded that he was very weak and infirm of body, needing fresh air, and was allowed to go to a country house. Thereafter the others were sent to counties far from their own, the sheriffs being responsible for them. Grantham was sent first to Dorset and then to Kent. Armyne, like Sir John Eliot, did not go as directed, and was required to explain his disobedience. The lieutenant of the Tower reported that visitors to his prisoners included Thomas Hatcher and, he believed, Armyne.[5]

Nevertheless, with the need for a new parliament they were released in January 1628, and in March Lord Lincoln was allowed to leave the Tower.[6] During their confinement the county justices, called on to contribute a third of the charge of a ship of war, to be set forth at Boston, pleaded the general poverty occasioned by the late lending to the king, and prayed to be excused 'this unusual and unexpected charge'.[7] The city, however, paid in full.[8] When parliament met Sir William Welby and other deputy lieutenants of the county were charged with levying money for military affairs, and committing to Lincoln gaol those who refused to pay. Welby agreed

---

[1] A.P.C. June–Dec. 1626, pp. 134, 168, 388–9.
[2] C.S.P. Venetian, 1626–28, p. 119.
[3] Ibid. pp. 126, 128, 130, 154, 161.
[4] H.M.C. Skrine, p. 116.   [5] H.M.C. Cowper, 1, 383.
[6] A.P.C. Jan.–Aug. 1627, pp. 128, 240, 252, 338, 395, 430; A.P.C. Sept. 1627–June 1628, pp. 217, 350.
[7] C.S.P.D. 1627–8, p. 138.   [8] Ibid. pp. 257, 360, 418.

that he had no authority save an order of sessions. He was summoned to appear before the Commons, but was saved when the king ended the session.[1]

Lincoln had to face another expense. In April 1626 a writ of *Quo Warranto* was issued against the city, and the council, called on to defend its liberties, appointed attorneys to plead the existing charter, or, if they thought fit, to renew it. In November 1627 it was resolved to petition the king for a new charter, with a view to amending existing defects and obtaining such additions as should be thought needful and requisite. As this course would be expensive, it was decided to raise £200 (later raised to £250) on mortgage of corporate property (including St Mary Hall). Interest was to be paid at 8 %, to be deducted from the mayor's allowance for the venison feast, and the twelve aldermen were each to pay 10s. a year from their private estates.

A new charter was issued on 18 December 1628.[2] It is said that *Quo Warranto* proceedings were used at this period as a means of controlling and modelling corporations;[3] but the only material change at Lincoln lay in the appointment of the mayor and justices. The old rule had been that four justices should be elected in addition to the mayor; the new charter provided that the senior alderman who had not held office should be elected, and that he and all the aldermen who had passed the chair should be justices.[4] This emphasis on seniority ensured that the older, and, it was hoped, soberer, men would hold office; but it is difficult to believe that the chief reason for the proceedings was not financial, especially as another writ of *Quo Warranto* was issued in 1631, and the city had to produce the new charter in London. The proceedings cost at least £50. A little later the charters were produced again to sustain the claim to the office of escheator.

The king's needs compelled him to call a parliament in February 1628, and, as Rushworth remarks, those gentlemen who suffered for the loan were chiefly in the people's eye.[5] Armyne and Sir John Wray were returned for the shire; Sir Christopher Wray and Henry Pelham for Grimsby; Sir Anthony Irby secured a seat for Boston on petition; Thomas Hatcher sat for Stamford; and Grantham and Ayscough were returned by the city. There was no longer any question of a Monson or a Rutland nominee holding one seat. These men, linked by proximity and conviction, and many of them by kinship and marriage, played a notable part in this parliament, and the survivors of them a yet more notable part later.

[1] *C.J.* I, 894–5, 917–18.   [2] Birch, p. 200.
[3] W. S. Holdsworth, *History of English Law*, VI (1924), 57.
[4] Birch, pp. 218, 233.   [5] John Rushworth, *Historical Collections* (1659), I, 476.

Grantham, Sir John Wray, Armyne and Ayscough sat on the committee of privileges; Grantham and Wray in company with Pym and Hampden on the committee for searching records and precedents; Grantham on the committee to consider what course was fittest to take about tonnage and poundage; and he and Armyne conferred with the Lords on the Petition of Right, and with Ayscough attended the king with the petition on religion.[1] When the Houses were dissolved in 1629, there began the eleven years of rule without parliament which were the prologue to yet more bitter conflict.

Affairs in Lincolnshire became bound up with the stormy career of John Williams, a shrewd and supple young Welshman seeking a career in the church, who by winning the favour of James I had become dean of Westminster in 1620, and in the following year lord keeper of the great seal and bishop of Lincoln.[2] On the accession of Charles I he suffered a reversal of fortune, and was deprived of the great seal, and lived thereafter chiefly at Buckden. He sealed his disgrace by supporting the Petition of Right in the Lords. He incurred the bitter hatred of William Laud, bishop of London, who became archbishop of Canterbury in 1633; and he was charged with favouring puritans and nonconformists. It is clear that the puritan gentry were accustomed to approach him in questions of church patronage and order. In 1632 Sir William Armyne wrote to him commending a minister who wished to keep a lecture in Stamford, as being conformable and of a quiet and peaceable spirit; and in 1635 Sir Anthony Irby had a suggestion of a successor to a resigning vicar of Boston to make to him.[3] It was given in evidence against him in the Star Chamber that he discouraged Sir John Lamb and Dr Sibthorp—diocesan officials—from proceeding in ecclesiastical courts against puritans, 'and that the bishop asked Sir John Lamb what kind of people those Puritans were of whom he complained, and whether they did pay the loan-money? to which Sir John replied, They did conform upon that account and paid their Money: but nevertheless they were Puritans, not conformable to the Church: to which the Bishop replied, If they pay their Monies so readily to the King, the Puritans are the King's best Subjects, and I am sure, said the Bishop, the Puritans will carry all at last'.[4] There, if the testimony be true, spoke the realist politician.

In 1628 Williams was brought into the Star Chamber on a trumped-up charge of betraying the secrets of the privy council, about which nothing

---

[1] *C.J.* I, 873, 902, 912, 916, 923. For their family connections see the table at p. 127, which is taken from M. P. Moore, *The family of Carre of Sleaford* (1863).

[2] He was precentor of Lincoln, 1613–21; he was installed as bishop in 1628.

[3] L.A.O. Cor. B./3/ff. 28, 37. [4] Rushworth, op. cit. II, 417.

happened for several years. Later he committed himself to upholding the credit of John Pregion, the principal registrar of the diocese and one of his witnesses, who had a bastardy order made against him. His intervention seems to have gone beyond the bounds of the legitimate, and he laid himself open to a new charge of tampering with the evidence. He was heavily fined and sent to the Tower, and he was later convicted of libel and fined again. He lay in the Tower until he was summoned to resume his seat in the House of Lords in the Long Parliament.

There was proceeding concurrently a bitter quarrel between the ecclesiastical lawyers of the diocese, who pursued one another through every available civil and church court with a zeal that to a less litigious age seems to be a shocking exhibition of malice and greed. The two quarrels, the greater and the less, became intermingled, and while Pregion relied on Williams, the other party, Sir John Lamb, Dr Farmery (the chancellor of the diocese) and others, looked to Laud for protection. The justices who heard the bastardy proceedings against Pregion were Sir John Monson, Farmery, and Charles Dalison, who became recorder of Lincoln.[1] Monson and his father Sir Thomas were supporters of Laud, to whom Sir John wrote in 1636 offering that his father, though aged and unfit for travel, should attend on him at Oxford, though he himself would not dare to appear 'for the declining of observation', a phrase with sinister suggestion of archiepiscopal collusion.[2] Sir Thomas gave evidence against Williams in the Star Chamber,[3] and Sir John Monson received 1000 marks damages against him.[4]

Most of the clergy sided with Laud. Dr Marshall, the precentor, gave an unedifying account of his visit to Mrs Pregion in Lincoln in an attempt to trap her into admissions, while her son lurked behind the hangings in the room; and he describes also how Dr Meres, the chancellor, had searched for Pregion's papers while Pregion was in the hands of a messenger. The city of Lincoln buzzed with the news of the varying turns of fortune in the prolonged struggle. The same report shows Williams using Sir Edward Ayscough as his agent.[5] Quarrels broke out again in Laud's metropolitical

---

[1] Dalison, one of the Laughton family, seated also at Greetwell as tenants of the dean and chapter, became one of the city's counsel in 1631 and recorder in 1637. He married Elizabeth, daughter of Robert Smith of Lincoln, and at the time of the civil war was a papist.

[2] Lambeth MS. 1030, no. 48.   [3] Rushworth, op. cit. I, (ii), 424.

[4] See *C.S.P.D. 1635*, p. 405. Sir Thomas Monson had been charged with complicity in the Overbury poisoning case in 1615, and only secured pardon in 1617 after the death of his enemy Sir Edward Coke. In 1633 he was trying to procure a barony, relying in part on the influence of his son's mother-in-law Lady Oxenbridge of Broxbourne, Herts, (L.A.O. Monson, 19/7/1). There is a portrait at South Carlton.

[5] Lambeth MS. 1030, no. 46.

visitation in 1634; Farmery suspended Pregion, and Williams later tried to suspend Farmery. In this struggle the parties were aligned exactly as they were in the great political questions of the day.[1]

Williams's attitude to puritans, and his endeavours to help a much distressed city[2] brought him many friends. Ambitious, hasty, and vindictive to his enemies as he was, he was a man of common sense and good nature, lavish in expenditure, and he enjoyed being a patron. He rebuilt the bishop's palace in Lincoln. It had not been lived in since the Reformation had stripped the diocese of many endowments; the rents that remained were not enough to keep it warm. In three years he restored it, and bought a library to instal there. 'But unkind troubles', wrote his biographer, 'that came thick upon the main Founder, stopped the advance of it so long, that the timber came into the hands of the soldiers to make fortifications: and the books became a prey to every vulture that could catch them.'[3]

In 1634 Laud asserted his claim to visit the diocese, and in spite of Williams's resistance he made the claim good. He sought an initial report on the diocese from Farmery, who alleged great defects in attendance and performance at divine service at the cathedral; with the general observation that the sort of people that ran from their own parishes after affected preachers were the most troublesome of the ecclesiastical inquisition.[4] In September, Laud's vicar-general, Sir Nathaniel Brent, who conducted the visitation, made his report. At the Minster he found the communion table not to be very decent, and the rail worse. The organs were old and naught, the copes and vestments had been embezzled, and there were prebendaries who had never seen the church, and who appointed insufficient men to preach for them. The churchyard was made offensive by the presence of alehouses, hounds and swine.[5]

He might have added that the fabric itself of the Minster was in disrepair. At this time Laud was collecting money for the repair of St Paul's, and evidently Sir John Monson was engaged locally on his behalf. Monson

---

[1] Williams was evidently in Lincoln in 1633, when presents were sent to him by the gentry. The rewards given by Pregion on the bishop's behalf to the servants who brought them were perhaps in proportion to the value of the gifts, and so to the esteem the donors felt for the bishop. The countess of Warwick's keeper for a fat doe received 6s. 8d.; Sir John Wray's keeper 6s. 8d.; Sir John Bolles's servant 5s.; Sir Thomas Monson's servant 1s.; Lord Castleton's keeper 6s. 8d.; Sir Edward Ayscough's servant 9s.; Dr Lincoln's servant 2s. (L.A.O. Bp. Acct. 23/1).

[2] See below, pp. 136–7.

[3] John Hacket, *Scrinia Reserata: A Memorial offered to the Great Deservings of John Williams, D.D.* (1693), II, 34. The bishop's manor house at Nettleham was taken down about 1630 after being deserted for over 60 years (*C.S.P.D. 1629–31*, pp. 166, 190); and tile, brick and wood were brought thence to the palace at Lincoln (L.A.O. Bp. Acct. 23/1).

[4] *C.S.P.D. 1634–35*, p. 149.   [5] Ibid. p. 204.

wrote that he had not been very successful, adding that he did not think the people were so much frozen in their zeal to so good a work, as deterred with a more near approaching mischief in the decay of their own mother church.[1]

Each year Laud reported to the king on the state of the several dioceses, and he notes in 1634 that his vicar-general certified that in Lincoln itself there were many anabaptists, led by one Johnson, a baker. He added that in divers parts of the diocese many both of clergy and laity were excessively given to drunkenness. Williams visited the diocese personally in the following year, which he claimed no predecessor of his had done for a century; by 1637 he was suspended, and Laud noted in the following year that there were many miserable poor vicarages and curateships, to redress which was beyond episcopal power.[2]

The anabaptists in Lincoln were presumably a community founded by John Smith. A letter from the London anabaptist congregation to Amsterdam in 1626 mentions a church at Lincoln as one of five in the kingdom, and the Lincoln church themselves wrote to Amsterdam in 1630.[3] They were no doubt marked down for attention by Laud, as was the puritan preacher Edward Reyner, who was ordered by the Court of High Commission to certify his conformity. In 1639 he was invited to Arnhem. He did not go, and in the troubles then beginning he escaped attention.

The king resorted to the expedient of ship money writs in October 1634. Only London disputed the legality of the tax without parliamentary sanction. Lincoln was more concerned with two subsidiary questions; how the cost of the ship charged on the county should be apportioned, and whether the share laid on the city should be borne by the corporation or levied from individual citizens in the first instance. The common council sent the mayor and others to London to treat about the provision of the ship charged on Lincoln and other places, which no doubt means about the apportionment; and they resolved that the burden of the tax should be borne by the corporation 'unless by the king's majesty's writ for that purpose some other course can be had and taken for the raising of that charge'. Precedents were searched for and ordered to be recorded. It is perhaps significant of feeling in the Outer House that—contrary to custom—eight common councilmen were placed on the committee for the search with the mayor, aldermen and sheriffs. In the following March the high

---

[1] *C.S.P.D. 1637*, p. 512.

[2] *Works of...William Laud*, ed. W. Scott (1853), v, pt. ii, pp. 325, 333, 356. The visitation book records 20 anabaptists in St Swithin's parish (L.A.O. Vj/30/3v–5).

[3] B. Evans, *Early English Baptists* (1864), ii, 26, 41–4. Champlain Burrage, *Early English Dissenters* (1912), I, 273; II, 233, 243.

sheriff's favour was acknowledged with a present; perhaps he had secured a favourable apportionment.

The second ship-money writ was issued in April 1635. The Lincoln council sent two aldermen to London to petition the privy council for confirmation of an assessment agreed upon for Lincoln and five other corporations in the county. They succeeded. The county assessment being £8000, Lincoln paid £200.[1] The mayor and sheriffs sent up their schedule, pointing out that they had left the clergy and residents of the Close to the discretion of the dean.[2] Inquiries about this second levy went on for many years, not for political reasons, but because of the behaviour of the high sheriff, Sir Walter Norton of Sibsey. Lord Lindsey and others complained of his conduct of the business; and when bidden to inquire into it, Lindsey reported that he had done his best to trace out Norton's intricate and inimitable ways, but Norton had hitherto refused attendance.[3] Six years later Norton was brought to the bar of the House of Lords as a delinquent for abusing the county when he was sheriff, and levying £4000 more for ship money than he had warrant to do, and putting it in his own purse. He was admitted to bail.[4]

The king issued the third ship-money writ in October 1636. It seems that its issue was the occasion of a visit to the city of Lord Lindsey, who received a present, and the high sheriff, who was entertained, when they came 'about the affairs of shipping'. Out of its quota of £200 the city accounted for £193. 6s. 8d. in May 1637.[5] The small balance was not forthcoming, and in May 1639 the privy council wrote to Mr Kent, who had been mayor when the levy was made, complaining that many of the persons charged were in arrears, attributing this to the coldness and slackness of Kent, and censuring him for his neglect. Kent had said that being no longer mayor he had not the power to levy money, and the privy council ordered that the then mayor should give him authority.[6] On 15 June the mayor and sheriffs reported that £3. 9s. 4d. was still unpaid, and urged that the matter should stand over until they should find sufficient goods belonging to the defaulters on which to distrain.[7] Clearly there was resistance from a tiny minority, and payment was being exacted from all those assessed as a matter of principle. The collection of £3 had

---

[1] £3900 was laid on Lindsey, and a like sum on Kesteven and Holland, the former bearing four parts and the latter three parts of it; within the divisions, Grimsby £20, Boston £70, Stamford £53. 7s. 4d., Grantham and its soke £159. 4s. od. (C.S.P.D. 1635, p. 367).

[2] C.S.P.D. 1635–36, p. 258.

[3] H.M.C. Cowper, II, 138, 142–3; C.S.P.D. 1635, p. 480; C.S.P.D. 1635–36, passim.

[4] L.J. IV, 158, 224, 225, 227, 263, 275, 297.   [5] C.S.P.D. 1637, p. 104.

[6] C.S.P.D. 1639, p. 191.   [7] Ibid. p. 317.

caused sufficient expense for the common council to pass a resolution that the cost of its collection should be borne by the corporation. Unhappily the common council book for the period beginning in 1638 is missing, and many things which it would be most interesting to know are now not likely ever to be known.

As trouble approached, the oversight of the trained bands became more important. In 1637 the deputy lieutenant of the county certified to Lord Lindsey that there was a magazine of powder, match and shot within the county to the value of £200, and there were in readiness 200 horse and 1800 foot, well-furnished and able men.[1] The king's Scottish ecclesiastical policy brought him into a conflict with the Scots which seemed bound to issue in war. On 11 January 1639 the king ordered Lindsey to muster the trained bands; and the fear of war so caused was increased by a sudden order to Lindsey to go to the Court. He was bidden embark at Grimsby with his levies, and for Berwick, where he was to take command. By April they were on board;[2] but before that could happen there had been much stir and bustle. On 21 March Sir William Pelham wrote from Lincoln to Lord Rutland, 'here are many captains come to receive command of the trained bands; some captains willingly resign, others challenge a right to their commands. The alteration is much disliked, and many think that the soldiers will not be easily persuaded to go from home under the command of strangers.' Pursuivants were busy, some looking for delinquents and some for ship money, and there was a rumour that an attorney who owed but 3s. 4d. was forced to give security to attend the Lords.[3] Those whose sympathy was with the king had much to make them anxious.

The dispute with the Scots was patched up, but it soon broke out again. Preparations were being made in May 1640, and the Lincolnshire contingent was to go by land. The county preparations were not very forward by September.[4] It was on this occasion that 500 arms were taken out of the county for the expedition to the north, under the king's promise to restore them. The promise was not redeemed.[5]

[1] C.S.P.D. 1637, p. 443.
[2] C.S.P.D. 1638–39, pp. 179, 307, 322, 404, 626; C.S.P.D. 1639, p. 49.
[3] H.M.C. Rutland, I, 503; H.M.C. Cowper, II, 209, 225.
[4] C.S.P.D. 1640, p. 247; C.S.P.D. 1640–41, p. 47.
[5] L.J. v, 8, 154–5.

THE RELATIONSHIPS OF PARLIAMENTARY LEADERS IN THE COUNTY

Names of those indicted by the Royalists for high treason, 1643, are printed in italics

Anne Ayscough, burnt at Smithfield 1546

Sir Francis Ayscough, Kt., of South Kelsey

Sir Edward Ayscough, m. Hester, daughter of Thomas Grantham, Esq., ancestor of *Thomas Grantham, Esq.*, of Goltho, 1643

Edward Ayscough, of Cotham, was ancestor of Sir George Ayscough, Kt, Admiral of the Fleet, in the Parliament service

William Ayscough, m. Katharine, daughter of W. Heneage, Esq.

Sir Nicholas Clifford, Kt., of Bobbing Court, Kent, and of Brackenborough, first husband; in descent from the Lords Clifford =Frances Drury, sister and co-heir of Sir Robert Drury, of Hawstead

=*Sir Edward Ayscough*, Kt., of South Kelsey, M.P. (member impeached by the Army)

Frances Clifford, daughter and heir

Katharine, m. *Colonel Tho. Hatcher*, M.P. for Stamford, Parliamentary Commissioner

Lucy, daughter of Sir Edward Montague, Kt., first wife =Sir William Wray, Bart., of Glentworth, M.P. for Co. Lincoln, second husband

Sir John Wray, M.P., one of the Parliamentary Commissioners for Co. Lincoln

Sir Christopher Wray, M.P., Colonel and Parliamentary Commissioner, Father of Colonel Wm. Wray, M.P. for Grimsby

Frances, m. *Sir Anthony Irby*, M.P., Parliamentary Commissioner

Elizabeth, m. half-brother of the Earl of Manchester, General of the Parliamentary Army

John Wray, Esq., of Glentworth

Frances, m. *John Hotham*, Esq., M.P., son of Sir John Hotham, Kt. Father and son beheaded, 1 and 2 Jan. 1644

Anne, m. *Colonel Edward King*, of Ashby, M.P., Sheriff Co. Lincoln, 1643. (In 1660 'first to move the Restoration of Charles II'. He was also allied to *Robert Caudron*, Esq., Hale; *William Thompson*, Esq., Roxholm; and *Sir Hamond Whichcote*, Kt., of Sleaford

CHAPTER VII

THE EARLY STUARTS: ECONOMIC AND SOCIAL AFFAIRS

THE growing demand for the long fine wool of the Lincolnshire sheep from the clothing towns of the West Riding—Leeds, Wakefield and Halifax—has already been mentioned.[1] There were brokers constantly riding through the county to buy from the farmers, for it seems that there was no Lincolnshire wool market, and the farmers would be long before they learned to stand together. By the 1630's they may have been getting some benefit from the competition of southern clothiers, men of East Anglia, who bought up all they could, with the result that the price rose from 8s. or 9s. per stone in 1610 to 14s. in 1638.[2] It may be doubted, however, whether this rise did more than keep pace with the general rise in prices.

The developing trade brought a renewed importance to the Fossdyke, which provided, or should have provided, water transport to the Trent and so to the Aire and Calder. It must have been about this time that John Taylor, the self-styled Water Poet, wrote *A Very Merrie Wherry Ferry Voyage*, which at least has some topographical interest:

> From thence we past a Ditch of Weeds and Mud,
> Which they doe (falsely) there call *Forcedike* Flood;
> For I'l be sworne, no flood I could find there,
> But dirt and filth, which scarce my Boat would beare.
> 'Tis 8 miles long, and there our paines was such
> As all our travell did not seem so much,
> My men did wade and draw the Boate like Horses,
> And scarce could tugge her on with all our forces;
> Moyl'd, Toyl'd, myr'd, tyr'd, still lab'ring, ever doing,
> Yet were we 9 long hours that 8 miles going.
> At last when as the day was well nigh spent
> We gat from *Forcedyke's* floodlesse flood to Trent.

To which he added a footnote: 'It is a passage cut thorow the Land eight miles from *Lincoln* into *Trent*, but through either the people's poverty or

---

[1] See above, p. 84.
[2] H. Heaton, *Yorkshire Woollen and Worsted Industries* (1920), pp. 118, 205; the West Riding clothiers complained of the increase (*V.C.H. Yorks.* II, 413, 415). When the Yorkshire clothiers petitioned parliament in 1641 the knights and burgesses of Lincolnshire were put on the Commons' Committee (*C.J.* II, 201). In the years immediately before the Civil War John Hatcher of Careby in south Kesteven was selling wool to buyers from Suffolk and Essex (L.A.O. Holywell, 22).

PLATE 11

JOHN WILLIAMS

By permission of the Dean and Chapter of Westminster

negligence, it is growne up with weedes, and mudde, so that in the Summer, it is in many places almost dry.'[1]

In his different fashion Serjeant Callis, who was a commissioner of sewers in Lincoln, passed a similar judgement on the canal in his famous *Reading upon Sewers* in 1622:

this Ditch is at this day a current and passage for Boats of small burthen in Winter, but in Summer none at all; though of late great sums of money hath been expended thereupon *Sed tamen ad huc nihil inde boni venit*: at the best it is the worst in all that country, and is of so slow a current *ut non videtur currere omnino*. It serves in many places for a fence to divide Lordships, and is a great trough to swallow up waters thereabouts, which otherwise would lie upon the Level, and of it I say no more, but *Spero meliora et expecto*.[2]

Before the works referred to were undertaken it must have been at least slightly worse. The first reference to the project of improvement occurs in February 1616. Some county notables had submitted to the king a 'certificate' declaring the great benefit that might arise to the city of Lincoln and the country thereabouts, by opening and scouring the Fosse for passage by water from Lincoln to maritime towns and ports, to the inlarging of trade for the help and commodity of the city, and the relief of all parts adjoining the river. Their proposals (which are not specified) for raising money to this end were not approved by the privy council, but the idea of spending £3000 to open the channel was approved; and his Majesty 'in his princely favour to that citty, which heretofore was one of the cheifest of the kingdome, but now decayed for want of trade, and become poore and one of the meanest', commanded the privy council to recommend the scheme to the earls of Rutland and Lincoln, the two Lords Willoughby, and the baronets, knights and gentry of the county, with a view to collecting the money in the county and within reach of the river. 'Wherein', they added, 'wee make soe little doubt of any man's backewardnes, that is well affected to his contry, as we rather expect that there will be some found, that for the advaunceinge of soe worthie a worke will disburse moneis aforehand, to be repaid by suche duties as shal be reasonably layd upon the shippes and boates when the river is open and made free for passage.'[3]

In the following March the king, on his way to Scotland, visited the city he so favoured; it was the first visit of a ruling monarch since that of Henry VIII (his arms in stone were placed on the south face of the Guild-hall in 1605: they are still there). He hunted along the heath from Grantham, was met in the highway near Cross of the Cliff by the sheriffs—this was the limit of the liberties of the city—and escorted to his lodging at

[1] Quoted in L. T. C. Rolt, *Inland Waterways of England* (1950), p. 21.
[2] 1st ed. 1647, p. 58.   [3] *A.P.C. 1615–16*, pp. 414–15.

St Katharine's, where he was the guest of Sir Thomas Grantham. The next day his coach was received by the mayor, recorder and aldermen at Bargate, where the recorder on his knees made a speech; then the king went in state to the Minster, where the dean said prayers, returning thereafter to St Katharine's. After an eight-day stay, spent in cocking at the George by the Stonebow, fencing at the Spread Eagle, and hunting on the heath, he went on to Newark. He was escorted to the farther end of Bracebridge bridge by the city sheriffs, and was there met by the high sheriff. In taking leave of the mayor and his brethren he thanked them all, saying that if God lent him life he would see them oftener; which he evidently meant, for one of his party wrote to Secretary Carleton that 'he was so in love with the country about Lincoln, that he intends to spend part of his winters there'.[1] The new king, Charles I, had this in mind in August 1625, when Secretary Conway wrote to Rutland about preservation of game about Lincoln, as the king intended to repair there that winter.[2]

In some serious interval during the royal visit opportunity was taken to petition the king for aid for the Fossdyke; he wrote from Newark to Rutland recalling that some beginning had been made of the work, but that it stayed for want of means. He was asked to advise with the deputy lieutenants and commissioners of sewers how the £3000 needed could be raised.[3] Collections were begun, and some moneys collected were acknowledged by alderman Robert Morcroft.[4] In January 1618 the common council were sending messengers to the President of the Council of the North and the archbishop of York with the king's letters to them under the privy seal, and letters patent for a collection for Fosse. In February they were sending like letters to the judges of assize in the eastern counties. In May a coffer was ordered to be made to hold all moneys received from the county other than from city, Bail and Close, and treasurers were appointed. They were to pay workmen and labourers on their bringing a note under the hand of two overseers, of whom Morcroft was to be one.

So vast an undertaking would not have been started without a prime mover and a compelling cause. The prime mover was Morcroft; it was at

[1] *C.S.P.D. 1611–18*, p. 460; The Venetian Secretary reported to the Doge that the king found Lincolnshire the most delightful county in his kingdom. *C.S.P. Venetian, 1617–19*, p. 26.

[2] *C.S.P.D. 1625–26*, p. 90. In 1619 steps were taken by the nobility and gentry to preserve the game and wild fowl about Lincoln and Ancaster heath for the king's sport (*H.M.C. Rutland*, I, 456). Horse racing and bull baiting were established sports in Lincoln. The races were much patronised by the nobility and gentry; the duke of Buckingham, who had married Rutland's daughter and bought a house at Burley on the Hill, was there in 1621 (*C.S.P.D. 1619–23*, p. 243).

[3] *H.M.C. Ancaster*, p. 390.   [4] *C.S.P.D. 1611–18*, p. 482.

his expense that the king's letters authorising a collection for Fosse were procured. Another aspect of his enterprise is soon to emerge.

Where Morcroft came from is unknown, possibly from the West Riding. He was admitted freeman of the city by purchase in 1598, and was already referred to as 'Mr Morcroft', implying some special consideration. He was sheriff in 1600, coroner in 1604, and mayor in 1607. The cordwainers' minute book records that he was entertained to dinner by the company, and became a member; and he took the lead in persuading them to seek a new charter from the judges of assize, and promised to give towards the expenses if necessary. He was elected mayor again in the year of enterprise, 1617, and was the guiding spirit throughout. Although he was away from the city a great deal he was always elected a justice, and a substitute appointed to act in his absence.

Contributions began to come in. Sir John Wray paid £20. The mace-bearer was sent to York to the recorder there to collect money. Rutland promised £100 on condition that the channel was made navigable within three years, and the city agreed to enter into a bond with penalties to repay the money if the work was not complete within that time. The other nobles and gentry were more leisurely. Having received the king's letters for the raising of money, they appointed a committee to view the river and to satisfy them of the possibility of the work, and of what further good might come thereby. They were not unanimous. One of the commissioners of sewers, speaking for himself and some of his brethren, put the case against the enterprise to Lord Willoughby:

As touching the cutting and opening of the Fosse, being a matter of great consequence, of benefit and profit (as is pretended) to the movers and followers of it, but of apparent peril and danger to us and others, if great care be not had in provision to avoid it; far be it from us in a matter of other men's benefit either to hinder or neglect it, not coming with our hurt and prejudice; but in regard to our and other men's danger,

they suggested that an equal number of commissioners of both sides should determine the matter in a way that would neither hurt the one nor hinder the other. They remembered that this was not the first attempt made by men of great wisdom, understanding and authority, and yet given over.[1]

Here spoke the landed interest, concerned with land drainage and prevention of flooding, and therefore concerned to keep down the water level; the conflict with navigation interests, which want to keep the water high, constantly recurs. Nevertheless, the committee found the project to be possible, likely to be commodious to the city and adjacent neighbours, and hurtful to none. The nobles and gentry then 'condescended to procure'

[1] *H.M.C. Ancaster*, pp. 392–3.

£300 if the city would raise the like sum. Such an offer was not to be missed, and the common council decided to resort to its usual expedient and deduct £50 from the annual allowance of six successive mayors; and the king, 'further to manifest his affection to perfect and profitable work did grant to the said city the making of three baronets' and appointed Morcroft to be treasurer of the Fossdyke funds. Whether the baronetcies were sold, and if so who bought them and at what price, are matters concealed from an inquisitive posterity.

The work, however, began. Morcroft found a skilful workman to undertake it, but the workman died before its completion. Moreover, Morcroft grew sick and old, and there was such opposition, as there always was, to the deduction from the mayor's allowance that the resolution to deduct was repealed in 1623, and the late mayor was given his money.

It was no accident that about the same time there was a project for making the Aire and Calder navigable.[1] These were the rivers which led to the Yorkshire cloth towns. Nor was it any accident that, the export of wool having been forbidden, the merchants of the staple were licensed to buy wool in specified places, near the clothing countries, and (to reduce the risk of illicit export) remote from the sea. All fellmongers within twelve miles of the appointed town must bring their fell wool to be weighed and registered. Among the appointed towns were Wakefield, Halifax, and Lincoln.[2]

The control of the wool trade in the staple towns was in the hands of the staple company, who appointed a weigher and searcher of wools sold there. Some of the buyers and sellers including some glovers who frequented the market, omitted to have their wools weighed and viewed by the officer. The merchants of the staple petitioned for relief, and the privy council ordered the mayor of the city to command the offenders to conform, and to report those who failed to do so. The mayor replied that the wool dealers of Lincoln were willing to admit the company's officer as weigher of wools in Lincoln, though by ancient custom the weigher should be elected by the council of the city. He asked that the city privileges should be respected, and—the exclusiveness of the staplers clearly being resented —asked that the rates of admission into the company should be reduced, as they were so high that none in Lincoln could become freemen of it.[3]

In the following year several of the citizens approached Mr Attorney of

---

[1] *H.M.C. 3rd Rep.* (Northumberland), p. 67.

[2] *A.P.C. 1616–17*, pp. 178–81.

[3] *A.P.C. 1618–19*, p. 374; *C.S.P.D. 1619–23*, pp. 19, 35. In 1617 there had been six admissions to the freedom of the city by purchase, including William Kent, merchant venturer, and Nicholas Hole, late apprentice to Robert Burton, glover. George Wragge, merchant, was admitted in 1619.

the Staple Company, who reported to the Company's Assembly that they sought a staple government in the city, and offered to bring in three persons as members of the company. They hoped that the company would allow others of the city to be assistant to the said three solely for the purpose of making a quorum. A fortnight later Robert Morcroft attended and offered to pay £50 in the making free of the said three persons. Morcroft was then appointed lieutenant of the Company for the city for a year, and was desired to submit the names of twelve sufficient and discreet persons out of which the Company might choose nine to be a quorum. The nine were to be sworn to performance of their duties before the mayor of Lincoln.

Morcroft, having taken his oath, at once informed the court that Robert Bartholomew, Robert Kelke, and Robert Richardson, all glovers of the city, and certain others who were not free of the Staple Company did without licence trade in wool there to the prejudice of the company; and he was asked to send in the names of all offenders to the end that order might be taken for their punishment and restraint.[1]

Whether Morcroft succeeded in securing a virtual local monopoly does not appear, and no more is heard of the Lincoln organization of the company. Perhaps it declined with Morcroft, who, however, lived on into the Civil War. In 1625 a wool market was proclaimed to be held at the Friars, but no further reference to it occurs, and it probably failed. The woollen industry itself was suffering from depression, owing both to the growing manufacture abroad and to the continental wars which hampered trade.

The Fossdyke scheme itself led to violent quarrels. On 7 December 1633, Morcroft obtained a letter from the king to the mayor and aldermen. It said that Morcroft had deposited £247. 11s. 3d. in the common chamber of the city, and that gentry appointed by the king found a sum of £88. 14s. 4d. to be due to Morcroft. The city was ordered to pay this, and mayors who had received their allowances in full (though they had not kept the freemen's feasts according to custom) to pay £50 each. This money, with the balance in hand, and anything that be raised by benevolence or otherwise, should be paid to collectors and the work completed.[2]

This letter was produced by Morcroft at a meeting of the common council on 27 February 1634, and the recorder having been sent for, it was publicly and solemnly read in both Inner and Outer House. But two

---

[1] B.M. Add. MS. 43849, ff. 5, 6b; E. E. Rich, *Ordinance Book of the Merchants of the Staple* (1937), p. 99 n. Robert Kelke is described as a fellmonger in the inventory of his goods, taken at death; he had in wool and skins about £100 (L.A.O. Lincoln Inventories, 144/208).

[2] *C.S.P.D. 1633–34*, p. 317.

aldermen, Richard White and Robert Marshall, and two ex-mayors who were called on to refund their £50 each, had known what was going on, and had not been idle. They produced a letter from the privy council, setting out a Star Chamber order of 24 January, appointing a committee to investigate the whole of the Fossdyke affair, and pending its report all action on the king's letter was stayed. This letter also was published, and no further proceedings were then taken.

The next year Rutland obtained judgement against Morcroft for the refund of his £100, apparently on the ground that as the work had not been completed in the specified three years, he was entitled to recover his money. The corporation sent a deputation to settle with him on the best terms possible, and eventually settled with his executors. So ended in failure a very gallant effort to re-establish the city in the wool trade.

Indeed, the economic condition of Lincoln was one of increasing gloom. In the first decade of the century, when prices remain fairly steady, the minutes of the council have nothing to say about poor relief; and their silence suggests that there was no need to supplement the activities of the parishes, which were being carried on under the new Poor Law Act of 1601. The presence of plague in 1610 called for a special assessment upon persons of ability and worth in aid of those shut up in their houses, and other needy folk.[1] The parishes were aided again in 1611 by the issue of a mayor's warrant for levying cessment to help the plague-stricken. The power to levy a city rate was challenged by the chamberlain of the east ward, who told the mayor to his face that he might be ashamed to make out such a warrant, which was more than he could justify. He was ordered to humble himself and pay a fine or be disfranchised; and all freemen who did not pay were threatened with the same penalty, which was generally effective.

The problem of vagrancy was clearly growing worse, and from 1615 onwards there was increasing stringency in dealing with beggars. A marshal or beadle was directed daily to patrol the parishes, and bring beggars in to the house of correction and spinning school. The parish constables were sworn to patrol their parishes with halberds to the like purpose. Further measures were taken in 1619. All strange poor were to be kept out, and newcomers must give security against becoming burdens on the parishes.[2] It seems that plague was present again in 1624, and an officer was appointed

[1] Perhaps on account of this distress the city was excused payment of a fifteenth and tenth in November 1610 (*C.S.P.D. 1603-10*, p. 644). There was plague at Sempringham in that autumn, when Lord Lincoln excused himself to the Lords (*L.J.* II, 668).

[2] In 1617 St Martin's parishioners agreed that none should be allowed to come to dwell in the parish unless they obtain the goodwill of the parishioners or give a bond to discharge the parish.

to prevent inordinate assemblages of beggars, and strangers were invited to make gifts for poor relief.

One of the ways in which the poor were allowed to help themselves, 'as in charity and by ancient custom of this Christian kingdom they ought to be allowed', was to glean in the open fields after harvest. When the husbandmen who worked the arable complained of the damage done by disorderly gleaners, the mayor and his brethren stepped in to protect the poor, and ordered that no swine, sheep or cattle should be allowed on any land in the field until it had been gleaned by the poor, on penalty of imprisonment and impounding of cattle.

The room under the free school at the Greyfriars was assigned for a house of correction. In 1615 a number of citizens combined to buy wool to set the poor on work there. Various efforts were made: money was lent and lost; and in 1624 Gregory Lawcock, a freeman, offered, if he could have convenient stock, to set the great number of beggars on work, to spin, knit stockings, weave garterings, and make woollen goods, and out of the profit to clothe the poor, giving to the mayor for this purpose a quantity of cloth which was never fixed. He was to have £20 of capital and £10 yearly to teach the young spinners, the mayor's allowance being reduced for the purpose. To provide a market for the goods made, the inhabitants were bidden to wear at least one suit of apparel and one pair of stockings of cloth or stuff so made. The attempt failed. Money was not to be made out of poor relief. By 1629 there was a 'general dislike' between all parties, and Lawcock claimed to have sustained great losses. His claim was settled for £30, and the city took over his looms and tools and wound up the venture.

These years saw the beginnings of a foundation which was to have a very different history. Richard Smith, a native of Welton by Lincoln, who was widely connected with gentry and citizens alike, practised for many years as a physician in London. Having lived near Christ's Hospital, founded by Edward VI, he resolved to found a like hospital in Lincoln and endow it with the manor of Potterhanworth. He died in 1602, and after long delays the hospital was incorporated in 1611.[1] It was to provide for twelve boys, five from the city, one from the Close or Bail, three from Potterhanworth and three from Welton. They were to be maintained up to the age of 16 and then bound apprentice. The school was first housed in St Mary's Gildhall; the schoolmaster was paid £5 a year and allowed 12d. for a week's diet for each boy.[2] Cloth for the boys' uniforms and their bedding came from London, deal planks for the beds were put on the boat at

[1] C.S.P.D. 1611–18, p. 42.
[2] This was in 1614; the figures were at once raised to £6. 13s. 4d. and 18d.

Boston, a cow was allowed to the matron towards keeping the boys, and she was occasionally allowed the cost of sending a boy to court to be touched for the king's evil; the cost was 10*s*. The boys were presently installed in a house in St Michael's churchyard, a site on which they remained until the dissolution of the hospital. Agricultural improvements and additional endowments enabled the hospital to become much larger in later days.[1]

There was plague in Lincoln in 1625. News of it reached London, and the Tuscan Resident reported to the duke of Florence that twelve persons died in one week in Lincoln, but that he believed that the real numbers of deaths were concealed, and were really more numerous.[2] That year regulations were drawn up by the bishop of Lincoln and the justices of the peace at Lincoln assizes for prevention of plague and the government of the people.[3] Plague raged again in 1630, and kept the registrar of the diocese away,[4] and in 1631, when because of the grievous contagion the dean and chapter could not get at their common seal in the chapter house.[5] That year Lord Strafford, who was President of the Council of the North, wrote to Secretary Dorchester that plague infection had spread from Lincolnshire and Lancashire into Yorkshire. Public fairs had been inhibited, watches were well kept, the passages from Lincolnshire by water had been stopped as far as possible, and visited persons provided with necessities and drugs.[6] Bishop Williams was busy again: on 12 September Dorchester wrote to him to say he hoped Williams had found the effects of the endeavours used with the king for his poor town of Lincoln;[7] in October Williams wrote, apparently to the dean, saying he had been charged with the matter by the king, who had been pleased to commiserate the lamentable case of the city, for a long time heavily visited with the sickness, and adding that as he was much interested in the plan he hoped for all possible aid;[8] in November Williams wrote to Archbishop Laud thanking him for furthering the king's charity to 'that most commiserable poor city of Lincoln' and, saying that but for his own illness he would have had the aldermen write to Laud.[9] In the following January Sir William Armyne wrote to the bishop acknowledging his extraordinary care that the money given to the

---

[1] The first account book of the hospital was lost, probably in the Civil War; it is now MS. Rawl. D687 in the Bodleian Library. For the founder see Kate Naylor, *Richard Smith, M.D.* (1951). At the metropolitical visitation of 1634 there were only nine boys, two without coats, and all six beds were very old and defective (L.A.O., Bp. Reg., Red Book, 1611–93, f. 191 b).

[2] *H.M.C. Skrine*, p. 6.   [3] *H.M.C. Rutland*, i, 473.
[4] L.A.O. Red Book, f. 124 b.
[5] Lincoln Diocesan Record Office Report 1946–7.
[6] *C.S.P.D. 1631–33*, p. 150. He feared lest it visit Halifax and Leeds.
[7] Ibid. p. 143.   [8] L.A.O. Cor. B/3/f. 50.
[9] MS. Lambeth 1030, no. 7.

city should be well disposed of, though there were still doubts whether the poor had been so well dealt with as they should have been.[1]

In that spring collections were being made in London and elsewhere for the relief of Lincoln and other infected places in the county. In St Margaret's parish the burials rose from the customary dozen in a year to forty-five in 1631, nearly all between July and October. On 4 December Steven Feild was buried; 'this was the last that died of the sickness in this parish.'[2]

The ordinary poor rate must have been heavy indeed, and the common council stood behind parish officers who were resisted in the levying of distress for non-payment. The influx of poor from other districts was an aggravation, and the parish underconstables were ordered weekly to notify the mayor or a justice overseeing the parishes of all persons seeking settlements, with a view to their removal. Landlords letting houses to non-inhabitants without the consent of the mayor and the majority of the parishioners were heavily fined; and if the landlord was not himself an inhabitant then the forfeiture was to be levied on the goods of his tenant. Poor persons were forbidden to take small sums of money to educate poor children who would become chargeable to the parishes. Parish officers provided materials for setting the poor on work.

The moneys collected elsewhere by letters patent were made the subject of a trust deed dated 10 January 1634 between Bishop Williams of the first part, the mayor and commonalty of the second part, and Sir John Wray, Sir William Armyne, Sir John Bolles, Sir John Monson and Serjeant Callis, all county justices, of the third part. It recited that £1000 had been raised to relieve the grievous visitation of pestilence in Lincoln, and that the bishop had placed the money in the hands of Robert Marshall, alderman and mercer. It had been decided, for the relief of poor decayed tradesmen and the settling of many disorderly poor in city Bail and Close, to find undertakers to lay out £400 in setting the poor on work and providing wool, thread, hemp and flax for the purpose; the undertakers allowing to the masters of the poor £4 yearly out of each £100, and buying the products at reasonable prices so that the poor might be paid their wages. There having been a great shortage of coal and its price having become excessive, £200 was to be lent out for provision of coal at the best rate, with a limit of 12d. a bushel. The remaining £400 was to be lent to tradesmen at £10 apiece to help them to maintain their trade. All poor were to be

---

[1] L.A.O. Cor. B/3/f. 28.

[2] At St Peter at Gowts the burials averaged 10 per year; there were 18 in 1630, 24 in 1642 and 20 in 1644, all plague years. The registers of both parishes have been printed by the Lincoln Record Society. Pest houses on the Carholme were being repaired in 1634.

sent in, the idle and refractory compelled to go in according to the poor
law, and they were to be surveyed quarterly to ensure that all were at work
and being paid. All this was to continue for the perpetual good of the city.
The copy of the deed in the Bishop's Red Book is endorsed with payments
of the first £400 to a woolman, a baker, a mercer and a chandler, no doubt
the undertakers, and loans to ten tradesmen.[1]

Whatever relief these measures may have effected, they did not solve
the problem of coping with the influx of poor from outside. In 1636 the
council sent for a copy of the rules adopted in Grantham to deal with this
problem; and they presently made orders to the same end which were confirmed by the judges of assize. The building of cottages, the conversion of
barns, stables and outhouses, and the division of houses had facilitated
'a great confluence and resort of poor people from foreign places', with
the result that the inhabitants were overburdened, the risk of pestilence
increased, idleness nourished, and strangers trying to make a living were
infringing the rights of freemen who were entitled to a monopoly of retail
trade. The remedies adopted were to prohibit anyone from taking a
stranger in as a tenant without the written consent of the mayor and
council; no inhabitant might build, convert or divide buildings for the
poor without like consent; persons who had been admitted to such quarters
within seven years must be removed and buildings restored to their former
state; the trading rights of freemen must be enforced. Unhappily the surviving minutes of the common council break off in 1638, and there is
nothing to show how far these measures were effective.

One, and perhaps the chief, cause of distress was the continuing rise of
prices. In the last decade of Elizabeth the average price of corn was 28s.
a quarter; between 1601 and 1610 it was 30s. 5d.; 1611–20, 36s. 9d.;
1621–30, 34s. 7d.; 1632–7, 42s. 10d. In the same period peas and beans
rose from 17s. to 20s. Though these averages bring out the general trend
of prices by levelling out fluctuations due to good and bad harvests, they
conceal the peak years which must have caused intense hardship. At
Michaelmas 1622, for example, corn ranged from 53s. 4d. to 40s. for inferior
grain; malt rose from 14s. to 28s. and barley from 13s. 4d. to 23s.; peas and

---

[1] *C.S.P.D. 1633–34*, pp. 408–9; L.A.O. Red Book, f. 151 a. The handling of this money
was to become one of the grounds of complaint against Williams by his enemies. On
18 September 1637 Sir John Lambe wrote to Laud: 'I was told by the Chancellor of
Lincoln that there was £1600 or £1700 collected for the relief of the infected people of
the city of Lincoln, when the plague was there, which was paid to my Lord Bishop, and
not above £1000 or £1100 paid in by him, and that since the plague ceased, whereupon
it was settled for the use of the poor; but the Chancellor saith that the rich men keep it in
their hands, and the poor have little benefit by it. It were good that it were seen into
both for the poor and for the sum remaining' (Lambeth MS. 943, p. 555).

beans from 16s. to 24s. Oats alone remained steady at 8s. From 1612 onwards wheat was generally over 40s., and it can hardly be a coincidence that the price of rye was first returned at the Michaelmas leet in 1617. It was 26s. a quarter, and did not fluctuate much. The poorer folk, probably accustomed to flour made wholly or partly of wheat (perhaps mixed with barley, peas or beans), were doubtless forced to oatcake, ryebread or bread made of peas.[1]

In 1623 the county justices were compelling farmers to bring their corn to market,[2] and several orders were made by the common council in 1625 which indicate anxiety about food supplies; the meal market must be held on the old market hill, and neither meal nor any other grain might be sold in shops or other private places, but only in open market; and new rules were made for better market government. One Fowkes was brought by the mayor into the Star Chamber: having 400 quarters of old malt and 300 of barley, he brought little of it to market, but bought other barley as it was coming to market; having malted above 200 quarters, he sent a little of it to market, but set on it so high a price that he brought it away unsold. For these offences of engrossing and forestalling he was committed to the Fleet, fined £1000, and ordered to acknowledge his offence at the city and county assizes.[3]

In 1630 and 1631 prices were not recorded at the leet at all. They were famine years. The county justices, under orders from the privy council, were securing corn to supply the markets and relieve the poor. Oatmeal was declared to be their greatest relief. As farmers' surpluses were forced on to the market prices fell, but in May 1631 wheat was still 53s. to 56s. the quarter. In the following year the plague was so virulent that the justices could not meet.[4]

It is not easy to say how far inclosure of land contributed to the distress, but there was enough feeling on the subject to provoke riots in 1607 in Northampton, Leicester and other counties, and the trouble spread into the adjoining part of Lincolnshire. Here the responsible justice was Sir William Armyne, and to him in June 1607 a correspondent in Staple Inn wrote:

I acquainted my lord Eure that I heard the Grantham men were up again on Friday, and that I met Richard Clark your man, who told me he had heard the king's majesty was angry in respect there was so great force used against

---

[1] Thorold Rogers, *History of Agriculture and Prices*, v (1887), 46. According to Gervase Markham, peas were being made into bread in Lincolnshire and some adjoining counties (ibid. p. 45).

[2] *C.S.P.D. 1619–23,* p. 553.

[3] John Rushworth, *Historical Collections*, III (1659), App. p. 58.

[4] *C.S.P.D. 1631–33,* pp. 35, 56, 59, 380, 387, 389, 419.

them in Northamptonshire: whose opinion was it was dangerous saying so, and then enquiring further of his Lord what course was best to deal with them, he holdeth it was good not to use over great commiseration towards them, if they would not otherwise be stayed. You had need be careful in these affairs, for all your countrymen's eyes here, as I hear as well in London as at home, are upon you for your good course taking therein, to cause them to surcease their courses. We hear and think how some of the judges come forth of London on Friday next into North: War: Leic: and Lincolnshire for the better course taking therein. We hear the liberties of North: shall be seized.

On 8 June the privy council sent down a proclamation to be used if necessary; on the 26th Armyne was told by his brother-in-law Ralph Eure that the lords of the council had a very good opinion of him for his care in pacifying the tumults; and on 23 July the council wrote to tell the lord lieutenant that the king had ordered a commission to inquire into unlawful inclosures, such as had been pretended to be the cause of the late grievances, with a view to preventing further trouble.[1] The only other hint of attempt to foment trouble in Lincolnshire is a paper dropped in Caistor church which was sent by Sir Ralph Maddison to Sir Thomas Grantham, passed to Sir William Pelham and then to the lord lieutenant. It purported to be from 'the poor man's friend and the gentleman's plague' to 'you gentlemen that rack your rents and throwe down land for corne'. and was directed against rack renting and inclosing of land.[2]

A surviving abstract of the returns of the depopulation commission of 1607 has been summarised by Mr J. D. Gould. Referring to that part of the return headed 'great depopulations and decays of husbandry', he says that twelve villages in Kesteven and seventeen in Lindsey were completely or largely depopulated. Yet save in the headings the word 'depopulation' is used only twice, and even so, it is clear that it is used to signify reduction in population. It is used of Sapperton in Kesteven, 'the whole town depopulated...and the land converted into pasture', seven cottages and the parsonage house alone remaining. This is a figure which tallies with a return of twenty-two communicants in the parish in 1603. It is also used of the whole town of Walesby in Lindsey, where there had been thirteen farms; yet there were 100 communicants in 1603.[3] All the other entries relate to 'decay', a word clearly used not only of the physical condition of the buildings but also of the economic injury inflicted on them. A farmhouse was 'decayed' by being turned into cottages or by having its land taken from it. Those farmers who stayed on may have become labourers and so lost in social status; whether they lost financially is not so clear. The

[1] Dr Williams's Library, Morrice MSS. xi, 15, 2, 23.
[2] H.M.C. Rutland, i, 406.
[3] C. W. Foster, State of the Church (L.R.S. 1926), p. 327.

owners may have been compelled to take over their land, and farms of 10 or 18 acres, to quote two instances, can hardly have provided a good living. Of substantial decline in population, however, such as would have aggravated the urban problem, there is little evidence. Mr Gould charges the earl of Lincoln with 'depopulation' of Tattershall: the return says that 'he pulled down 20 small farmhouses then having about 10 acres apiece belonging to them, and hath converted 120 acres of arable into pasture'. Yet Lincoln's action is put into perspective when it is found that the area of Tattershall parish is (since drainage) 4580 acres, and that it had 400 communicants in 1603 and 100 families in 1705.[1]

The other owners specially mentioned by Mr Gould are Sir Christopher Wray, the lord chief justice, and his son Sir William. At Grainsby they 'decayed' eight farms and converted 230 acres from arable to pasture. In 1562 it had twenty-one families, and in 1705 twelve. At Stainton with Langworth Sir William Wray and Sir Nicholas Saunderson 'decayed' four farms: the parish had 106 communicants in 1603 and thirty-five families in 1705. At Calceby the Maddisons 'decayed' five farms and Sir Christopher fifteen; it had thirty-five communicants in 1603, and had shrunk to three families in 1705.

The impression these examples give of a slight fall in population conforms with Mr Gould's total of land affected. The area converted from arable to pasture probably did not exceed 17,500 acres, which out of a county area of 1,700,000 acres is a modest total. A 'depopulation' of the kind indicated above on, say, 1·25 % of the land cannot have been serious. Furthermore, the conversions complained of covered a number of years. Several of the owners reported against were dead; the inclosures at Blyborough had been the subject of inquiry by the privy council 25 years before;[2] and the returns mention that one 'decay' (Sapperton) was 40 years old.[3]

Nevertheless, the gradual process continued. In 1635 the lordship of South Hykeham was being inclosed, and tillage turned into pasture, and the parson complained to Laud that his tithes were diminished.[4] There must have been other such complaints, for the lords of the treasury directed a commission to inquire of depopulations since 1588 in Lincolnshire and

---

[1] Foster, op. cit. p. 400; *Speculum Dioeceseos Lincolniensis 1705–1723*, ed. R. E. G. Cole (L.R.S. 1913), p. 125. Thorpe Tilney, also quoted against him, is not so clear, as it is a hamlet in Timberland parish.

[2] *A.P.C. 1580–81*, p. 334; *1581–82*, pp. 257, 336, 345; *C.S.P.D. 1581–90*, p. 104.

[3] For the abstract of the returns, among the Sir Julius Caesar papers, see B.M., Add. MS. 11574, ff. 70–98; J. D. Gould, 'Inquisition of depopulation of 1607 in Lincolnshire', in *E.H.R.* LXVII (July 1952), pp. 392–6.

[4] *C.S.P.D. 1635*, p. 125.

other counties.[1] When Sir George Heneage wrote his account of the family estates in 1625 he mentioned houses and mills decayed and land inclosed. He certainly was not charging himself and his family with anti-social conduct.[2] No doubt he and the Wrays and Lord Lincoln would have made a good case of economic necessity. They could hardly have described the countryside more vividly than did Sir William Pelham of Brocklesby to his brother-in-law Sir Edward Conway in 1623. He wrote that his private affairs

were never so burthensome unto me as now. For many insufficient tenants have given up their farms and sheepwalks, so that I am forced to take them into my own hands, and borrow money upon use to stock them....Our country was never in that want that now it is, and more of money than corn, for there are many thousands in these parts who have sold all they have even to their bedstraw, and cannot get work to earn any money. Dog's flesh is a dainty dish, and found upon search in many houses, also such horse flesh as hath lain long in a *deke* for hounds, and the other day one stole a sheep, who for mere hunger tore a leg out, and yet the great turn of scarcity not yet come.[3]

Another witness speaks of the throwing up of farms. In December 1640 Sir Ralph Maddison of Fonaby near Caistor published a tract called *England's Looking In and Out*, addressed to the Long Parliament. Economists must decide whether his diagnosis is correct; he was at least shrewd enough to forecast the ills that impended:

Wherefore (seeing our merchants have no care nor regard of this) it behoveth our State (which you represent at this present) to have a special regard and care unto, which I most humbly present to your grave consideration; lest the want of moneys (when you stand most in need of it) now flying away from us do still continue the fall of wools yet lower, with all other commodities, and your rents and livelihood to fall, which will be the undoing of your tenants (turning up your farms) impoverishing all trades and handicrafts, in the whole kingdom exceedingly in general, which (in truth) is the mother of Rebellion, procured through a general decay of all estates, every man being ready to strike the next above him or about him.[4]

---

[1] *C.S.P.D. 1634–35*, p. 597. Whatever the degree of inclosure and depopulation may have been, the measures taken by the privy council were chiefly prompted by the need for revenue. Sir John Monson was charged with depopulation conversion in Cherry Burton, Owersby and Broxholme; but for £300 he was granted a pardon and licensed to retain his houses and land in their decayed state, any law to the contrary notwithstanding (L.A.O. Monson 19/7/1 (8)).

[2] J. W. F. Hill, 'Sir George Heneage's Estate Book, 1625' in *L.A.S.R.*, 1 (1938), 35–84.

[3] *Lincs. N. & Q.* 1 (1888–9), 16. In 1621 the commissioners for the subsidy wrote that the general decay of rents and estates made it impossible to bring the subsidy up to the last (*C.S.P.D. 1621–23*, p. 305).

[4] P. 21. He republished his tract in 1655 under the title *Great Britain's Remembrancer*, with a dedication to the Lord Protector and Parliament. See also *C.S.P.D. 1619–23*, p. 417.

To all these discontents must be added those due to disturbances caused by drainage operations in the flat lands. Several projects were set on foot in the reign of Charles I. Sir Anthony Thomas and others had a scheme for the Welland area, and the king directed them to meet the commissioners of sewers and the men of the country.[1] Later Sir John Monson undertook the Ancholme Level; by 1639 he claimed that he had fulfilled his part, and that the commissioners had approved it. Bishop Juxon, lord treasurer, was not so sure, as judgement had been passed in a dry season; he objected to there being no benefit to the king, though the matter having gone so far he did not know how to make stay of it.[2]

But the project which caused the most noise was that undertaken by the Dutch engineer, Cornelius Vermuyden, in 1626. He was to drain Hatfield Chase near the Isle of Axholme, himself receiving a third of the drained lands. The commoners were hostile, and in 1628 the privy council ordered proclamation forbidding the inhabitants of the Isle to oppose the works.[3] The following August Wentworth, President of the North, reported that there had been no disturbance in Yorkshire; Lincolnshire was outside of his commission.[4] By 1633 Vermuyden was a prisoner by commandment of the Lords for having refused to contribute towards 'that new work the proportion which their Lordships have ordained', in another letter called his draining debts.[5] That year it was complained that the people in Lincolnshire had risen in troops and threatened to kill the servants of the Dutch, rip up their bellies, and throw their hearts in their faces. A serjeant at arms was sent down, and the power of the county summoned.[6] The commissioners of sewers were very critical of the operations. They found a number of townships injured by the stoppage of the ancient river Idle, and made a new law for opening it with qualifications.[7]

The city of Lincoln was more concerned than might at first sight appear.[8] In 1632 the commissioners of sewers for the county ordered that the fens from Saxilby town on both sides the Fossdyke and Witham river to Langrick Gowt were to be viewed so as to make a bargain with such as would undertake the draining thereof.[9] Any measure that would have lowered the level of the water in the Witham, and still more important the Foss-

---

[1] C.S.P.D. 1629–31, pp. 44, 116.   [2] H.M.C. Cowper, II, 225.
[3] C.S.P.D. 1628–29, p. 338; A.P.C. Sept. 1627–June 1628, p. 497.
[4] C.S.P.D. 1629–31, p. 35.   [5] H.M.C. Cowper, II, 17.
[6] C.S.P.D. 1633–34, p. 145.   [7] Ibid. p. 537.
[8] In 1631 Thomas and his fellows began to drain the East and West fens on the lower Witham, and three years later the work was adjudged complete (H. C. Darby, The Draining of the Fens (1940), pp. 46–8; W. H. Wheeler, Fens of South Lincolnshire (2nd ed.), p. 207; G. M. Hipkin in A.A.S.R. LX (1931), 225–6.
[9] C.S.P.D. 1631–33, p. 419.

dyke, would have prejudiced the city. The conduct of the inhabitants of Torksey, whose interest was similar, showed that they were in no doubt about the matter. They threatened to kill the workmen, threw some of them into the river and kept them under water with long poles, and at several other times, upon the knelling of a bell, came to the works in riotous and warlike manner, filled up the ditches and drains, and burned the working tools of the undertakers. The defendants were committed to the Fleet and many heavily fined.[1] The activities of the earl of Lindsey in the fens between Glen and Kyme led to much disorder in the early days of the Long Parliament.

The feelings of the fenmen and commoners, who lived by fishing and fowling and selling willows for basketmaking, were expressed in a ballad which runs as follows:

> Behold the great design, which they do now determine,
> Will make our bodies pine, a prey to crows and vermin;
> For they do mean all fens to drain, and waters overmaster,
> All will be dry, and we must die, 'cause Essex calves want pasture.[2]

---

[1] J. Korthals-Altes, *Sir Cornelius Vermuyden* (1925), p. 106.

[2] Sir William Dugdale, *History of Imbanking* (1662), p. 391; S. R. Gardiner, *History of England* (1884), VIII, 292–5; Samuel Smiles, *Lives of the Engineers* (1861), I, 54, for the whole ballad.

PLATE 12

SIR JOHN MONSON

From a portrait by Cornelius Jansen, by permission of Lord Monson

CHAPTER VIII

THE CIVIL WAR AND INTERREGNUM

AFTER eleven years of rule without a parliament Charles's necessities, enlarged by the Scottish war, compelled him to call another parliament. There, in the Short Parliament, all the discontents, religious and political, were to focus upon the unpopular ministers, Strafford and Archbishop Laud. In the Lincolnshire elections both points of view found expression. The knights of the shire were Sir John Wray, whose attitude was already well known, and Sir Edward Hussey, who was later to be a great sufferer in the royalist cause.[1] The city returned Dr John Farmery, the chancellor of the diocese and bitter enemy of Bishop Williams, and Thomas Grantham, son of Sir Thomas, who was dead. Thomas the son was described by Mrs Hutchinson as 'a fine gentleman bred beyond the seas according to the best education of those times'.[2] Other names already familiar occur: Sir Anthony Irby for Boston, Thomas Hatcher for Stamford and Sir Christopher Wray for Grimsby, all of them appointed members of the Committee for Privileges.[3]

The king soon dissolved the parliament, but by November 1640 he was compelled to call another, which became famous as the Long Parliament. The movement of opinion against him is indicated by the substitution of Sir Edward Ayscough for Hussey in the election for the shire, and by John Broxholme—one of a family of gentry settled in St Peter at Gowts parish—who was to side with the parliament, in place of Farmery for the city. This time the two Wrays, Irby, Ayscough, Hatcher and Grantham were all members of the committee to deal with elections and privileges.[4] Sir William Armyne, son of Hugh Tuke's protector,[5] had been excluded from the Short Parliament because he was high sheriff of Huntingdon, and he did not secure a seat in the Long Parliament until he came in for

---

[1] His views were probably known already, for his election was challenged by Sir Edward Ayscough (*C.J.* II, 10).

[2] *Memoirs of Colonel Hutchinson*, ed. Sir C. H. Firth (1906), p. 41; in 1626 he was given leave to travel abroad for three years with three servants, provided he did not go to Rome or to the King of Spain's dominions (*A.P.C. 1625–26*, p. 348). He had just laid down the office of high sheriff, in which he had been busily engaged in collecting shipmoney (L.A.O. Aswarby, 9/1/20).

[3] *C.J.* II, 4. The other member for Grimsby was the royalist Gervase Holles, whose *Church Notes* (ed. R. E. G. Cole (L.R.S. 1911)) have endured longer than his political activities. He allowed his views to peep out in his reference to Sir John Wray as 'an owle and changeling' (op. cit. p. 64).

[4] *C.J.* II, 20–1.   [5] See above, p. 113.

Grantham on the death of Thomas Hussey in 1641. Here were the puritan families who had appeared a generation earlier, only the St Pauls (whose line died out with Sir George) being missing. They were knit together by religion and kinship; from the start they took a prominent part in the business of the commons; and when warlike preparations began they were able to move quickly. There was no such cousinage of royalist gentry in the county; Lord Lindsey was to be busy outside it, though he could count on Sir John Monson and some members of the Pelham, Hussey, Heron, Scrope and Thorold families and the papist recorder of Lincoln, Charles Dalison.[1]

In the first days of the Long Parliament petitions were presented from various counties, setting forth the burdens and oppressions of the people during the long intermission of parliament, in their consciences, liberties and properties, and as to this last especially in ship money. Sir John Wray handed in the Lincolnshire petition, which the House much approved,[2] and Boston presented its own through Sir Anthony Irby. In the various committees county members took a full part. The course of events and the hardening of opinion is shown in a few speeches of Sir John Wray which have been preserved. As the speeches were no doubt much discussed by his friends and studied in the shire it is worth while to consider them. The first speech, on religion (12 November) was an exhortation to unity, with loyal references to the king. On the 20th, following the report of the committee on religion, he goes further:

You may see to what an exorbitant height Popery is grown; and yet how slowly we goe on to suppress it...the only way is to fall to our work in earnest, and lay the Axe to the root, to unloose the long and deep Fangs of Superstition and Popery: which being once done, the Barke will soone fall down...I shall humbly move that the groves and high places of Idolatry may bee removed, and pulled down, and then God's wrath against England will be appeased; until then, never.

On 15 December, of the spiritual engineers who were undermining the foundations of religion, to establish their tottering hierarchy in the room thereof, it

will never bee safe, nor well at quiet, untill these heavy drossy Cannons with all their base mettle, be melted, and dissolved: let us then dismount them, and destroy them, which is my humble motion.

On 21 January 1641 he spoke of a settlement with the Scots; and on 26 February on the impeachment of Strafford and Laud:

Wee have had thus long under our Feathers many Estriges Egges, which as some observe are longest in hatching, but once hatched, can digest Iron; and

---

[1] See *L.J.* v, 375; *C.J.* II, 791.   [2] Ibid. p. 424.

wee have many Irons in the fire, and have hammered some upon the anvill of justice into nayles; but wee have not struck one stroak with the right hammer, nor rivetted one nayle to the head...if we faile in this our pursuit of justice, it is time to look about us: for then I feare that wee ourselves shall hardly scape scot-free.

A third speech on Strafford gives even stronger expression to the sense of urgency:

Truth is the daughter of Time, and experience the best Schoolemaster, who hath long since taught many men and estates the sad and woefull effects of an halfe-done work...Have we not then, Mr Speaker, a wolfe by the eares? is there any way to goe scot-free or wolfe-free, but one?

The last of the recorded speeches, on 3 May, was on 'a loyal covenant'.[1]

On that day a protestation was adopted. It was taken by the knights for Lincolnshire, the city members, and most of the other county members.[2] The temperature continued to rise through the year 1641, until on 1 December the Grand Remonstrance was presented to the king; Sir Christopher Wray was on the committee for the purpose.

By March 1642 the king was at York. According to one tract a petition had been presented to him at Newark from 'his loving subjects in the county of Lincoln', and he promised to deliver his reply thereto at York. The spokesmen of the petitioners certainly appeared there, and perhaps they presented it again, along with those of other counties.

Lincolnshire, Sir Richard Erle delivered it with some twenty gentlemen of quality, who were scoffed at by the courtiers and citizens and called Roundheads; they lay in York on Sunday, being coronation day, where was bonfires made and much disorder; and about midnight that night, about threescore persons with clubs and bills assaulted the house where they lay, and swore they would have the bloods of them; the gentlemen being up, and the rogues got into the house, they were forced to put out their lights, and betake themselves to their swords, which done, the unknown rascals departed, giving threatening speeches that they would cut the throats of them that came next; yet I praise God we (the Nottinghamshire spokesmen) had reasonable quarter from them.

The king replied to both Nottinghamshire and Lincolnshire to the effect that he had been driven from parliament, to whom they should address their petitions.[3]

---

[1] *Eight Occasional Speeches made in the House of Commons this Parliament, 1641* (1641).

[2] John Rushworth, *Historical Collections* (1659), IV, 244. On 5 May there was a rumour that the army was to be used to overawe the houses, and Sir John Wray, with the thought of a second Guy Fawkes in his mind, called out that he smelt gunpowder. There was a panic, the trained bands turned out from the city of London to succour the members, to find when they reached Covent Garden that they were not needed (Gardiner, *History of England* (1884 ed.), IX, 359).

[3] Quoted in Hutchinson, *Memoirs*, ed. Firth, pp. 389–90.

Meanwhile the Commons drew up a list of persons recommended to the king as fit to be entrusted with the militia; and on the king's refusal both houses passed the militia ordinance appointing lords lieutenant, Theophilus Earl of Lincoln for Kesteven, Holland and the county of the city of Lincoln, and Francis Lord Willoughby of Parham for Lindsey.[1] Lincoln asked to be excused on the ground that the county was divided, and Willoughby was authorised to act for the whole of it.[2]

In April the king demanded admission to Hull, and was denied by the governor, Sir John Hotham. (He was connected by marriage with the Wrays.) The Houses declared the royal demand a breach of their privileges, and issued an order to the sheriffs of Yorkshire and Lincolnshire, and all other royal officers, requiring them to suppress all forces that should be raised in those counties, either to force the town of Hull or to stop passengers to and from it.[3] The reinforcement of Hull had to be undertaken from the Lincolnshire side of the Humber, and there was much coming and going in the process. Willoughby, Ayscough, Christopher Wray and Hatcher were sent down to the county and told to go to Hull as required; several of them wrote from there. Money was sent down and troops raised for its defence.[4]

A parliamentary committee to ensure the execution of the militia ordinance took up its duties in the county. It included Willoughby, the members for county and city, Irby, Hatcher, Armyne and Christopher Wray.[5] All the chief constables of the hundreds were summoned to meet at Lincoln on 31 May. They attended in strength to the number of nearly four score, only two or three being absent. The king's proclamation had been fixed on the gates of the very inn where the committee was sitting, but it had no deterrent effect, nor had the news that the Earl of Lindsey had been appointed the king's lieutenant for the county. The committee found in the city the trained bands and a like number of volunteers completely armed.[6]

As to the city meeting, Willoughby and his deputies met at Lincoln on 6 June to take the view of arms. . .

in which service the mayor and his brethren were very forward, and the city of Lincoln, with the towns belonging thereunto, came in willingly and readily, only the Bail of Lincoln and most of the Close of that great Church neglected to appear, for which the constable made this pretended excuse, that the sickness being below the hill (where the view was taken) they durst not come down thither; but the truth is (as we conceive) that the Recorder of the City, whom

---

[1] 5 March 1642 (*A. & O.* i, 2; *L.J.* iv, 578, 587; *C.J.* ii, 426).
[2] *L.J.* iv, 674; *C.J.* ii, 497.   [3] Ibid. p. 547.
[4] *L.J.* v, 20–1, 27, 71, 82, 87–8, 114; *C.J.* ii, 548, 551, 568, 588, 608, 658.
[5] Ibid. p. 589.   [6] *L.J.* v, 104.

we may justly suspect not to be well-affected to the service, and some others of his leaven (Popishly inclined) near the great Cathedral, were so far from sending in their own arms, or giving any countenance to the business, that we rather apprehend they endeavoured to dishearten others therein as much as in them lay.

The lord lieutenant sent for them, but they were not to be found.[1] By 22 June Willoughby could report that he had carried out the militia ordinance in the county, had received a declaration signed by many thousands of hands, and was assured of fidelity and affection.[2]

Willoughby also reported that he found the Lincoln trained bands in a good posture, far beyond his expectation, considering the sickness in the town, and he sent up to London copies of a letter he had received from the king, ordering him to give over meddling with the militia; and of his reply, saying that he was carrying out the ordinance of parliament, which was held to be legal by eminent lawyers, and impudently pleading that 'the want of years will excuse my want of judgment'. Both Lords and Commons approved of his conduct and that of his deputies.[3]

In an attempt to arrest parliamentary activity in the county, Charles had written on 28 May to the high sheriff, Sir Edward Heron, requiring him to take effectual care that the stores of ammunition in his custody should not be taken by order of parliament without order from the king or Lindsey. The letter was reported to parliament; the Lords declared it a breach of the militia ordinance, and ordered the high sheriff to apprehend Lindsey as a public enemy.[4] Lindsey was expected in the county upon the mustering of the trained bands, but had quitted it before he could be taken. He was soon to die of wounds received at Edgehill. The county magazine, held by Sir Philip Tyrwhitt and Sir William Pelham, was denied to Willoughby.[5]

When the mayor of Lincoln, John Becke, received the king's proclamation forbidding the muster of the militia, he complied with the request of the parliamentary committee and refused to publish it; furthermore, he handed the key of the city magazine to Willoughby, who placed a guard over it. Thereupon the king sent a messenger to summon the mayor to York to answer for his disobedience. The parliamentary committee arrested the messenger and sent him under guard of twelve horses and pistols to London, and the mayor agreed on their advice to go to London and place

---

[1] Ibid. p. 131. [2] Ibid. pp. 154–5, 169.

[3] *Lord Willoughby of Parham to an Hon. Member of the House of Parliament; the King to Lord Willoughby; Lord Willoughby to the King. Ordered to be printed by the Lords in Parliament. 9 June 1642.* (*L.J.* v, 115–17.)

[4] Ibid. pp. 102–3; *C.J.* II, 611. [5] *L.J.* v, 127–8.

himself under the protection of parliament. By the time they reached
Grantham the mayor, by persuasion of the messenger, had changed his
mind, and both escaped to York. There the mayor submitted to the king,
and was pardoned on condition that he returned to Lincoln and published
the royal proclamation. This he did, thereby incurring the displeasure of
the parliamentary committee.[1]

On 4 July the king issued commissions of array to a large number of the
gentry of the country and others including the mayor and sheriffs of
Lincoln.[2] On the 9th he made another attempt to stop the exercising of
the militia by issuing his warrant for the arrest of Alderman William
Watson and Sheriff Edward Emis (a shoemaker), who were taken to
Beverley and kept in custody. Parliament declared their arrest to be a
breach of privilege, and the Lords eventually obtained their release by
writ of *habeas corpus*.[3] Their fate and that of the mayor vividly illustrate the
dilemma confronting all men holding posts of local responsibility; however much they acted under duress from one side they were bound to fall
foul of the other.

Charles, having failed to take Hull, decided to visit the counties of
Lincoln and Nottingham in the hope of arresting disaffection there. The
nobility, knights, gentry and freeholders of Nottingham were summoned
to meet him at Newark on 12 July, and those of Lincolnshire at Lincoln
on the 13th. The parliamentary leaders were not yet prepared for a direct
clash, and Willoughby and the committee retired to London.

Accounts of the king's visit to Lincoln have been preserved by both sides.
The royalist version dwells on the immense crowd which gathered in spite
of short notice, and on the great demonstration of loyalty; the other
version points out that when all the people came together 'not one in
twenty had so much as a sword about them', inferring therefrom that they
came not to fight. The king's speech was delivered by Sir John Monson.
The knights, gentry and freeholders of the county were assured of the
defence of their religion, liberty, their common interest and the law of the
land. The militia ordinance was denounced, as was the king's exclusion
from Hull, and his hearers were promised that the county would not
become a seat of war, as this could only be where persons rose in rebellion
against him. He called on them to respond to his commission of array.

The spokesman of the city was Charles Dalison, the papist recorder.
Rather oddly, he first offered to his majesty his 'selfe, Estate and Fortune',
and then made the like offer on behalf of the mayor and corporation, who

---

[1] *C.S.P.D. 1641–43*, p. 342; *H.M.C. 5th Rep.* p. 141.
[2] L.A.O. Ancaster, xii/A, no. 4.
[3] *L.J.* v, 216, 227; *C.J.* ii, 682.

attended with the city trained band. Dalison was knighted; he was to serve with the royalist horse throughout the first Civil War.[1]

By the following day there was drawn up a petition of 'divers baronets, knights, esquires, gentlemen, clergy and freeholders of the county' to the Commons. It boldly asked that the king should have Hull, the militia be disbanded, and Church Government as it then stood put into execution. No Lincolnshire member was available to present it, and it was therefore sent with a covering letter to the Speaker, telling him that upon the king's summons the greater and more considerable part of the county had appeared at Lincoln, and that they hoped the petition would not miscarry, as they heard some others had. It was despatched by Sir Edward Heron, the high sheriff. In due course the House resolved that the petition was false, scandalous and seditious, and ordered the sheriff's arrest.[2]

The gentry offered to form a troop of horse to serve for three months, and the king accepted the offer. A commission was issued to Lord Willoughby de Eresby to raise a troop of eighty horse, and to command troops raised by Monson, Sir Charles Bolle and Sir William Pelham.[3] The dean promised four horses, the precentor and the chancellor three each and the archdeacon two. Farmery promised four and Dalison four. Altogether 172 horsemen were promised by seventy-five subscribers. Secretary Nicholas reported that the county had shown itself beyond all expectation affectionate and ready to serve the king.[4]

After staying in Lincoln for two days the king went to Beverley, but apparently he passed through the city again a few weeks later, drawing some of the arms of the trained bands 'of that country' for the use of his troops.[5] He was on his way to Nottingham, where, on 25 August, he raised his standard. Volunteers came in to him there, and to arm them he disarmed the trained bands of several counties.[6]

While the king was at York (1 August) the Lincolnshire gentry had presented another petition to him, promising to concur with neighbouring counties in defence measures, and asking for protection against the county

---

[1] *His Majestie's Two Speeches: One...Newark, The Other To the Knights Gentlemen and Freeholders of the County of Lincoln at Lincoln. London, 1642* (Royalist). *A True Relation of His Majestie's Reception and Royal Entertainment at Lincoln* (Royalist). *An Extract of All the Passages from Hull, York and Lincolnshire being taken out of Sundry Letters sent by the Last Post. Being a True Relation of His Majestie's Proceedings in those Parts* (Parliamentarian).

[2] *C.J.* II, 689.   [3] L.A.O. Ancaster, XII/A/5, 6.

[4] *Declaration of Divers Knights...to Lord Willoughby, Lord Lieutenant of the County of Lincoln and Lincolnshire, subscribed by Many Thousand Hands* (C.S.P.D. 1641–43, p. 359).

[5] Clarendon, *History of the Rebellion* (1849 ed.), II, 316.

[6] Francis Maseres, *Tracts* (1826 ed.), I, 53. Thence he sent urgent letters to Farmery asking for loans from the clergy of the diocese (L.A.O. Bp. Reg. Red Book 1611–93, f. 226a).

becoming a seat of war. This nervousness boded ill for the king. A tract followed on 15 August. It professed to speak for the greater part of the gentry who had promised horse. It said that having done their duty they had resolved to keep their forces in the county: the people in the north were in fear of attack from Hull, the reins of government had slackened and been cut to pieces, a maritime county was exposed to invasion from abroad, neighbouring counties were full of troops, they desired the prosperity of both king and parliament; in short, there was every reason for doing nothing.[1] Another tract was published to the like effect.[2]

Soon after the king's departure from Lincoln the city returned to parliamentary control, and elected a new mayor, William Marshall, of the parliamentary party (14 September). On the same day the Commons ordered the impeachment of Lindsey, his son Willoughby, Monson, Heron, Dalison and Scrope, and on 8 October Heron was brought to the bar of the House. Examined about the petition drawn up when the king was in Lincoln, he said that a first draft by Scrope was not approved, and Monson, aided by Dalison, then drew a new one. A royalist captain had broken in Captain Lister's door, arrested Lister, and sent him to the king's council at Nottingham. The under-sheriff, sent for, confessed that he took all the arms from Sir Edward Ayscough's house, and was promised protection by Dalison and Monson. The arms were laid up in the bishop's palace. Heron was committed to the Tower for high treason, and the sheriff bidden to move his prisoners from the castle to the palace, Lord Lincoln being told to hold the castle for the safe keeping of the city. Dalison was discharged from the recordership, and Broxholme directed so to inform the city.[3]

Battle was joined at Edgehill on 23 October, and the real war had begun. Christopher Wray and Hatcher, who had both been given commissions, were given leave to go to their troops.[4] After Edgehill, Essex, the parliamentary general, sent an appeal to the deputy lieutenants of Lincolnshire for men, horses and arms to be sent at once, calling on the whole county to rise with their tenants and servants, and come in to help.[5]

Lincolnshire was from the first associated with the northern counties on the parliamentary side. Irby was serving in Yorkshire under Fairfax, where Lincolnshire moneys were sent to him. The war came nearer when

---

[1] *True Intelligence from Lincoln-Shire Discovered by a Letter to a Private Gentleman. Presented to the View and Consideration of the Peaceably Minded.*

[2] *Joyfull Newes from Lincoln-shire, or the Resolution of the Gentry and Commonalty concerning the King's Most Excellent Majestie and the High Court of Parliament.*

[3] *C.J.* II, 791, 805, 811, 816, 882, 894, 921.

[4] Ibid. p. 772; L.A.O. Holywell, H93, no. 10.

[5] *H.M.C. Savile Foljambe*, p. 141.

the royalists began to muster at Newark and turn it into a stronghold. It had 500 foot, three troops of dragoons, two troops of horse, and seven pieces of ordnance,[1] and it was to Fairfax that the Lincolnshire committee appealed for protection against them.[2] On 9 January 1643 the Lords and Commons passed a declaration and ordinance for the defence of the county. It declared that papists and other wicked persons had traitorously combined together, and were then in a great body under William Earl of Newcastle in the counties of York and Nottingham, and directed that Willoughby of Parham and the parliamentary committee should raise forces of horse and foot in the county.[3] On the other side the king associated the counties of Leicester, Derby, Nottingham, Lincoln and Rutland, and appointed Colonel Henry Hastings to be their colonel general.

That spring Captain John Hotham, son of the governor of Hull, made a general of the parliamentary forces in Lincolnshire through his Wray connections, was in secret correspondence with Newcastle. On 14 April he wrote from Lincoln telling Newcastle that

I have since I came into this town dealt with some of my friends that they would not be so violent against his Majesty's service, and was bold to promise them a pardon if they would retire and give way, that this country might be wholly at his devotion, the gentlemen are so considerable that of my knowledge, if they desist, there shall not a man here to hold up his hand against his Majesty; I was so earnest with them that I am confident it will be done, if your Lordship will be pleased to return me an assurance that they shall have his Majesty's favour and pardon. The gentlemen are Sir Christopher Wray and Sir Edward Ayscough, men as considerable as any in the North....

On the 18th he wrote that he hoped to gain Lord Willoughby and all those that had either power or reputation there. In spite of his assurances there is no sign that the local parliamentarians ever wavered. At the same time he was openly joining with Wray and Ayscough in writing to Speaker Lenthall upon the position in the county.[4]

Meanwhile the parliamentary forces in Nottingham resolved to attack Newark before it was too strong, and they invited the forces in Lincoln and Derby to join in the attack. There was, it seems, a delay of a month, after which the Lincolners advanced as far as Collingham and then withdrew.[5] Later they came up to Newark, and during the combined attack actually entered the town (28 February). But their commander, major-general Ballard, who later became a royalist, and who was determined to

---

[1] *L.J.* v, 527.   [2] Ibid. pp. 473, 527, 538, 588.
[3] *A. & O.* i, 58.
[4] *H.M.C. Portland*, i, 701–6; *C.J.* iii, 75, 146, 152, 155. His double-dealing was to bring him to the scaffold (C. Dalton, *History of the Wrays of Glentworth* (1880), ii, 24–62).
[5] Sir William Dugdale, *Short View of the Late Troubles in England* (1681), p. 47.

ruin the project, withdrew his troops. On 9 March, Sir John Henderson, commanding in Newark, had another brush with Lincolnshire roundheads; he stormed Grantham, and swept up to the walls of Lincoln. The whole county lay open before him.

It was about this time that a protestation and declaration of knights, esquires, gentlemen and freeholders of Lincoln and Nottingham against the 'unjust oppressions and inhumane proceedings' of Newcastle and his cavaliers was issued. It set out that the royalists were billeted in Nottinghamshire, whose male inhabitants had either to leave their wives, families and homes, or submit to indignities. Their sheep and cattle were driven away, plate money and goods exposed a prey to the soldiers, and their persons ill used. Divers of them were making inroads upon Lincolnshire, whose inhabitants could only expect to be treated with almost Turkish inhumanity. They protested their obedience to parliament and Lord Willoughby. In all this propaganda there was doubtless some truth.

Some of the parliamentary committee were being accused of want of diligence.[1] Hotham was arrested and taken to Nottingham castle, whence he escaped to Lincoln and so to Hull. He wrote to Queen Henrietta Maria that Hull and Lincoln should be surrendered. He and his father were, however, arrested and sent to London. In May there was a report that royalists had taken the Close of Lincoln,[2] and in July a Newark party, disguised as country folk, were admitted to Lincoln and took shelter in the deanery, but the attempt on the city failed.

Lincolnshire was a frontier county. On the north-west and west were the royalists, and to the south were the parliamentary forces. Alternate waves were to pass over the city several times within the year. Cromwell was engaged in East Anglia, and by the end of April 1643 had stamped out royalist forces there. In May he advanced to the north, defeating a party of royalists in a skirmish two miles from Grantham on the Newark road; it was of that engagement that Gardiner, with perhaps some exaggeration, said that the whole fortune of the Civil War was in that nameless skirmish.[3] It enabled Sir Edward Ayscough and John Broxholme to write from Lincoln to Speaker Lenthall on 3 June that

the cloud which hath long hung over this county, it hath pleased God...in some measure to disperse. For the malignant party at Gainsborough, being assured that the strength of our horse was joined to the great body about Nottingham, were puffed up with such boldness as...to range over the county to assess towns,

---

[1] Carlyle, *Letters and Speeches of Oliver Cromwell*, ed. Lomas (1904), I, 132 n.; perhaps they were influenced by the younger Hotham (see above, p. 153).

[2] *H.M.C. Hastings*, II, 100.

[3] *History of the Great Civil War* (1894 ed.), I, 143.

to take prisoners and to drive men's horses, and this course being long held by them, the 1st June with some troops and horse and dragoons they passed to Market Rasen and from thence to many other places in this county, still doing their pleasure to the prejudice of the people. 2nd June they marched to and lodged at Louth. Their leaders were Sir John Brook, Sir Charles Dallyson and Captain Whichcoat. We being advertised of the way they took, and assisted with 300 horse brought out of several parts to this town the day before, sent our men to waylay them in their return homewards, but such was the valour and vigilancy of the commanders and soldiers, as without rest to themselves or ease to their horses they arrived at Louth very early this morning, which they entered and subdued, and have this day by noon brought hither near 100 prisoners and as many horses with some arms and other considerable booty. The chief commanders of the enemy saved themselves by flight.[1]

On 24 July Cromwell stormed Burghley House and cleared the Stamford district. Farther north, on 20 July, Willoughby surprised Gainsborough, and Cromwell marched to his support. They defeated the royalist horse a little to the north of Lea. They then found that they were facing Newcastle's whole army, and they had to withdraw.[2]

Later Willoughby, his forces melted away, had also to abandon Lincoln and retire to Boston, whence he wrote to Cromwell on 5 August that

Since the business at Gainsborough, the hearts of our men have been so deaded as we have lost most of them by running away, so as we were forced to leave Lincoln on a sudden, and if I had not done it, then I should have been left alone in it. So as I am now at Boston, where we are but very poor in strength; so as without some speedy supply, I fear we shall not hold this long neither.[3]

Newcastle entered Lincoln with his army

without great difficulty, and placed also a garrison in it, and raised a considerable army, both horse, foot and dragoons, for the preservation of that county, and put them under command, and constituted a person of honour commander in chief (Lord Widdrington), with intention to march towards the south, which, if it had taken effect, would doubtless have made an end of that war.[4]

On 6 August Newcastle wrote from Lincoln to summon Nottingham to surrender.

Little is known of events in Lincoln during Newcastle's occupation. The mayor, William Marshall, left the city, and the royalist Richard Somerbie was installed in his place. Edward Reyner, the puritan rector of St Peter

---

[1] *H.M.C. Portland*, I, 712.

[2] Reports of the battle were sent by Cromwell, Ayscough and Broxholme to Lenthall, and by Cromwell, probably to Sir John Wray (Carlyle, op. cit. App. 5; W. C. Abbott, *Writings and Speeches of Oliver Cromwell* (1937), I, 240–4; *C.J.* III, 180, 188).

[3] Carlyle, *Letters and Speeches of Cromwell*, I, 146; *H.M.C. 7th Rep.* p. 558b; *C.J.* III, 198; *L.J.* VI, 173.

[4] Margaret, Duchess of Newcastle, *Life of William Cavendish Duke of Newcastle*, ed. Sir C. H. Firth (1886), p. 56. Dugdale, *Short View*, p. 189, says that Lincoln was taken forcibly.

at Arches, had his goods plundered, and was in danger of being shot in his church. He fled and settled first in Yarmouth and then in Norwich.[1]

The need to recover lost ground, and to overcome local jealousies, prompted Parliament on 25 July to appoint Lord Manchester, who was a cousin of the two Wrays, commander-in-chief of six eastern counties, and on 20 September to attach Lincolnshire to them.[2] Whilst Manchester advanced into the county,[3] Newcastle was being pressed by the king to march south but by the Yorkshiremen to return to that county for its defence. An attempt by Sir Thomas Fairfax on Stamford Bridge near York decided him upon the latter course, and he besieged Hull. Fairfax's horse became useless there, and he joined Manchester in Lincolnshire.[4] Sir John Henderson with 5000 men from Newark wished to prevent their junction, but failed. In the battle of Winceby near Horncastle on 11 October the royalists were routed.[5] On the 17th Newcastle wrote from York to Hastings asking him to spare what forces he could for the relief of Lincoln, promising to send what he could spare. It was too late. Manchester entered the city on 20 October, and Bail, Castle and Close surrendered, with colours, arms and ordnance.[6] His forces settled into winter quarters, but Sir John Meldrum went to Gainsborough; according to a chronicler he stormed it at noontime. 'Lincolnshire', he added, 'is at liberty. The Lord Willoughby, Sir John Wray, Sir Edward Ayscough, Sir Christopher Wray and Sir Anthony Irby, are now by an orbicular providence, by an admirable revolution, reinstated, re-entered, relincolnshired again.'[7]

The supersession of Willoughby by Manchester after the loss of the county caused much recrimination. Willoughby sent Manchester a challenge, but the House of Lords intervened and eventually found in Manchester's favour.[8] Cromwell attacked Willoughby in the Commons for deserting Gainsborough and Lincoln, leaving arms and ammunition which the enemy made use of. He was also charged with having loose and profane commanders under him; meaning apparently Christopher Wray and two other Wrays.[9]

[1] Edmund Calamy, *Nonconformists Memorial* (1775), II, 151.
[2] *A. & O.* I, 215, 291. The mayor, the two M.P.'s for the city, and aldermen Morcroft, Wilson and Dawson, were appointed collectors for the Eastern Association levy.
[3] See *L.J.* VI, 225, for Manchester's capture of Bolingbroke (12 October).
[4] *H.M.C. 5th Rep.* p. 107; *H.M.C. 7th Rep.* p. 564b.
[5] Maseres, *Tracts*, II, 433; Carlyle, *Letters and Speeches of Cromwell*, I, 163–5; *H.M.C. Hastings*, II, 105, 107.   [6] *C.J.* III, 287.
[7] *Mercurius Britannicus*, 28 December 1643; C. Dalton, *History of the Wrays of Glentworth* (1880), I, 215; *C.J.* III, 351.
[8] *L.J.* VI, 405, 414–15. Willoughby also had a quarrel with Col. King which continued to take the Lords' attention until they settled it in Willoughby's favour (ibid. p. 575).
[9] *C.J.* III, 387.

Before his supersession Willoughby had been engaged with forces from Leicester, Nottingham and Derby in the siege of Newark, which had been exposed to attack by Newcastle's retirement. All the Lincoln garrison and the available parliamentary forces in the county were there, and the town was hard pressed.[1] In March came the news that Prince Rupert was on his way to relieve it.[2] The parliamentary commander Meldrum was urged to fall back on Lincoln, but he resolved to stand fast. In the struggle that followed he was defeated, and signed terms of surrender on 22 March. Lincoln was occupied on the 23rd, 2000 arms being taken there; Gainsborough was slighted, and Sleaford abandoned.[3] Lincolnshire was royalist again.

Rupert was not, however, able to exploit his victory, and by 25 April he was back in Oxford. Sir Francis Fane, the royalist governor of Lincoln, was left with only a handful of men to meet a new advance by the forces of the Eastern Association, whose commander Manchester had orders to march to York to join Fairfax and the forces besieging Newcastle there. By 5 May a royalist at Welbeck reported that Lincoln was besieged by Manchester and Cromwell, who were said to have 6000 men and horse; the Close was well manned with 2000 men and good store of provision and ammunition. 'On the Thursday night they killed threescore of the rebels who came near the works.'[4] Yet on 6 May the city was stormed. Manchester's report records that he entered the lower part of the city on the 3rd after some resistance, the enemy betaking themselves 'to their upper workes, to the Minster, and to the Castle, which they conceived to be impregnable'. On the 4th, rain stopped any advance, 'it being so slippery it was not possible for our Foot to crawl up the hill to come to their works, where the Mount whereon the Castle stood, being near as steep as the eaves of a house'. Cromwell was sent to stop a relieving force of royalists; and between 2 and 3 o'clock on the morning of the 6th the Foot all fell to work, and within a quarter of an hour they got up to the works, 'which would have been enough to tire a horse'. As scaling ladders were being set up, the defenders ceased firing, and threw down great stones, which caused more hurt than all their shot. The ladders were too short, but the attackers managed to get up, and the defenders fled, crying for quarter and protesting that they were poor Array men. The royalists lost about fifty men killed; the parliamentarians eight killed and about forty injured. Sir Francis Fane the governor, Dalison the former recorder, with

[1] *H.M.C. Hastings*, II, 120, 124.   [2] *H.M.C. 7th Rep.* p. 446 b.
[3] *H.M.C. 7th Rep.* p. 447 a; A. C. Wood, *Civil War in Notts.* (1937), pp. 80, 83. On 8 April Essex wrote to the Lords 'Newark is not taken, Lincolnshire is lost, Gloucester is unsupplied, and the last week there was but a step between us and death, and, what is worse, slavery' (*L.J.* VI, 505).   [4] *H.M.C. Hastings*, II, 128–9.

other officers and 650 men were taken prisoner, and all the arms captured. The sinister note is added, even in the victors' report, that all the pillage of the upper town was given to the troops. Manchester was thanked for his victory by the Committee of both Kingdoms.[1]

He was still in Lincoln on the 22nd, when he reported to the House of Lords his preparations for advance. He had four regiments of foot,

> and have quartered four more at Gainsborough, Torksey Bridge and Saxilby, being in readiness to march towards the Scottish army, upon certain notice of Prince Rupert's marching that way. Most of my horse are already joined with the Scotch horse, and lie quartered on the other side of Trent. The Derby and Nottingham horse intend to join with them. Those on the other side Trent will make near 6000 horse and dragoons. I keep on this side with my foot and 1200 horse. I lie only in expectation of an enemy, having my chief respect to the security of the Scotch army before York. We are not willing to draw near each other until some appearance of Prince Rupert, lest we should prejudice one another in the position of our armies. Colonel Whyte I know will give a full account of the condition of the Scotch army. The great rains in these parts have so raised the Trent as it hinders my marching as yet.[2]

The Trent was crossed at Gainsborough, and Manchester marched to join Fairfax and the Scots in the defeat of Rupert and Newcastle at Marston Moor on 2 July. On the 16th York surrendered, and the whole of the north was in the hands of the parliamentary forces. By 6 August Manchester was back in Lincoln. There he lingered for a month without, as Cromwell complained, 'attempting anything either to reduce Newark or to secure the country against it'.[3] The truth was that Manchester, a presbyterian grandee of moderate views, had lost heart in the struggle. During the delay in Lincoln he gave some attention to the work of removing ministers 'that are scandalous in their lives, or ill-affected to the Parliament, or Fomentors of this unnaturall Warre, or that shall wilfully refuse obedience to the Ordinances of Parliament, or that have deserted their ordinary places of residence, not being imployed in the service of the King and Parliament'. He had been directed to appoint committees to carry out this work in each of the seven counties of the Eastern Association; and he issued his commissions on 24 February 1644.[4] On the findings of these

---

[1] *A True Relation of the Taking of the City Minster and Castle of Lincoln, with all their Ordnance Ammunition and Horse. By the Rt Hon the Earl of Manchester on Monday 6 May 1644* (*C.J.* III, 486); *C.S.P.D. 1644*, p. 154; John Vicars, *God's Ark*, pp. 218–20. On 3 July the House of Commons ordered that Dalison be not released without their consent (*C.J.* III, 550).

[2] *H.M.C. 10th Rep.* App. VI, p. 152. Sold at Sotheby's, 19 February 1947. Now in my possession.

[3] *Manchester's Quarrel with Cromwell*, ed. J. Bruce (Camden Series, 1875), p. 80.

[4] *A. & O.* I, 371.

commissions he ordered the ejection of a number of clergy. Among them was Dr Hurst, parson of Barrowby and Leadenham, charged with preaching a sermon comparing the four horns of the Book of Daniel to four parliamentary commanders, Essex in the south, Fairfax in the north, Waller in the west and Cromwell in the east, saying, moreover, that Cromwell was 'the greatt and terrible horne and that he was not worthie of the name of Christian'. Perhaps Manchester relished being exempted from attack in favour of his junior as the eastern horn; but he did not spare Hurst, who was ejected as a notorious fomentor of the war.[1]

On 3 July Parliament had passed an ordinance for putting the counties of the Eastern Association in a better posture of defence,[2] and on 2 October provided for weekly assessments in them for the upkeep of Manchester's forces. The sum of £1218. 15s. 0d. was to be raised weekly in the county of Lincoln and the city. On 22 August Manchester, as serjeant major general of the Association, had issued a commission to Thomas Hatcher, appointing him governor of the Bail, Close and city of Lincoln and the parts of Holland and town of Boston. He later appointed him captain of a troop of horse and issued blank commissions for the posts of lieutenant, cornet and quartermaster in the troop.[3] On leaving Lincoln Manchester moved slowly southwards to the indecisive second battle of Newbury and his quarrel with Cromwell. In the following April both Essex and Manchester resigned their commissions, and Cromwell's New Model Army was constituted in time to win the decisive battle of Naseby.

Newark still held out for the king, and in the winter of 1644–5 the Lincolnshire horse under Colonel Rossiter and the Nottinghamshire horse under Colonel Thornhagh had brushes with the cavaliers. On 20 April a Newark party surprised the fort at Trent Bridge at Nottingham, and threatened the town itself.[4] On the 26th the Committee of both Kingdoms wrote to Hatcher, saying that he knew the consequence of the fort to the passage to the north-east, and also to the safety of Nottingham; and desiring him to afford all assistance to the town until the fort could be recovered. According to Mrs Hutchinson the fort was recaptured in about a month.[5]

[1] J. W. F. Hill, 'Royalist clergy of Lincolnshire', in *L.A.S.R.* II (1938), 73. Later the Lincolnshire committee reported against the famous Michael Hudson, rector of Uffington and scoutmaster to Newcastle's army, who accompanied Charles I to Newark in 1646. Scott told the story of his death in *Woodstock*, following Peck, *Desiderata Curiosa* (1779 ed.), pp. 378 and 347–66.   [2] *A. & O.* I, 462, 515–16.

[3] L.A.O. Holywell Collection, H93, nos. 11–16. For Hatcher, see *D.N.B.* and *Lincs. N. & Q.* I (1888–89), 31, 62.

[4] *C.J.* IV, 118; Wood, *Civil War in Notts.* pp. 89–90.

[5] *Memoirs of Colonel Hutchinson*, ed. Firth, p. 229; L.A.O. Holywell Collection, H93, no. 20.

By September 1645 Hatcher had been succeeded as governor of Lincoln by Colonel Browne,[1] who was given command of the county in the absence of Rossiter, who had joined Cromwell in order to take part with him at Naseby. To Browne at Lincoln were to be sent 800 horse, with power to call on a further 400 stationed at Grantham.[2] After Naseby Rossiter resumed his old duty of watching Newark, to which royalists had rallied from various parts of the country, making it the strongest garrison remaining to the king. Constant raids into the surrounding country produced floods of complaints and pleas for help. In August the king marched northwards; at Welbeck (captured by Newarkers) he received reinforcements from Newark; thence he passed to Doncaster with intent to join Montrose in Scotland. He was, however, too close to the Scottish army and the forces of the northern counties under Colonel Poyntz, which Rossiter hastened through the Isle of Axholme to join, and he retreated through Belvoir and Stamford, followed by Poyntz. Rossiter was ordered to accompany the latter with 1000 Lincolnshire horse.[3] Defeated at Chester, Charles made for Newark again, arriving on 4 October. Prince Rupert, having surrendered Bristol after an heroic defence, and being dismissed for his loss of the town by the king, went to Newark to make peace with his uncle. He was attacked by Rossiter and driven into Belvoir for safety. Rupert and others were allowed to leave the area, and later the king also escaped from the forces around Newark. He reached Oxford on 5 November.

Troops were closing in on Newark, but in December 1645 and January 1646 the garrison could still raid almost as far as Lincoln.[4] By March it was closely invested by troops of the surrounding counties and the Scots army. The commissioners for its reduction, Lord Rutland, Lord Montagu, Sir William Armyne, William Pierpoint, Sir Edward Ayscough and Hatcher, lay in Lincoln. Thence, on 14 March, Rutland wrote:

The affairs before Newark (through God's blessing) go on well. Colonel Ledgerde regiment is come from York to us. The officers and soldiers are all as one man, to perform the service they are appointed; full of courage and healthful. Half the line we hope will be finished on Wednesday next and the other will with all possible speed. One of the bridges over Trent against Winthorpe was

[1] Appointed 9 May (*C.J.* IV, 137).

[2] *C.S.P.D. 1645–47*, p. 109.   [3] Wood, op. cit. p. 96.

[4] Wood, op. cit. p. 109. Among the Monson papers is a testimonial from officers of the garrison of Pontefract castle testifying to the loyalty and courage of Thomas Farmery, who during the two sieges there and before was 'a great furtherer of the services in bringing in of provisions, overseeing the works and workmen and discharging such imployments as have been committed to his care and industry' (17 Jan. 1646); on the strength of which apparently Lord Bellasise, governor of Newark, appointed him muster-master-general of the garrison there (21 March; L.A.O. Monson Deeds, no. 201–2).

PLATE 13

The right Honourable the Lord Willoughby of Parham etc

FRANCIS, LORD WILLOUGHBY OF PARHAM

From an engraving in Ricraft's 'England's Champions'

ready three days since. The Trent there divides: the other will be finished in a day or two. We have brought a pinnace musket-proof within half a mile of Newark, wherein are two guns, and which will hold 4 musketeers. The whole cannon from York is come to Winthorpe. One strong fort is made to secure the bridge. Another is preparing nearer the enemy; great service. The whole culverings and mortar piece is come to Balderton and Farnton. The great mortar piece is to be riven on Wednesday at Nottingham. We hope in God to lose no time nor omit any opportunity in reducing Newark, and to give your lordships a good and speedy account thereof.[1]

On 5 May 1646 the king, accompanied by Michael Hudson, quondam rector of Uffington, arrived at Southwell to surrender to the Scots. Newark surrendered,[2] and the royalist troops marched out on 8 May. The surrender of Oxford on 20 June brought the first civil war to a close.[3]

The maintenance of armed forces was a heavy financial burden, and in March the city of Lincoln had asked to be excused from collecting and paying an assessment for the relief of the armies in Ireland; to which request the parliamentary committee replied that the necessities of the armies there were so great and cried so loud that they supposed none could be insensible of them; and that if the rebels were not prosecuted they were likely 'to infest us at home and lengthen out our troubles, which otherwise are in a hopeful way of a good and speedy end'. The committee thought the assessment was light and would not be burdensome if fairly distributed.[4]

The city was to experience a short sharp period in the second civil war.[5] The prospect of Scottish help for the king inspired cavalier risings in various

[1] *H.M.C. 10th Rep.* App. VI, p. 164. Now in my possession. The besiegers were exhorted by 'Orders from the Lord of Hosts', delivered by Reyner, at a public Feast and solemn Humiliation. (Copy in Nottingham Public Library.)

[2] After the surrender of Newark the mayor and aldermen of Hull sent to Lincoln for the return of the great guns belonging to Hull, lent for the siege. *Yorkshire Diaries*, ed. C. Jackson (Surtees Society, 1877), p. 142.

[3] Sir John Monson was one of the commissioners for the surrender of Oxford. Among the Monson papers is a draft clearly intended as his *apologia*: 'he that bids me when persecuted in one citye fly to another commands me only to beare with submission what I cannot avoide bye lawfull providence, and not by a rash boldness provoke danger, splitting my vessel upon a roke wheare I may recover a harbour though torn and weatherbeaten; which would rather prove self murther than martirdom...religion nature reason doe al dictate self preservation in all lawful waies' (L.A.O. Monson 19/7/2 (4)). Some of the argument recurs in his *A Short Essay of Afflictions* (1647); compare p. 73. See *D.N.B.* and for his publications *Short Title Catalogue*, which attributes to Dalison *The Royalist Defence* (1648), a robust legal argument against William Prynne. Toughness is not among the qualities suggested by Cornelius Jansen's portrait of Monson at South Carlton.

[4] *C.S.P.D. 1645–47*, p. 376.

[5] See E. W. Hensman, 'The East Midlands and the Second Civil War', in *Trans. Royal Historical Society*, 4th series, VI (1923), 126–9.

parts, and on 5 June 1648 Parliament sent Rossiter down to the Newark area, and bade the parliamentary committees of Leicester, Derby, Nottingham and Lincoln to send forces to serve under him.[1] On 30 June a message reached Lincoln that a royalist force of 400 horse dragoons and 200 musketeers had crossed the Trent at Gainsborough and were marching on the city. Word was at once sent to Rossiter at Belvoir, but too late to defend Lincoln, which was occupied the same day. Captain Bee, with thirty men, withdrew into the bishop's palace, the only defensible place which had so far escaped damage. The royalists, under Sir Philip Monckton, stormed it and set fire to part of it, raided the houses of known parliamentarians and plundered the city. Bee offered to surrender on terms which provided for his own protection, and the royalists agreed, but after his surrender they seized him and other officers and soldiers, the mayor (alderman Emis) and alderman Dawson, and took them away as prisoners.

Rossiter arrived within three miles of Lincoln on 3 July, to find that Monckton had retired to Gainsborough, though before doing so he had released all the prisoners, criminal and political alike, in the castle. Rossiter overtook him at Willoughby near Nottingham, gained a complete victory, and released all Monckton's prisoners. So ended the misadventures of the city in the civil wars.[2]

During this raid Reyner, back in Lincoln after two years' absence, was again singled out for maltreatment by the royalists. He fled into the Minster library, where they followed him with drawn swords, swearing they would have him dead or alive. He opened the door, and having been stripped of his coat and purse, was led off in triumph. Luckily for him one of the royalist captains had been his pupil when he was a schoolmaster at Market Rasen, and he espied and released him.[3]

The damage caused by the wars cannot be calculated. The injury to timber buildings must have been very great, and there were losses due to plunder by troops of first one side and then the other. Loss of trade was probably limited to the relatively short periods of active fighting in the neighbourhood, though food supplies must have been affected, especially when the Newark garrison was foraging for supplies. There is a hint about pillage by Manchester's troops in 1644 in an order issued by the Commons on 27 June—some weeks after the taking of the city—forbidding the removal of lead or bells from churches or houses in Lincoln on any pretence whatever.[4] A survey of parish churches gives a few bald facts

---

[1] *C.S.P.D. 1648–49*, pp. 99, 103.

[2] *H.M.C. Portland*, I, 477; *Memoirs of Colonel Hutchinson*, ed. Firth, pp. 439–41; *Monckton Papers*, ed. E. Peacock (1884), pp. 22–3, 177 et seq.

[3] Calamy, *Nonconformists Memorial*, II, 152.   [4] *C.J.* III, 543.

about the damage done to them. St Nicholas and St Peter in Eastgate were destroyed in 1643, probably by Willoughby because they were too near to the city walls. St Swithin was burnt on 5 May 1644, the day before Manchester's assault, and it seems that St Bartholomew was burnt on the same day. After the Restoration the churches of St Michael, St Mary Magdalene, St Paul and probably others were either roofless or their roofs were in need of repair. St Botolph and the tower and nave of St Benedict had fallen.

The Minster suffered severely. Windows were broken, brasses torn up and monuments and statues mutilated or destroyed, and barge-loads of metal removed.[1] In fairness to the troops, however, it must be remembered that some of the responsibility for this destruction lay with parliament, which ordered the demolition of church ornaments and furniture on religious grounds. The charge that Cromwell, who was not in command, stabled his horses in the Minster comes only from a notoriously unreliable royalist pamphleteer, and can be dismissed. So also can the story, told half a century later to the diarist de la Pryme, that Cromwell contemplated the demolition of the Minster, and was only deterred from his purpose by a Lincoln citizen, Original Peart.[2]

Cottesford Place, in James Street, was ruined; it may have been singled out for vengeance because it had been the residence of Willoughby of Parham. The subdeanery was divided into tenements for the poor. The precentory was bought by the puritan John Disney, who built a house for himself among the ruins. The palace with its appurtenances was sold to Colonel Berry, later to be one of Cromwell's major-generals, whose purchase gave rise to a curious incident. During the war the Minster pulpit had, at the request of the minister and inhabitants, been removed from the choir to the bishop's late seat for warmth, as the Minster windows were broken. Berry held that the bishop's seat was one of the appurtenances of the palace that he had bought, and he wished to use the seat for his family. He applied to the magistrates for the removal of the pulpit, but in vain. On appeal to the Council of State, however, the removal of the pulpit was ordered, so that Berry might enjoy the seat according to his contract.[3]

The fact that this order was issued to the mayor and alderman indicates that with the abolition of the dean and chapter their jurisdiction within

---

[1] Evelyn, Diary, 19 August 1654.

[2] *Mercurius Aulicus*, 21 Sept. 1644; de la Pryme, *Diary*, ed. C. Jackson (Surtees Society, 1870), p. 158; *Lincs. N. & Q.* VIII (1904–5), 176–7. The story of de la Pryme is the subject of a window in the chapter house, showing Peart on his knees before Cromwell (Venables, 'Survey of Houses in the Minster Close of Lincoln', *A.A.S.R.* XIX (1887), 45).

[3] *C.S.P.D. 1655*, pp. 160, 205.

the Close was deemed to belong to the corporation. The common council were concerned to assert and defend their new sphere of authority. In 1657 they resolved that all warrants issued into the liberty of the Close and all officers employed by the mayor should be avouched and maintained by the corporation. Similarly, they asserted their rights within the liberty of Beaumont Fee, and prepared for litigation. In the previous year they had been laying out money in defence of their charters and privileges, but against whom is not clear. As in other ways, the Protectorate anticipated modern reforms, but having been effected hastily and with violence they were destined to be undone in a short space of time.

The ranks of the corporate body illustrate the way in which those citizens who had to choose a side were divided. The aldermen in office in 1642 during the king's visit showed by later actions that they were equally divided. The mayor, John Becke, supported parliament, to be ejected at the Restoration. His father Robert Becke (they were in partnership as woollen drapers) was mayor in 1640; he was ejected by the parliamentarians in 1647, and two other aldermen with him, for having been captains in the king's forces.[1] He was fined £60 by the committee for compounding, though he pleaded that his service had been forced by Newcastle. Aldermen Somerbie, Kent and Bishop were royal commissioners of array, and Blow pleaded that he had only repaired to Newark for safety. Aldermen Morcroft, William and Robert Marshall, Dawson, Bracebridge, Watson and John Becke sat on the parliamentary committee for the county. Not one of them has left any personal record to show how much of the issues he understood, or what were the considerations that weighed with him. During the war much of the ordinary public business must, except in periods of disturbance, have gone on automatically, though it is significant that no entries were made in the White Book of the proceedings of the city court between 1641 and 1650. The common council minute book beginning in 1638 has vanished, perhaps to destroy evidence which on some turn of fortune in the war or after would have become incriminating.[2]

The king was executed on 30 January 1649. Throughout the interregnum there remained a large minority of royalist sympathisers in the common

[1] L.P.L. MS. 5013, p. 37.

[2] In St Mary le Wigford's parish the election of churchwardens was recorded to 1643, with a vicar. There was a gap to 1649, when Nathaniel Clarke, minister, appears. In St Michael, parish accounts were taken in 1641, and thereafter not entered until 1653. At the Bluecoat School accounts were taken to 1642, and there is a gap until 1646. Arrears of rent were then being collected, money laid out for repairs and for writings that were plundered. The school had evidently been closed as there was no income until rents could be collected again. It was not until 1650 that rents from Newark could be got in. (Bodleian Library, Rawl. MS. D687) Income of Gales Charity, paid in December 1642, resumed in January 1646. (Accounts in my possession.)

council, and reaction against puritan rule and heavy war taxation no doubt brought them increase of strength. The death of the town clerk Thomas Peachell was the signal for a party struggle. The Cromwellian candidate Mason was elected, but shortly afterwards an aldermanic vacancy was filled by the royalists, who also won the following election of a common councilman. They then rescinded the election of the town clerk, and appointed their own candidate, South. They also captured the mayoralty. Their triumph was short-lived. Within a few days the Protector issued a proclamation continuing an Act of 1652 against the election of royalists, whereupon the outgoing mayor and his friends petitioned the Council of State, complaining of the election of a delinquent mayor and the 'outing' of the town clerk. The petition was referred to a committee, who recommended that major-generals Whalley and Berry should inquire and report.[1]

On 1 December Whalley wrote that it was a general complaint to him in Lincoln that wicked magistrates, by reason of their numbers, overpowered the godly magistrates, and that no sooner were alehouses suppressed than they were set up again. The major-generals were hampered through not having been appointed magistrates; Whalley also wrote that 'I was forced at Lincoln, for the composing of a long and hot difference there, betwixt the mayor and aldermen and citizens, to assume a little more power than (I think) belonged to me; and I hope God hath made major-general Berry and myself instruments to reconcile them, and to settle their government.' There was a shortage of magistrates, and he hoped to submit suitable names.[2]

The royalist mayor was displaced, but the royalist majority in the council refused to disturb their town clerk. Whalley suggested as a compromise that both elections to the town clerkship should be declared void, and proposed a third candidate, Perkins, who was a Cromwellian. The suggestion being refused, Whalley, 'by an usurped, illegal, pretended power', as the minutes boldly recorded, commanded the council to elect his nominee, threatening that if they refused he would take their sword and charter from them. Thereupon the council complied and carried submission further by admitting Whalley and Berry to the freedom of the city.

It may be that royalist activity in Lincoln had some underground connection with royalist plots, for in 1655–6 Lord Willoughby was said to be taking part in such a plot in Lincolnshire.[3] If so, however, such evidence

[1] C.S.P.D. 1655, pp. 364, 399.

[2] Thurloe Papers, ed. T. Birch (1742), IV, 197, 272. As to excess of authority, so might the regional commissioners have written in the Second World War.

[3] Nicholas Papers, ed. G. F. Warner (Camden Series, 1892), II, 218, 220, 222, 237; Cal. Clarendon State Papers, ed. F. J. Routledge (1932), III, 17.

as may have reached Berry did not impress him. He wrote on 27 June 1655 to the Lord Protector that 'the hearts of the enemy are fallen, and a word commands them, and all would be well here, had we a few honest men to bear rule and lead the people. Our ministers are bad, our magistrates idle, and the people all asleep; only these present actings have a little awakened.'[1] Whalley reported to the like effect in the following January that 'we are likewise very busy in casting out scandalous and ignorant ministers, suppressing alehouses, taking order that the poor in all places under our charge may be set a work, and beggars suppressed'. But he still flattered himself that he was doing a good and successful job: 'You cannot imagine what an awe it hath struck into the spirits of wicked men, what incouragement it is to the godly, yea, and I may say, through God's mercy, how it reconciles them amongst themselves, through our weak indeavours.'[2]

The wicked men were addicted (*inter alia*) to horse-racing. When Lord Exeter asked Whalley if he would permit Lady Grantham's cup to be run for at Lincoln, Whalley, with some hesitation, agreed, saying that the Lord Protector did not wish to abridge gentlemen of that sport, but only to prevent great confluences of irreconcilable enemies.[3]

Edward Reyner had long been re-established as preacher in Lincoln. In August 1644 the Commons asked the Assembly of Divines to think of two suitable ministers to be sent to the city of Lincoln to preach there at stipends of £150 each,[4] and £300 was appropriated out of the revenues of the cathedral church for this purpose.[5] Reyner was recommended in May 1645.[6] When in 1655 he republished his *Precepts for Christian Practice or, the Rule of the New Creature New model'd*, he mentioned in a dedicatory epistle to the Mayor and Aldermen 'with the rest of my Christian Friends in the City of Lincoln', that apart from about two years 'in the heat of the late unhappy broiles', he had worked in the city since he was called full 28 years ago by the general vote of all the godly in it. He was still in Lincoln in 1658,[7] but died in or about 1660.[8] He was joined at the cathedral by George Scortwreth in or before 1649. Scortwreth had been licensed to preach in the parish church of Alford—an endowed lectureship —by Bishop Chaderton in 1605;[9] he also died before the Restoration. He was followed by James Abdy, 'companion of Mr Edward Reyner whilst

[1] *Thurloe Papers*, ed. Birch (1742), III, 590.
[2] Ibid. IV, 434.   [3] Ibid. IV, 607.
[4] *C.J.* III, 597.   [5] *A. & O.* I, 663.
[6] *Minutes of Westminster Assembly* (1874), p. 87.
[7] Francis Peck, *Desiderata Curiosa* (1779), p. 508.
[8] A. G. Matthews, *Calamy Revised* (1934), p. 408. See below, p. 177.
[9] L. A. O. Cragg 3/1.

he lived; and a teacher of the remainder of his Flock, whom the Cathedra-lists had not scattered, after his decease'.[1]

As is so often the experience of reformers, the puritans found that they had to contend with others who were more to the left than they were. George Fox preached in the county in 1654, and that year John Whitehead

for bearing testimony in the High Place called the Minster in Lincoln that it is the Light of the Glorious Gospell that Shines in Man's heart and Discovers Sin, he was buffetted and most shamefully intreated, being often knocked down by the Rude and Barberous people, who were encouraged thereunto by Humphrey Walcott who was then in Commission to have kept the peace; but brake it by striking of the said John Whitehead with his owne hands, which so encouraged the Rude People, that so far as could be seene they had slaine the said John, but that God stirred some Souldiers to take him by fforce from amongst them.[2]

The most interesting of the quakers was, however, the pamphleteer Martin Mason, a scrivener and an able man who gives a number of glimpses of the various parties in the city of the Protectorate, in the customary phraseology. He began by reviewing Reyner's *Precepts* in a paper whose title began *The Proud Pharisee Reproved; or the Lying Orator laid Open*, saying that Reyner 'calls himself a Minister of the Gospel in Lincoln. But is found a Lyar by a Child of the Light.' It was addressed to his friends and acquaintances in Lincoln 'who yet love the Garlic and Onions of Egypt, better than the Milk and Hony of Canaan'. Mason was attacking a paid ministry. 'Peter could say, We have left all and followed thee. Canst thou say so? Thy Norwich journey will rise up in judgment against thee. ...Art not thou and thy fellow Priest paid for your preaching out of that yearly Revenue which was formerly paid to your Elder Brethren the Bishop Dean and Chapter of Lincoln £300 a year between you?' What they called the Assemblies of God's people were a mixed multitude of presbyterians, independents and cavaliers.

Mason then addressed himself to Scortwreth in *A Check to the Loftie Linguist. Or the Imprudency of a Smooth Tongu'd Pastour plainly made Manifest.* Amidst much abuse is the interesting charge that Scortwreth

was not long since fluttering among the Birds of the Independent Region, but then the Presbyterian Congregation (being the more numerous and Potentiall

---

[1] Calamy, *Nonconformists Memorial*, II, 154. James Pink, stonemason and carver, told E. J. Willson that when the wainscot screen at the Minster was taken down to give place to the present stone screen, they found painted on the old stone screen behind it a text: 'But if our gospel be hid, it is hid to them that are lost: In whom the God of this world hath blinded the minds of them which believe not, lest the light of the glorious gospel of Christ, who is the image of God, should shine unto them' (II Cor. iv, 3, 4) (Willson MSS. (Society of Antiquaries), XIII, 56).

[2] See *Journal of George Fox*, ed. N. Penney (1911), index; Emily Manners, *Elizabeth Hooton, first Quaker Woman Preacher (1600–1672)* (1914), p. 13.

Partie) lookt asquint upon Him, which this Ciceronian well perceiving, suffered himself to be befoold by the old Sophister, and so shak't hands with the linsie woolsie Presbyters, and is now by them esteemed a glorious Starre in that fading Firmament.

There is nothing to show whether Reyner and Scortwreth deigned to reply, but a baptist pastor, Jonathan Johnson, dealt with Mason in kind. Mason wrote a letter to him, and he replied; whereupon Mason printed *The Boasting Baptist Dismounted, and the Beast Disarmed and Sorely Wounded without any Carnal Weapon.* Johnson, however, found a more telling title: *The Quaker Quashed and his Quarrel Queld,* and after this Mason's *Sion's Enemy Discovered* is but feeble.[1]

Mason was right in saying that the presbyterians were gaining on the independents; and the surviving presbyterian leaders were leaning towards restoration of the monarchy. Many of the leaders of the wartime county committee were dead: John and Christopher Wray, Thomas Grantham, John Broxholme, Sir William Armyne.[2] Manchester, Willoughby of Parham and Rossiter were promising support to the future Charles II. Thomas Lister, Armyne's son-in-law, took Broxholme's seat in the Long Parliament, but after its dissolution the citizens were left to find their own representatives without the aid of the gentry. In 1654 they returned Original Peart, a city lawyer, and alderman William Marshall; in 1657 Peart and Humphrey Walcott, a presbyterian gentleman living in the Close; in 1659 alderman Robert Marshall and the young royalist lawyer Thomas Meres. In that year Colonels Hatcher and Rossiter replied to an inquiry that they were prepared to serve for the county: 'wherefore', said a circular letter,

it is the resolution of the gentlemen that have declared, and it is our interest, to procure them to be chosen before a third party (who agreed not with our declaration) that is now busy setting himself up against them and us at this election, and will be chosen if the declarers come not generally in for our two colonels only. Wherefore we desire you to move all the honest freeholders in your parts to appear at the next election so that none but their and their country's friends may be chosen. For our mutual good, and to preserve a good correspondence is this notice given to yourself and all others of best interest to inform all parts.[3]

They were elected.

---

[1] Copies of the pamphlets are in the Library of Friends' House.

[2] His funeral sermon is printed in John Wilford, *Memorials and Characters...of Eminent Persons* (1741), p. 520; his wife Lady Mary Armyne died in 1675. She was generous in giving books and money, endowed almshouses in three counties, and gave large yearly contributions to promote the carrying on of the work of converting the Indians in New England (ibid. p. 522).

[3] L.A.O. Holywell Collection, H 97A.

Events were on the move. The régime began to disintegrate after Oliver Cromwell's death on 3 September 1658. Royalist plans for insurrection, including schemes on Boston and King's Lynn, failed. On 9 August 1659 the Council of State ordered Captain Cust at Lincoln to recruit his troops to the number of 100. He was bidden to take Willoughby's engagement on his honour not to act against parliament or the state, and, if he refused, to secure him and report. He was also to send up his prisoners by a convoy to be provided, to forward money in the hands of the receiver at Lincoln, and to get such arms from Hull as the Lincolnshire commissioners should appoint. The following day it was reported that the arms in Lincoln were secured.[1] The royalists thought Willoughby backward, but he was forward enough to be detained in Hull. On 3 February 1660 General Monck entered London: the declarations presented to him asking for a free parliament, included one from Lincolnshire, presented by Rossiter. In April 1660 the county returned Rossiter and the royalist Castleton to the new parliament, and the city the royalists Meres and John Monson. On 29 May Charles II was back in London.

[1] *C.S.P.D. 1659–60*, p. 95.

CHAPTER IX

THE LATER STUARTS: RELIGION
AND POLITICS

CHARLES II entered London on 29 May 1660, and on 25 June he was presented with an address from the nobility and gentry of Lincolnshire, royalist and presbyterian alike.[1] They had been preceded by the clergy of the county, headed by Dr Robert Sanderson, on 23 May.[2] The welcome given to him was almost unanimous. The minister of Cawthorpe and Covenham may speak for the small minority. On the night when bonfires were made for the proclamation of the king, he kicked the fire about, and said, 'Stay, the rogue is not yet come over.'[3] That same December inquiries were being made about a puritan plot; Mr Marshall, perhaps the Lincoln alderman, was the only one distinctly accused, though according to the soldiers Mr Disney and one Harvey were deep in guilt.[4]

One of the first concerns of the new government was to secure the passing of the Militia Act, declaring the sole right of the militia to be in the king, and adding 'during the late usurped governments, many evil and rebellious principles have been distilled into the minds of the people of this kingdom, which unless prevented, may break forth to the disturbance of the peace and quietness thereof'. Almost at once steps were taken to raise the militia generally for 14 days in the year, and the deputy lieutenants were busy all over the county under the lord lieutenant, Lord Lindsey. The usual difficulties arose; as in August 1663, when the deputies wrote from Lincoln to assure Lindsey of their diligence, but asking that their men need not be drawn into actual duty until after harvest, unless there were danger.[5] When there was fear of invasion in 1666 orders were given for the more speedy and circumspect watch and regard to be given to fire beacons in the county.[6] A militia assessment for the city, Bail and Close which must relate to 1661 has survived showing leading citizens assessed at a pike or a musket or a proportion of one or other, the total being fifty-four muskets and twenty-six pikes.[7]

Petitions poured in to the king from royalists who had suffered during

---

[1] B.M., C. 112. h. 4(1).
[2] In spite of their financial difficulties the newly restored dean and chapter gave the king £1000 in 1661 (*H.M.C. Hastings*, IV, 112).
[3] *C.S.P.D. 1660–61*, p. 109.
[4] Ibid. p. 425.
[5] Univ. Lib. Cambridge MS. Dd. 9. 43, f. 43.
[6] Ibid. f. 95.
[7] Bodleian Library, Top. Lincs. MS. c. 3.

the interregnum. Lindsey sought to recover Belleau House near Spilsby which had been procured by the younger Sir Henry Vane, soon to die for treason.[1] The dispossessed recorder Dalison declared that he had sacrificed the benefit of his profession as a lawyer for 18 years, spent much money, and been surety in large sums for the late king, for whom he raised forces in the wars; he was often imprisoned, was one of the thirty-nine excepted from pardon, had lost £1000 in money and £400 a year in land, and compounded for his estates at half their value.[2] Sir John Monson said he had lost £30,000 in the royal cause and been faithful both in parliament and elsewhere; and he declared that the late king had intended for his service to make him a baron, but was prevented by leaving Oxford.[3] It was impossible for the king to make good the losses suffered during and after the war, and the bitter complaint that the Act of Indemnity and Oblivion was one of indemnity for the king's enemies and oblivion for the king's friends was perhaps the first expression of disillusion that followed upon the initial rejoicings.

Meanwhile the common council of Lincoln had resolved, on 19 June 1660, to address the king, accepting his pardon for being involved in the late general defection, and congratulating him on his escape from so many dangers and his restoration to his subjects. The fee-farm rent of £81 was returned to him, having been purchased 'from inevitable necessity and self-preservation' for £700.[4]

The victorious royalists, with the aid of Dalison, who resumed his office, at once began to assert themselves in the common council. William South claimed the town clerkship against Perkins, who had been elected at the dictation of Major-General Whalley.[5] The claim was referred to arbitrators, of whom Dalison and the presbyterian Humphrey Walcott were two; they declared the election of Perkins null and void, and ratified that of South. The blow was softened by the proviso that South should pay Perkins £20 a year for three years, and that Perkins should execute so much of the office as might be discharged by deputy.

But the puritans were still strongly entrenched in the council. William Bishop and Edward Blow, who had been ejected from the council seventeen years earlier, petitioned the king to command the corporation to restore them. They declared that they were plundered, imprisoned and sequestered in 1642–3, and were kept out of their places by their violent enemies.[6] On

[1] *C.S.P.D. 1661–62*, p. 409.
[2] Ibid. p. 185.
[3] Ibid. p. 213. The hint was lost: and it was left to George II, in very different times and circumstances, to redeem Charles's promise.
[4] *C.S.P.D. 1660–61*, p. 67.   [5] See above, p. 165.
[6] *C.S.P.D. 1660–61*, p. 246.

26 September 1660 they produced to the common council a writ commanding their restoration. It was resolved to signify, with the advice of counsel, why Bishop was not forthwith restored. The reason was not recorded. This produced a letter from the king, read on 28 November, expressly commanding that Bishop and Blow and such other aldermen and common councilmen as had been displaced 'in these late ill times' should be restored. In face of this direct command Bishop was restored to his aldermanry, and Blow and another to their places as common councilmen. It would seem that pressure was put upon the council to comply more fully than this with the royal command, for on 15 June 1661 the king's letter was again considered 'with a desire that the same be fully answered and obeyed'; and after leaving the matter to the next day, it was resolved that all persons unduly brought into the office of alderman or common councilman should be displaced, and Blow was restored to his full dignity as an alderman as the king had commanded. 'And they humbly hope', ran the minute, 'that they have herein fully answered and manifested their one obedience to his Majesty's said letter and command.'

Some of the more enthusiastic royalists wished to go further against the puritans. They brought charges of embezzlement against the mayor (William Suttoby) and some of the aldermen. The charges were heard by the privy council and dismissed; but the common council, determined for the sake of all parties to clear up the matter, resolved to inquire into the charges. Suttoby was called upon for an account; three years later he was still £15 in arrears, and it was ordered that he be sued at the assizes. William Marshall was called on to account for the sum of £800 within fourteen days, evidently in the hope that he would not be able to comply; his account was produced in the time prescribed. It was no uncommon thing in times when the mayor was treasurer during his year of office for an outgoing mayor to be late in submitting his account for audit, and in handing his credit balance to or claiming his debit balance from his successor. New rules of account were made in 1665 providing that if the mayor would not give security for moneys in his hands, the council should appoint two treasurers or stewards, apparently to be jointly responsible with him. This was done two years later, the Inner House appointing one, the Outer the other.

It was to be expected after a period of puritan rule that a council recruited by co-option should have a strong and perhaps a predominant puritan element; certainly the aldermen, who held the real power, were mainly puritan. This state of things was not peculiar to Lincoln, and it was to bring municipal corporations under the effective control of the court that there was passed in December 1661 an Act for the Well Governing and

Regulating of Corporations.[1] It provided that all holders of municipal offices must take the oaths of allegiance and supremacy and non-resistance to the king, make a declaration against the validity of the Solemn League and Covenant, and take the sacrament according to the practice of the Church of England. Of greater immediate importance was a provision that until 25 March 1663 the administration of the Act was to be in the hands of special commissioners nominated by the Crown, any five or more of whom might, should they 'deem it expedient for the public safety', by a majority remove from their offices any corporation office-holders, 'although such persons shall have taken and subscribed, or be willing to take and subscribe, the said oaths and declarations'. They were empowered to fill up all vacancies thus created from among existing or previous inhabitants, and such appointments were to have full effect as if they had been duly made according to charter. For fifteen months the corporations lay at the mercy of the Crown and its nominees who might approve or expel as they pleased; and who would clearly act on a review of the records of members of the corporations during and after the Civil War. The court might have gone even further, and secured that the powers of the commissioners became permanent but for the opposition of the borough members in the House of Commons.[2]

The commissioners appointed for Lincoln were the zealous Dalison, Sir Thomas Meres, Sir John Monson and other county gentry. Their measures were drastic and prompt. On 23 August 1662 they displaced seven aldermen,[3] both the sheriffs, one coroner, one chief constable, eight common councilmen, one chamberlain, the swordbearer and the macebearer. William South, lately restored to his offices of steward of the courts, common clerk and clerk of the peace, was ejected. The commissioners then proceeded to fill the vacancies so created. Edward Blow, Richard Wetherall and Robert Wrosse were given the same aldermanic seniority as if they had never been displaced. William Dawson was restored, and William Bishop was continued for his known loyalty and good affections. Three other aldermen[4] were continued after examination, though one of them, Dawson, was shortly afterwards displaced.

One of the least important but most interesting of the commissioners' appointments was that of macebearer. James Yorke was appointed. He was the author of the well-known heraldic work *The Union of Honour*,

[1] 13 Charles II, c. 1.

[2] See J. H. Sacret, 'The Restoration Government and Municipal Corporations', in *E.H.R.* XLV (1930), 247.

[3] Robert Marshall, John Becke, William Marshall, Edward Emis, William Hall, John Leach, William Suttoby.

[4] Thomas Dawson, Stephen Fowler and Samuel Lodington.

published in 1640. Yorke was a blacksmith living in the Bail, where he was a lessee of both corporation and the chapter.[1] He included in his work the arms of the gentlemen of Lincolnshire, noting against the arms of Monson that his duty bound him to acknowledge the favours he had received from the family in his work. Sir John Monson, who was one of the corporation commissioners, had no doubt nominated him to his new post.

Not all the commissioners' appointments worked well. John Babb had been chosen a common councilman. In 1669 the swordbearer reported to the council that when he summoned Babb to a council meeting, Babb gave this answer, or to the like effect: 'Trouble me no more, for I will come no more amongst them'; for which, and other opprobrious language, he was expelled. There is no hint that his attitude was due to religion or politics; perhaps he disliked his colleagues or was bored by the business, or, being a barber, he could not spare the time.

The purge was complete. All the office-bearers with any taint of puritanism were removed, and thereafter the council, recruited only by co-option, and protected by the oaths and declarations required of members, remained exclusively anglican until the municipal reforms of 1835. These defences did not, however, prevent the emergence of whiggism in following generations.

The Crown was also resorting to the old weapon of *quo warranto* writs, and it seemed now to be used for the purpose of substituting new charters for old ones, vesting in the Crown the appointment of recorders and town clerks, providing for parliamentary elections by members of the common council only, and generally bringing local government under the closer control of the court.[2] Many such writs were issued in the years after 1660. In 1663 such a writ was issued against Lincoln corporation, and the town clerk was ordered to attend the recorder in London thereon. The council wrote to him that it would be cheaper to buy a confirmation charter than to plead the old ones, but as they were 'at present out of moneys and incapable to raise any', they desired to have the matter postponed. The policy of delay and plea of poverty seem to have been wise, for no new charter was issued, and no more is heard of the writ.

Meanwhile the Church of England was being restored to its former place in the national life. Dr Sanderson was included in a first list of nominees to bishoprics at the request of Archbishop Sheldon, and on 28 October 1660 he was consecrated bishop of Lincoln. He was a man of saintly

---

[1] See E. M. Sympson, *Lincoln* (1906), p. 383. Fuller's comment on his book is that 'although there be some mistakes (no hand so steady as always to hit the nail on the head), yet it is of singular use and industriously performed' (*History of the Worthies of England* (1840 ed.), II, 295).

[2] See Sacret, op. cit. pp. 237 et seq.

character and great learning, later to be commemorated by a memoir written by Izaak Walton. He has a special claim to remembrance in a history of Lincoln. Christopher Hatton, comptroller of the household of Charles I, had appointed the antiquary William Dugdale to a place in Heralds' College. In 1641 Dugdale journeyed throughout England making notes of the ecclesiastical monuments which would be in peril in the political strife he saw approaching. In Lincoln he found Sanderson to do the work for him; and hence the Winchelsea Book of Monuments which is the only evidence of so many of the memorials in the Minster which perished in the Civil War.[1]

The re-establishment of the cathedral chapter presented some difficulties. The dean, precentor, chancellor and subdean had all died. There was living, however, Raphael Throckmorton, who had been appointed archdeacon of Lincoln, but not installed because of the suppression of the chapter. A mandate to instal him was accordingly issued by the vicar-general of the see of Canterbury, addressed to the dean, or in his absence to the subdean 'or to any other canon or prebendary who has or shall have power to instal him or his proctor'. The installation was carried out on 1 July 1660 on the authority of the king, 'exercising full right by reason of the vacancy of the see of Lincoln'; and a prebendary was found to do it. It is recorded in the first entry in the chapter acts after a lapse of twenty years. Other installations followed, among them that of Michael Honywood as dean.

Honywood was not a distinguished figure. Walker described him as 'an holy and humble man' and 'a living library for learning';[2] beside which may be placed the complementary notes of the worldly Pepys that 'he was a good-natured but very weak man, yet a dean, and a man in great esteem', 'a simple priest, though a good well-meaning man'.[3] Nevertheless Honywood deserves well of lovers of the Minster, for he initiated the long process of restoring it in fabric and in seemliness; and in particular he paid for the building of the library by Sir Christopher Wren over the ruined north cloister in 1674, and endowed it richly with books.

The restoration of the fabric was a formidable task, and a draft public appeal for funds in the hand of Sir Charles Dalison referred to the Minster's

---

[1] D. C. Douglas, *English Scholars* (1939), pp. 36–7; Browne Willis, *Survey of the Cathedrals*, III (1730), 4; Sir William Dugdale, *Life, Diary and Correspondence*, ed. Hamper (1827), p. 14. What must be Sanderson's index volume of a vast manuscript collection for the history of Lincolnshire is now in L.A.O. Monson 7/43. It is not known whether the collection has survived: for references to it see G. G. Walker's paper on Sanderson in *A.A.S.R.* XXXI (1911), 25–7.

[2] John Walker, *Sufferings of the Clergy* (1714), II, 269.

[3] Diary, 29 June and 6 August 1664.

'vast dilapidations'. Evelyn had noted in 1654 that 'the soldiers had lately knocked off most of the brasses for the gravestones, so as few inscriptions were left; they told us that these men went in with axes and hammers, and shut themselves in, till they had rent and torn off some barge loads of metal, not sparing even the monuments of the dead, so hellish an avarice possessed them'.[1] Most of the glass was broken, and the church furniture had no doubt been made away, and the place adapted for use as a puritan meeting-house. The chapter quickly voted £1000 for repair, and the St Mary's bells and Lady bells were ordered to be rehung. It was to be several generations before the work was complete; some of the damage was irreparable.[2]

By 1662 four of the parish livings in the city had been filled and later the others were filled by resort to pluralism.[3] In a wholesale resumption it was inevitable that some unsuitable appointments should be made. The cathedral organist, Mr Mudd, had bouts of tippling, abused the organ-builder, fell to singing aloud during a sermon, and had to be dismissed. The vicars were apt to come late to service or not at all. An enterprising clerk, the Rev. Hugh Walter, obtained a certificate that he was in the late king's service from 1642 until the end of the war, had behaved well, and was several times wounded, and that he had secured a party of ill-affected persons who were going to join Colonel John Lambert.[4] Thus he procured a letter from the king to the Master and Governors of the Lincoln Christ's Hospital setting all this out, adding that having been formerly elected reader in the cathedral church, he did (on the day of thanksgiving for the king's restoration) solemnize the divine service of the Church of England, which had not been read there by the space of sixteen or seventeen years. It continued that he had been deprived of his stipend, reproached for reading the Book of Common Prayer, and given notice to quit the place he had

[1] Diary, 19 August 1654. Browne Willis noted in 1718 that he counted about 207 gravestones that had been stripped of their brasses (*Survey of the Cathedrals*, III, 31).

[2] See J. H. Srawley, *Michael Honywood* (Lincoln Minster Pamphlets, no. 5, 1950). The fabric accounts have many entries for the casting of lead, work about taking up the great bell, work about the bishop's seat and the Close Gates, making a pinfold and walling up the Bight lane back door (D. & C. Bi/1/8). During the interregnum the common council assumed jurisdiction within the Close. For the reassertion of the rights of the dean and chapter at the Restoration, see *M.L.* pp. 124–6. To enable innkeepers in the Bail and Close to make their returns of ale brewed to the excise commissioners in Lincoln rather than in Wragby the Lindsey justices ruled in 1670 that the Bail and Close were within the old bounds of the ancient city of Lincoln and within the market town of Lincoln (Lindsey Sessions Minutes, I, 644b).

[3] L.A.O. Liber Cleri, 1662, ff. 33 and b.

[4] *C.S.P.D. 1660–61*, p. 147. Walter's fellow-vicars believed that he had keys to all three locks of their common chest, which was in his custody: in it were their writings and common seal. When he had been 'crost in his will' he '[in his fury and passion] threatened to set a fire to their writings' (L.A.O., D. & C., Civ. 14/2).

PLATE 14

LINCOLN CATHEDRAL LIBRARY
designed by Sir Christopher Wren

held as school master in the Hospital. It directed the Master and Governors to continue his stipend and office until the church was otherwise settled, and allow his wife and servant to be his assistants in the ordering and dieting of the schoolchildren.

The governors at once declared that Walter had been lying to the king, and they resolved to send a speedy reply to his Majesty certifying the whole truth of the business. This resolution brought the peccant petitioner to his knees. He begged them not to reply to the letter, as he wished to desist from all further prosecution thereof. The governors further recalled a rule made for them by Lord Ellesmere that there should not be a schoolmaster resident in the house, but decided that as Walter was destitute of any other habitation he should be allowed to remain for a short time and teach the boys until he could get another house. Two years later the governors examined the boys in arithmetic and found them totally ignorant. Walter having now become a senior vicar choral at the Minster, he was discharged. It is surprising that Walter, although he had been censured by the chapter for drunkenness, disobedience, and arraigned for rudeness to a lady in the choir, was reappointed schoolmaster in 1668 in place of one dismissed for incompetence; there must have been serious difficulty in finding anyone fit for the post.

By the Declaration of Breda Charles II had promised a liberty for tender consciences; no man was to be called in question for differences of opinion in matter of religion. It was no doubt in reliance on this promise that the common council, as yet unpurged, resolved, on the displacement of the puritan ministers from the cathedral, that Reyner and Abdy—Scortwreth was dead—should be paid a yearly stipend of £40, to take effect from the time when their allowance from the dean and chapter lands came to an end. This was on 26 September. On 25 October the king made his Declaration on Ecclesiastical Affairs, making concessions to presbyterians, but not to independents and baptists and other dissenters. The latter had therefore no protection, and even without regard to these royal assurances royalist magistrates were able to invoke the Elizabethan legislation imposing penalties on all who refused to hear divine service or attended conventicles. The anabaptists of Lincolnshire addressed the king protesting against his declaration, recalling his letter from Breda, and asking why the righteous should suffer with the wicked.[1] In March 1661 the quaker Martin Mason

[1] B.M. 669. f. 26 (59), *The Second Humble Address of those who are called Anabaptists in the County of Lincoln*, signed on behalf of the several congregations in the county by Thomas Grantham and 29 others. *The Third Address* was signed by Grantham and several others (B.M. C. 112, h. 4 (74)). A baptist prisoner succeeded in publishing *The Prisoner against the Prelate: or, a Dialogue between the Common Goal and Cathedral of Lincoln*, a dialogue in verse attributed to Thomas Grantham (apparently wrongly: see *Short Title Catalogue*).

addressed the judges of assize from the Lincoln city gaol. By then about 80 quakers were prisoners in the city and county gaols by virtue of 'that hasty paper called the King's Proclamation'. 'Yea, some of us were haled out of our houses and had to Prison before the Proclamation came amongst us, so mad was the multitude and some of the magistrates that they out-paced the Decree of Caesar in showing their teeth against the Innocent'.[1] There were so many quakers always in the castle that a special room was hired for them, and a loom provided by their Monthly Meeting so that the prisoners might earn a little money.

Parliament soon swept away all idea of even a limited toleration. The Act of Uniformity required uniformity of public prayers and uniform administration of the sacraments. Episcopal ordination was alone recog-nised as valid. Ministers who did not comply with the Act by St Bartholo-mew's day 1662 were to be deprived of their livings. About 40 were ejected in Lincolnshire, 26 of them in 1662.[2] That this was not thought severe is indicated by a report in November of that year that the fanatics in Lincoln increased by over-indulgence, but were quiet.[3] Edward Reyner escaped further adventures, for he was dead. Abdy remained in the neighbourhood, teaching those of his flock 'whom the Cathedralists had not scattered'. John Joynes having been presented to the rectory of St Peter at Arches, the common council voted him a salary of £20 a year for preaching afternoon sermons at St Peter's every Sunday, and the sermon at the mayor's election on Michaelmas day.

The Act of Uniformity was followed by the other repressive measures of the Clarendon Code. Persecution always produces a revulsion of feeling, and the sufferers, mostly humble folk, were not without friends. Among them was Colonel Edward King, who as M.P. for Grimsby had moved in parliament for the recall of the king. He was one of those people who are naturally against the government. He attended conventicles and aided deprived ministers, and in September 1665 was arrested by the deputy lieutenants of the county, who refused him bail. This at once caused a flutter. Secretary Coventry wrote to Arlington that King was demanding his *habeas corpus*. The Duke of York was anxious that Charles should con-sider the case, for it would test the validity of the King's intructions to his lieutenants.[4] Colonel King at once petitioned. He had been summoned, he said, by Sir Anthony Oldfield and Sir Robert Carr, two deputy lieu-

---

[1] Martin Mason Papers at Friends' House. It does not appear whether Mason was continuously in prison, but he was there in 1665 when he published some prison medita-tions, in which he denounced 'ignorant dreaming priests, and those devouring Cormorants [the Bishops Courts]'.

[2] A. G. Matthews, *Calamy Revised* (1934), p. xii.

[3] *C.S.P.D. 1661-62*, p. 540. [4] *C.S.P.D. 1664-65*, p. 565.

tenants, to sign a bond for £2000 to abstain from conventicles and do other things, and for refusing was sent to gaol and there continued in time of pestilence contrary to law.[1] He obtained his *habeas corpus*, though he was abused by lord chief justice Bridgeman as a turbulent fellow and an opposer of his prince. Some years later, in 1672, Sir Edward Lake, the chancellor of the diocese, complained that King had for many years tried to protect those questioned for nonconformity in the ecclesiastical court at Lincoln; that he had counselled or set on about 90 actions against Lake and the officers of the court, and dared to bring only four to trial, and was cast in them all, plainly endeavouring to ruin Lake for only doing his duty.[2]

The energetic William Fuller became bishop of Lincoln in 1667, and he did his best to enforce church order. Many charges of nonconformity were brought in the archdeacon of Lincoln's court: it is said that there were 1400 in two years.[3] In 1669 it was reported to London that the county grand jury, having found the good effects of the proclamation against conventicles, had drawn up a paper of thanks to his Majesty, which was read and subscribed in the county court. There had been a great conventicle held at Gedney, though three-fourths of those present had come from adjoining counties.[4]

Fuller conducted a visitation in 1671. He found evidence of malice at work. Money had been collected upon a brief for the captives—presumably of the Algerian pirates—but returned to the donors on a rumour spread all about Lincolnshire, which had crept into other parts of the diocese, that the brief was a cheat, and the money was to be otherwise employed. When the mistake was corrected the money was not given again.[5]

On the whole, however, he was pleased with his reception. In August he wrote from Stamford to Secretary Williamson:

I have now passed through five counties in my visitation, and though I have toiled like a horse from morning till night these 23 days, yet I am sufficiently rewarded by the love of the gentry and the kindness of the people, who, wherever I come, depart well satisfied with the severity of my proceedings, for I have sacrified some officers who exact fees, as well as debauched ministers and half-conformists, to the people's satisfaction, and it was time to do so. Old and young of all qualities are very desirous of confirmation, which I give wherever I come. You would wonder at the vast numbers I everywhere confirm, which I note to

[1] *C.S.P.D. 1665–66*, p. 36. [2] *C.S.P.D. 1672*, pp. 536–9.
[3] F. Bate, *The Declaration of Indulgence* (1908), p. 59.
[4] *C.S.P.D. 1668–69*, p. 449.
[5] Another rumour believed in the diocese was that the king would seize unbranded cattle: 'the king is coming to take our cattle: his takers are in the next town' (*C.S.P.D. 1671*, pp. 59, 426).

confirm your opinion that the people, if left to themselves, are strongly for the present Church government. The noise against it proceeds from not many mouths—I will show you a list of parishes where there is not one separatist.

He added that he encouraged catechising rather than preaching.[1]

The bishop, like all others concerned with church order, was confronted in 1672 by problems arising out of the king's Declaration of Indulgence. This document was issued without parliamentary sanction under the claim that the king could suspend the laws. Under it, licences might be issued to persons named in them to preach in certain places, and some houses might be licensed for preaching without a particular preacher being named in the licence. Sir Robert Carr, one of the knights of the shire and a deputy lieutenant, combined an expression of dislike of the indulgence with full submission to the king's will when he wrote: 'I pray God they make no ill return for this generous declaration of his Majesty, which, it being his pleasure, I am highly satisfied with, but I know no other thing could have made it relished well with me, who have upon all acts of grace found them highly ungrateful, but whatever my private opinion was before the declaration, I am sure now I am of opinion with it.'[2]

Fuller, lately so optimistic, was reduced to despair. He wrote: 'Many in my diocese pretend to have licences to preach, who, I think, have none. I entreat you to send me a list of those licensed in my jurisdiction.'[3] Sir Edward Lake, the chancellor of the diocese, met some novel legal arguments based on the declaration. It was contended that it was to be interpreted as against all ecclesiastical laws; a parishioner at Boston, legally questioned by Lake for begetting a bastard child, confessed the fact, and being enjoined the usual penance, pleaded that the declaration tolerated the fact.[4] By the autumn the bishop wrote to Williamson acknowledging the list of licensed teachers, but asking whether those licensed for one place could preach in another licensed place. 'Five houses are licensed in Lincoln for Anabaptists, but no preacher named: pray let me know who are licensed for those five? All these licensed persons grow insolent and increase strangely. The orthodox poor clergy are out of heart. Shall nothing be done to support them against the Presbyterians, who grow and multiply faster than the other?'[5] Another time he wrote: 'Both Presbyterians and Anabaptists, with the Quakers, are exceedingly increased: Insomuch that if there be not a sudden stop put to their daring growth, I dread to write the consequence.'

Four of the Lincoln baptist conventicles can be identified. They were held in the houses of Roger Fawnes, Nicholas Archer, Elizabeth Lylly and

---

[1] *C.S.P.D. 1671*, p. 426.
[2] *C.S.P.D. 1671–72*, p. 215.
[3] *C.S.P.D. 1672*, p. 264.
[4] Ibid. pp. 536–9.
[5] Ibid. p. 589.

PLATE 15

FRONTISPIECE OF *THE PRISONER AGAINST THE PRELATE:*
DIALOGUE BETWEEN THE COMMON GOAL AND
CATHEDRAL OF LINCOLN

John Anderton. The first licence to be issued for Lincoln was for the house of John Disney the presbyterian, and another authorised James Abdy, who had once preached at the Minster, to preach in the house of Mr Powell.[1]

The situation soon changed again. The declaration aroused such hostility in parliament that the king was forced to abandon it, and he broke the great seal upon it on 7 March 1673.[2] Presently an order in council was issued commanding that effectual care be taken for the suppression of conventicles. But the king could not undo the results of the declaration. Sir John Reresby, looking back, wrote that 'all sectaries now publicly repaired to their meetings and conventicles, nor could all the laws afterwards, and the most vigorous execution of them, ever suppress these separatists or bring them to due conformity'.[3]

It would be easy to draw from the foregoing narrative a wrong impression of the strength of nonconformity, and it is fortunate that a sense of proportion can be ensured by the results of a census taken in 1676 on the orders of Archbishop Sheldon of conformists, popish recusants or persons suspected of such recusancy, and other dissenters 'which either obstinately refuse or wholly absent themselves from the Communion of the Church of England at such times as by law they are required'.[4] The returns given are as follows:

	Conformists	Papists	Nonconformists
Eastgate	134	0	0
St Paul in the Bail	162	6	0
St Michael on the Mount	150	3	20
St Martin	348	1	23
St Peter at Arches	206	1	17
St Swithin	304	7	14
St Benedict	178	2	8
St Mary le Wigford	126	7	8
St Peter at Gowts	148	1	12
St Mark	67	0	6
St Botolph	106	0	8
St Mary Magdalene	304	2	2
Newport	76	0	4

The figures are not to be taken as strictly accurate, for several reasons: the mere inquiry would frighten weaklings back into the Church; presbyterians who sometimes attended the parish church were not counted as nonconformists; and many of the so-called conformists did not receive the sacrament.[5] The great preponderance of anglicans is not however in doubt.

[1] Ibid. pp. 380, 475, 515, 579. At his death Abdy's goods were valued at £126. 7s. 0d. of which £40 was in books. L.A.O. Inventories, 174/34.
[2] C.S.P.D. 1673, p. 24.   [3] Memoirs and Travels (1904 ed.), p. 150.
[4] Lincs. N. & Q. xvi (1920–1), 43–4, 50. A return of papists made in 1680 names ten men and one woman in the county of the city, each no doubt representing a household (H.M.C. House of Lords 1678–88, p. 226). For estimation of numbers of Conformists, Protestant Nonconformists and Papists in 1693, see C.S.P.D. 1693, pp. 448–9.
[5] See A. Browning, Thomas, Earl of Danby (1951), I, 197–8.

The chance survival of the city quarter sessions books for the period 1677–85 throws a little light on the operation of the repressive laws. First, in 1679, a number of suspected popish recusants appeared in court voluntarily and took the oaths of allegiance and supremacy; then the oath of supremacy was tendered by the mayor and other justices to a number of persons believed to be recusants, who refused to take it, though many of them took the oath of allegiance, and the result was reported to lord chief justice Scroggs and the rest of the justices. In 1683, before the mayor and two aldermen, information was laid upon oath touching an assembly in part of the house of John Lupton, a baker of Bardney, in St Swithin's parish on the Lord's Day. The court held it to be an unlawful meeting, and adjudged Richard Sharpe of Lincoln, a cordwainer, who took upon him to preach or teach at the meeting under colour or pretence of some exercise of religion in other manner than according to the Liturgy and practice of the Church of England, to have offended. Both he and Lupton were fined £20. Lupton appealed to quarter sessions and was found guilty. The mayor was directed to pay the fines into court, to be disposed, as the Act directed, a third to the sheriffs to the king's use, a third to the overseers of the poor of St Swithin, and a third to the informers.

In 1685, at successive sessions, numerous persons were presented for not repairing to the parish church to hear divine service for three weeks, the usual fine being a shilling a week. Many of the same names appear each time. In April ten people, one of them Susanna Morrice, were indicted upon a riot. They submitted and were fined 5s. each, which they paid; and a number of people were fined for being present at an assembly in the house of an unknown person in Waddington in the county of the city.

An example in conformity was set by the corporation. In 1678 the justices, aldermen and common councilmen were ordered to attend the mayor to St Peter at Arches church on Sunday afternoons in their gowns, and there take their places in the aldermen's seat and common council loft, on penalty of a shilling for attending without gown. The macebearer was made responsible for the collection of fines. In 1681 the town clerk was the offender, and he was admonished to attend in his gown, and take his seat in the loft. (In 1701 the loft was thought to be too small, and the mayor and aldermen were bidden consult together about a new loft on the north side of the church.)

In matters political in the county the central feature was the rivalry between Lord Lindsey and Sir Robert Carr. Carr belonged to a family settled at Sleaford, and after being returned as a knight of the shire on a casual vacancy in 1665 he secured his advancement by a marriage with the sister of Henry Bennet, Lord Arlington, a member of the Cabal

Ministry. Carr was a great racing man and a deep drinker.[1] In 1672 he was appointed Chancellor of the Duchy of Lancaster, and as his brother-in-law was soon to fall from power, it was fortunate for him that he had a life patent.[2]

Robert, third Earl of Lindsey, succeeded his father in 1666, and became a privy counsellor and lord lieutenant. Like Carr, his position in the political world was largely determined by a marriage. His sister Bridget married Sir Thomas Osborne, whom Burnet describes as 'a gentleman of Yorkshire, whose estate was much sunk'.[3] But if the lady married beneath her her husband was to raise her later in life, for Sir Thomas became Earl of Danby and Lord Treasurer, and lived to make her Duchess of Leeds.

The rivalry between Lindsey and Carr showed itself in the elections at Boston and Stamford, and still more at Grantham. When Sir William Thorold, one of the members for Grantham, died in 1677, the candidates were Lindsey's nominee Sir Robert Markham and Carr's nominee Sir William Ellis. Markham was returned, having been helped, on Lindsey's orders, by a parade of the militia. The matter was brought before the House of Commons, who referred it to the Committee of Privileges. The court party supported Markham, and the country party tried to bring in Ellis; they were indignant that the king should speak to all he met, and set his servants to solicit help in the matter, which at bottom, reported Sir Robert Southwell to Ormonde in Ireland,

is a high contest of that country between Lord Lindsey and Sir Robert Carr, each drawing in all their strength and relatives to support it, and so growing up in the House as a trial of strength, and to decide the fate of the session. But the court was so worsted upon several divisions that having sat till one in the morning, it was urged by them to be irregular, and a new day come on, which the House had not appointed. Whereupon all that side went forth and away to bed, trying thereby to dissolve the assembly as unlawfully met. But the other gentlemen departed not till they had voted all things as they pleased.

Before the matter passed to the floor of the House Carr had secured the support of the country party on a promise that he would expose the whole business of the election, the drawing up of the militia by Lindsey to over-awe the electors, and other things that would have sounded ill. When the

---

[1] Pepys, Diary, 29 July 1667; C.S.P.D. 1682, p. 116.

[2] C.S.P.D. 1671-72, pp. 135, 149. Mr Justice Milwood remarked that it was a pleasant office, and honourable, with £1200 a year, and admitting of much ease and quiet.

[3] Burnet, History of his own Time (1828 ed.), II, 12. See Letters from Dorothy Osborne to Sir William Temple, ed. Sir E. A. Parry (1888), p. 128.

time came, however, Carr hesitated to go so far. 'Taking calmer advice,'
wrote Southwell, 'he would not be provoked into it when it came to the
push.' After a long and fierce debate, Markham was declared to be well
elected. The country party were angry with Carr for not laying open
Lindsey's enormities as he had promised, doubtless thinking to lay up
credit with the king for his silence. But he had lost one side's support without gaining the other, for the king ordered his name to be struck out of the
privy council books. Carr was so mortified that he was not seen in the
House for some days.[1] Lindsey and his friends gave themselves up to
rejoicing.[2]

In the Convention Parliament of 1660 the city had returned Thomas
Meres and John Monson (son of Sir John). At the election of 1661 Meres
was returned again, his colleague being Sir Robert Bolles, who had served
on the grand jury at the trial of the regicides in 1660. Bolles died in 1663,
and Monson took his place. Thereafter Meres and Monson represented
the city until 1681, save that on John Monson's death in 1674 his son
Henry Monson followed him.

Henry Monson was regarded by Danby as a non-official supporter
worth remembering, and a report made to him in 1676 added: 'Mr Chyny
must take care of this gentleman, and that most particularly, for he is very
uncertain unless one is at his elbow.'[3]

Meres cut a larger figure. He was a son of Dr Robert Meres, chancellor
of the cathedral, and a lawyer. He was returned to parliament at a very
early age—he was born in 1635—and he played many parts in local life.
He combined with his parliamentary duties the captaincy of the city
trained band, and was an active county magistrate. (He lived in Deloraine
Court—not yet known by that name—and gave the large candelabra in the
cathedral choir.) Pepys admired his good sense as a speaker, but he
acquired the name of a great talker, and was too changeable to be really
trusted. Lindsey wrote to Danby of those who enriched themselves as
'Sir Thomas of my country does by the sale of a penned speech pronounced
in Parliament'.[4] He was a strong Churchman, opposing the Declaration
of Indulgence, and in 1685 proposing a bill in parliament to compel all
foreigners settled in England to adopt the English liturgy.[5] He was
mentioned as a possible Speaker or Secretary of the Treasury under Danby.
Later he was, like Carr, associated with Arlington, and Danby wrote of
him in 1675 that he was 'at all times at the head of all opposition to your
Majesty's service, and whose business has been to possess all men that

---

[1] *H.M.C. Ormonde*, IV, 429, 431, 433.   [2] *H.M.C. Rutland*, II, 51.
[3] Browning, *Thomas, Earl of Danby*, III, 82, 96.   [4] *H.M.C. Lindsey*, p. 377.
[5] *Lives of the Norths*, ed. A. Jessopp (1890), III, 180–1.

I drive all the designs of the late Lord Treasurer, only in a more dangerous manner'.[1] In the following year a report was made to Danby that it might be possible to give a further account of Meres before Michaelmas. 'Colonel Whitly can do much with him, and has hinted to me something of that nature as if Sir T. might be treated with'.[2] Whitly was an Excise pensioner, and Meres was for a time an Excise Commissioner. He was to wobble several times in the coming years. Professor Feiling sums him up: 'Always mentioned as a coming man, but never quite arriving, never a whig but never quite a tory, Meres survived until 1710 to represent a pre-party age and the middle school of the Restoration.'[3]

The country presently flamed with the excitement of the Popish Plot. Angry parliamentary debates on successive Exclusion Bills intended to take the catholic Duke of York out of the succession to the throne were creating the tory or royalist, and whig or opposition parties. There were two general elections in 1679, followed by a third in 1681, in all of which the whigs had great successes. In Lincolnshire the tory cause was Lindsey's, and Carr's influence coincided with that of the whigs. At the elections for the county Lord Castleton and Carr held the seats. Castleton counted for nothing: he was a nonentity who was said to believe that the Duke of York was married to the pope's eldest daughter.[4] Sir Thomas Meres had a hard fight in Lincoln at the first election;[5] the fact that the court unsuccessfully nominated him as Speaker in 1679 suggests that he was regarded as standing in the court interest.[6] No doubt Carr's party pressed him hard. His colleague in the two elections of 1679 was Henry Monson, who wrote, probably to Mr Hatcher, thanking him for persuading Sir Thomas Hussey not to oppose him at Lincoln.[7] In 1681, however, Hussey supplanted Monson. Both, probably, were on the court side.[8]

---

[1] Browning, op. cit. III, App. I, p. 2.
[2] Ibid. p. 110.
[3] K. Feiling, *History of the Tory Party 1640–1714* (1924), p. 147.
[4] *Letters to Sir Joseph Williamson*, ed. W. D. Christie (1874) II, 27.
[5] *H.M.C. Fitzherbert*, pp. 12, 13.
[6] Burnet, *History of his Own Time*, II, 195.
[7] L.A.O. Holywell Coll. H/97/C. For the Duke of York's passage through Lincolnshire in 1679 and his treatment of Lindsey, Carr and others, see a letter from Lindsey to Danby in *Lincs. N. & Q.* XVIII (1924–5), 147–50, now L.A.O. Cragg 2/30.D.
[8] The number of persons admitted to the freedom in time to vote at a parliamentary election gives some idea of the energy with which the candidates and their agents pursued their campaigns. At the by-election in April 1675 following the death of Sir John Monson, thirty-four were admitted by birth and fifteen by servitude. In Jan.–Feb. 1679 thirty-eight were admitted by birth and twenty-four by servitude; in August 1679 ten by birth and eight by servitude; in February 1681 sixteen by birth and ten by servitude; in March 1685 twenty-three by birth and eight by servitude. Presumably the candidates paid the fees on admission: when other inducements were first added does not appear.

Charles unexpectedly dissolved parliament in 1681. There followed a rapid reaction against whig violence and in favour of the Crown. Lindsey, although he had been left out of the privy council in 1679,[1] entered with zest upon a purge of whig justices of the peace, and so short of justices did the parts of Holland become that the clerk of the peace complained that no sessions had been held for six months, that Spalding gaol was full of malefactors, and that active and useful magistrates were left out of the commission and others put in who refused to act.[2]

At this time, with Danby in the Tower, himself out of the privy council and his brother Charles Bertie, Danby's secretary, in disgrace,[3] Lindsey made his discontent plain to the king. In reply Secretary Jenkins wrote that 'the King has in his thoughts what will remove all those grounds of dissatisfaction that may lie somewhat uneasy on you at this time. I have communicated to Mr Peregrine Bertie all that his Majesty has let me know of that matter. He spoke with all affection of your family and with a great esteem of yourself.'[4] Lindsey was sent a prompt reply by, as Jenkins described them, 'two worthy gentlemen that go on the Church of England and the Old Cavalier principles which, according to my poor understanding, are the only principles that are safe for the Government and comfortable to the conscience.' Lindsey used a striking phrase: he said he had passed over the Rubicon. The king liked the phrase, and promised to support him with all his forces.[5]

The phrase seems to mean that Lindsey recognised the king's intention to establish himself as an absolute monarch, and had committed himself to the same enterprise. In the autumn of 1681 he was still busy getting rid of deputy lieutenants and justices who refused to join in an address to the king. He wrote to Jenkins that he hoped there was no thought of courting Presbytery, whose principles were inconsistent with monarchy. He could not answer for the militia without purging it: he hoped there would never be an occasion for its service, but it would be an ill time to model it when the enemy was in the field.[6]

Lord Willoughby and Charles Bertie were in touch with the king, and on the other side Carr was trying to justify the malcontents.[7] Lindsey tried to persuade a county grand jury to express its abhorrence of the traitorous Association, but an address was rejected: and so, at the next sessions, a jury specially chosen by the high sheriff resolved to address the king. 'The Presbyterians and the Dissenters', wrote Lindsey, 'are much dissatisfied, and by what I can conjecture daily lose ground in these parts, and my

[1] *H.M.C. Var. Coll.* II (Wentworth), 394.   [2] *C.S.P.D. 1680–81*, p. 141.
[3] *H.M.C. Lindsey*, p. 407.   [4] *C.S.P.D. 1680–81*, p. 354.
[5] Ibid. p. 376.   [6] Ibid. p. 409.   [7] Ibid. pp. 442, 466.

opinion is, if some justices that favour the factions were removed, this county would absolutely be at the King's command, and the royal party might once more hope to carry elections if his Majesty should have occasion of the Parliament.'[1] On 30 October 1682 he was still complaining of obstructive justices, who were strong both in the country and in the corporations, because they were encouraged by the Chancellor of the Duchy (Carr). He added that several trials were impending between informers and nonconformists and therefore a Church of England sheriff was important.[2]

The Rye House Plot to kidnap the king and the Duke of York was one of the symptoms of rebellious feeling, of which there are a few hints in Lincolnshire. At a meeting of a few of the capital burgesses of Stamford, one of them remarked 'The king is a rogue', and an informer who reported the remark to the mayor was himself described as a rogue: 'so', it was said, 'there will be whiggish dealings if left to themselves'.[3] In an alehouse conversation at Epworth, one Holgate having refused to drink the Duke's health, discourse arose of the disloyalty of some inhabitants, and it was reported to be publicly said by several present that they hoped suddenly to see a change, and that his Majesty should not live long. That Holgate declared that one Wilson, there present, was the Duke of Monmouth, and that if he were given the course he would sound a trumpet and bring 500 of the inhabitants to fight for him against the king and the duke.[4] Searches for wanted persons and arms were going on. Lindsey wrote to Jenkins of the principal suspects. There was Sir William Ellis, nephew of the Ellis who had been the Protector's solicitor; he was heir to a great estate, had voted for the Exclusion Bill, and married the daughter of John Hampden, who was involved in the plot. 'So', said Lindsey, 'that it seems strange to me that he is not in the conspiracy with his wife's brother, the Hampden now in the Tower. I am credibly informed the Duke of Monmouth made frequent visits to him. He is the head of all the Presbyterians in the county, and, I presume, will stand for the shire if a parliament is called.' There was also Sir William Yorke, who had been Member for Boston, a gentleman of £500 a year, as disaffected as Ellis; and Sir Richard Cust, with £1000 a year, of whom Jenkins would often have heard in the House. Lindsey had made search at the house of Sir Drayner Massingberd, son-in-law of Henry Mildmay, who committed suicide to escape execution for complicity in the plot. Massingberd was active in the late wars, and a dangerous person. 'Other persons', said Lindsey, 'are scarce considerable. It is observable they deal much in blunderbusses, for most of the three

[1] *C.S.P.D. 1682*, pp. 137–8.   [2] Ibid. p. 514.
[3] *C.S.P.D. Jan.–June 1683*, p. 13.   [4] *C.S.P.D. July–Sept. 1683*, pp. 31–2.

former mentioned knights had blunderbusses. I do not doubt, if they intended to raise an insurrection in this country, most of their arms are hid underground, and so not to be discovered.'[1] By the end of the year Lindsey was asking whether he might return the arms he had seized: he was presently ordered to send them to Boston.[2]

The city of Lincoln, of which no overt acts are recorded, presented an address to the king, congratulating him on the discovery of the plot for the assassination of himself and his brother. But a severe strain was soon placed upon the common council's loyalty. The city of London and other towns having become strongholds of opposition, Charles II set about securing the surrender of the charters. Where London succumbed, lesser towns could not hope to hold out. In Lincolnshire the charters were surrendered to Judge Jeffreys, who was on circuit, and who, said Roger North, 'made all the charters, like the walls of Jericho, fall down before him, and returned laden with surrenders, the spoils of towns'. The city of Lincoln, knowing who was the real power in the county, offered the recordership to Lindsey. He wrote to ask the king's approval of his acceptance, saying 'it being the metropolis of this country I could not with civility refuse'.[3]

The letter of surrender, dated 11 July 1684, addressed to Jeffreys, then gone on to York, thanked him for the honour of his visit, and said that according to the loyal inclination then manifested they had resolved to surrender the charter of his late Majesty King Charles the First of blessed memory: lack of unanimity was indicated by the addition *nemine contradicente*. Jeffreys replied that he had given the king an account of their loyal and prudent behaviour, and he gave them instructions as to procedure. The deed of surrender runs: 'Know ye that we considering how much it imports the Government of this Kingdom to have men of known loyalty and approved integrity to bear offices of magistracy and places of trust'; and petitions for a regrant of such liberties as the king should judge most conducive to the good government of the city, with such reservations as the king should appoint. The surrender was made by the mayor and others to the king at Whitehall on 2 November 1684. Jeffreys presented them, and 'his Majesty was pleased to receive them very kindly and promise them a new charter'.

It arrived on 1 January 1685. The mayor and corporation walked to St Katharine's, and there, upon the green, the mayor received it from Sir Thomas Hussey, to whom it was sent by Lindsey, the new recorder. The party then returned to the Guildhall in state, where Mr Mayor was sworn mayor and justice of the peace. There were great rejoicings. The

---

[1] *C.S.P.D. July–Sept. 1683*, p. 180, and see p. 251.
[2] *C.S.P.D. 1683–84*, pp. 171, 216; *C.S.P.D. 1684–85*, p. 27.   [3] Ibid. p. 186.

conduits ran claret, and the mayor and the company drank the healths of the king and the duke.

There was nothing to rejoice about. The charter had been costly. The bishop subscribed £20, and Sir Thomas Hussey, Sir Henry Monson, Sir Thomas Meres and Henry Stone of Skellingthorpe £10 each. Its point was contained in a proviso that the king might at any time remove the mayor or any other officer of the corporation by order of the privy council; and an addition to the clause excluding justices of the county of Lincoln at large from entering the city and interfering with the city justices, which read 'without the special commission of us our heirs and successors first had and obtained for that purpose'.[1] It was assumed that the new recorder would act by deputy. (The mayor and town clerk went to London to swear him as a governor of the Bluecoat School, though he never attended a meeting.)

Within a month Charles II was dead, and the accession of the romanist Duke of York as James II must in itself have inflamed the fears of many people. Nevertheless the royalist reaction held, and, aided by the recasting of the corporations, James secured a compliant House of Commons. Sir Robert Carr had died in 1683, and his influence vanished. As knights of the shire Lord Castleton and Sir Thomas Hussey were returned. At Boston the whigs Irby and Yorke lost to Lindsey's two sons Lord Willoughby and Peregrine Bertie. At Grantham, after some manoeuvres, Markham, who was branded as an excluder, withdrew, and two court candidates were elected.[2] At Stamford, where Lindsey himself was active, his two brothers Charles and Peregrine Bertie recovered the seats they had lost in 1679. At Lincoln Meres and Sir Henry Monson were returned.

There are odd hints of opposition opinion in the city. When the Reverend John Curtois, rector of Branston, preached in the Minster against treason and rebellion, his sermon was on the whole kindly received, but there were a few much disgusted by it, who on coming out of church fell to calumniate and belie the preacher.[3] One Phillpotts, a Lincoln resident, wrote to the king to report that a Lincoln gentleman, Cornwallis, being in a coffee-house, said the king broke his word given in his declaration, and violated his coronation oath. The witness, Mr Kent, made oath to this effect before Mr Rider, the recorder (doubtless the deputy), a man sometime famous for breaking open a letter directed to a catholic there. As Cornwallis was believed to have been a confidant of Sir Thomas Meres, to whom the matter would be directed, there might be partiality in the

[1] Birch, pp. 272, 275.
[2] *H.M.C. Rutland*, II, 85–7.
[3] *A Discourse shewing that kings*... (1685). From a copy in L.P.L.

cause.[1] During the Monmouth rebellion Gervase Disney, son of the Lincoln puritan, had a letter of his intercepted by the Nottingham magistrates, which was suspected of being Monmouth's Declaration; he absconded, but presently surrendered, and was released on giving sureties. His cousin W. Disney, who printed the Declaration, was executed.[2]

James made himself a military despot by raising and maintaining a regular army on Hounslow Heath; and in a bid for the support of the dissenters to a policy for the relief of catholics he issued a new Declaration of Indulgence. An instance of concession to dissent occurs in a letter from the king to the mayor and corporation of Lincoln ordering them to admit the Lincoln quaker, Abraham Morrice, to the freedom of the city. The king dispensed him from the necessity of taking the oaths. The common council complied with the order.

But James most directly damaged his own cause when he alienated the nobility and gentry. The process is neatly illustrated by his treatment of the Bertie family, who had done more for his father and his brother than any other family in the county. On 17 December 1685 Charles Bertie wrote to his niece Lady Rutland 'my nephew Willoughby, my brother Dick and brother Harry—the three battering rams of our family—are all turned out of their employments as captains'. His nephew Peregrine, a cornet, was also dismissed, 'so that they have cleared the army of our whole family'. Bridget Noel wrote to her that the greatest news was of the disbanded officers.[3] Sir Thomas Meres, for refusing to support the repeal of the Test Act, was removed from the commission of Foreign Plantations and the commission of the peace.[4] Many clergy of the diocese refused to read the Declaration of Indulgence in spite of the bishop's orders,[5] and the dissenters were not prepared to accept freedom for themselves at the price of assent to the royal policy of encouraging romanism.

With encouragement in high places, romanism prospered. A Jesuit priest was in Lincoln in 1680, and by 1685 there was a catholic chapel, small but much frequented, where a sermon was preached on Sundays and holidays. The number of missioners grew to three. There was also a school, whose scholars so increased in number that it was proposed to buy larger premises, and an agreement to buy one of the principal houses in the city was only stopped by rumours of the approach of the Prince of Orange.[6]

Men's thoughts had turned to William of Orange, the protestant champion, husband of James' elder daughter Mary, who was next in

---

[1] MS. in my possession.
[2] *Some Remarkable Passages in the Holy Life and Death of Gervase Disney Esq.*, ed. D. Disney (1692), pp. 78–91.   [3] *H.M.C. Rutland*, II, 97.
[4] *H.M.C. Portland*, III, 406.   [5] Ibid. III, 406.
[6] *Records of the English Province of The Society of Jesus*, v (1879), 619.

succession to the throne. Already in 1687 William's emissary Dykvelt had been in consultation with leading statesmen, including Danby, who was free after five years in the Tower. On 30 June 1688 the famous letter of invitation to William was sent, Danby being one of the signatories. James issued a proclamation for defence of the realm, and Danby, still cautious, wrote to his wife that it gave them a happy opportunity of arming for defence of their country, and that the gentlemen of the county would meet at York to consider how to do it in the best manner. 'I desire you will use some means', he continued, 'if you have no other, that you will send a man purposely upon pretence of seeing your brother Lindsey or Lady Rutland to bring you notice when any horse or dragoons pass by Newark, and what number they are, and by whom commanded, and to inquire what more are following them, and at what distance.'[1]

On 20 November Danby was in arms, and by 1 December in York, and with him Lord Willoughby, the two younger Berties serving as messengers to William of Orange, who had landed at Torbay. On the 10th Lindsey wrote to his sister Lady Danby to tell her of an impending meeting of Lincolnshire gentry, 'who, I believe, will act conformably with the gentry of Yorkshire. Castleton stays all the time out of the county, and I guess will not act against the Court, for we shall be divided into two factions again, Presbytery and Church of England.'[2] Lindsey also wrote to Danby that the meeting of gentry was appointed at Sleaford, and 'if Sir Thomas Hussey weds the cause, his interest will do much to make this country unanimous'.[3] Hussey, of the Doddington family, was knight of the shire with Castleton. Whether the meeting was unanimous does not appear, but the lord lieutenant and others signed an address to the Prince of Orange.[4]

There was a little trouble in the county. Lincoln marked the revolution by attacking the papists. At the beginning of the alarm, the mob, incited by some protestant minister, attacked chapel and school, vowing to tear the priest piecemeal, but the three priests had fled. The premises were nearly levelled, and a bonfire made of books and furniture. Some of the building material was sold by public auction. A flourishing Jesuit College was thus broken up.[5] Philip Bertie wrote of a body of 1500 horse who were firing all and putting everyone to the sword, and there were rumours of massacres at Grantham and Newark which proved to be unfounded.[6] In March 1689 James's dragoons met about 600 of Marshal Schomberg's regiment

[1] H.M.C. Lindsey, p. 447.　　　　　　　[2] Ibid. p. 452.
[3] H.M.C. Leeds, p. 28.　　　　　　　　[4] H.M.C. Waterford, p. 76.
[5] H.M.C. 5th Rep. p. 198; Records of the English Province of the Society of Jesus, v (1879), 619 et seq.　　　　　　　　　　[6] H.M.C. Leeds, p. 28.

at Spanby hedge on Swaton common. The king's men were taken prisoner and sent to Folkingham church.[1] About the same time statements were taken at Grimsby against Lord Lexington, Matthew Lister of Burwell and Mr Hilliard for swearing at King William (as he had become) and drinking to King James. Lindsey thought it best to hush the matter up.[2]

At the election of January 1689 the shire and the boroughs returned members who supported the offer of the throne to William. The most dramatic result was at Lincoln, where Meres, who had represented the city in every parliament since 1659, polled only 9 votes, the two winning candidates, Sir Henry Monson and Sir Christopher Nevile of Aubourn, each polling over 200.[3] Perhaps at the last moment Meres had adhered to the losing side; or it may be that he sat on the fence. When James had sent out a questionnaire to lords lieutenant to discover the attitude of gentry and justices towards the repeal of the Test Act and other matters, Nevile had replied that he was in favour of taking off the penal laws, Monson and Hussey against. Meres' reply is not recorded.[4] Meres cannot have been in serious disgrace, for he was made a deputy lieutenant in 1691.[5] The undependable Monson refused to take the oath to William and Mary and was discharged from parliament, Hussey being returned in his place.[6]

In one of his last bids for support James II had issued a proclamation for restoring the municipal franchises so lately tampered with. Whether for this or other reason the common council assumed that the charter of Charles II was null and that of Charles I in full force. Writing a century later, Samuel Lyon, the Town Clerk, said that this could only be accounted for upon the principle either that the surrender of the earlier charter was not valid, or that the surrender became invalid through its not having been enrolled in one of the king's courts of record. In 1784 counsel's opinion was taken on the question whether Lord Monson the recorder could appoint a deputy; he thought he could, for this was a corporation by prescription, and could act partly by charter and partly by prescription. The opinion depended on the view that the surrender of the charter of Charles I was void for lack of enrolment.[7]

---

[1] *H.M.C. Cowper*, II, 352.
[2] *H.M.C. Leeds*, p. 35. Lister's sentiments did not prevent him from writing to Lord Willoughby, asking Willoughby to solicit Danby for a place in the government service for him.
[3] There being virtual unanimity, there was no need to recruit new freemen.
[4] See G. F. Duckett, *The Penal Laws and the Test Act* (1882), pp. 145 et seq.
[5] *C.S.P.D. 1690–91*, p. 441.
[6] In May 1689 eighteen freemen were admitted by birth and fourteen by servitude.
[7] Lyon's 'Account of the Charters' (Lincoln Corporation MSS.).

PLATE 16

SIR THOMAS HUSSEY

From a portrait by Sir Peter Lely, by permission of Colonel C. F. C. Jarvis

Certainly Stephen Mason, who had been displaced from the recorder-ship by Lindsey's appointment in the later charter, was regarded as restored to his office, though for security and at his own request he was resworn. With equal promptness the council, recalling that Abraham Morrice the quaker had been thrust into the freedom of the city by James' exercise of the dispensing power, declared that the late king had by his declaration made the same void, and directed the town clerk to 'scrawle' out the order and put Morrice out of the rolls and records of the city.[1]

Feeling against the new government came out in various ways. The high sheriff was warned that Sir William Tyrwhitt and Mr Heneage of Lincoln were professed and known papists, and had in their possession good and able horse, so they should be watched.[2] Castleton, still knight of the shire, was discontented, and it was noted that he should be spoken to in relation to his carriage and behaviour.[3] In March 1691 several messengers were said to have gone into Lincolnshire to seize some persons that had appointed a great meeting on a pretence of a cock-fighting.[4] In 1693 Captain Stow, lately high sheriff, was taken for high treason.[5]

Although the legal disabilities of the romanists remained unchanged after the Revolution, the protestant dissenters, having for the most part joined the anglicans against James, received their reward. The Toleration Act of 1689 allowed them to have their own places of worship, provided that they met with unlocked doors and certified their places of meeting to the bishop or archdeacon, or to the justices. It was at about this time that the surviving quaker meeting-house was built in Lincoln on land bought as a burial ground in 1669; an emergency exit into the churchyard was provided at the back of the women's gallery for use in the event of a raid by the justices. The new liberty might prove precarious: no man so soon could say. Michael Drake, by then an aged man, who had been under

[1] A statute of 1696 (7–8 William III, c. 34) enabled quakers to make a solemn affirma-tion instead of taking an oath in certain instances. Thereupon Abraham Morrice once more sought admission to the freedom of the city, and sued out a writ of *mandamus* in the Court of King's Bench, addressed to the mayor, directing that he be admitted. After consulting counsel the corporation filed a reply admitting that Morrice had been apprenticed to a mercer for seven years, and had offered to make a solemn declaration in the words of the oath according to the Act; and that the mayor had refused to allow him to make the declaration. Chief Justice Holt quashed the *mandamus* for misdirection. The point was a technical one: the writ should have directed admission to the privilege, instead of to the place and office, of a freeman (*Lord Raymond's Reports*, I, 337; III, 203). Morrice was re-admitted on 30 July 1698, with another quaker, it being noted that they had made an affirmation in accordance with the Act. His son Abraham was soon after-wards enrolled as apprentice to his father.
[2] *C.S.P.D. 1689–90*, p. 272.
[3] *C.S.P.D. 1690–91*, p. 210.
[4] *H.M.C. Fleming of Rydal Hall*, p. 319.   [5] *H.M.C. Rutland*, II, 145.

arrest on suspicion of complicity in the Monmouth rebellion, was ministering to a presbyterian congregation in the Disney house.[1] About 1701 Joseph Veal built a meeting house for anabaptists at Brayford head, and at his death devised it to trustees, of whom Richard Sharpe[2] was one; it is now the Thomas Cooper Memorial Church.

In 1695 William III visited Lincoln: it was the first visit of a reigning monarch since that of Charles I. He was met up Cross Cliff Hill by the sheriffs, and at Great Bargate by the mayor, recorder and corporation. After the mayor had offered the great state sword to the king (which the king returned), and the recorder had made a speech on his knees, the mayor rode on horseback, wearing the hat of maintenance and carrying the sword, before the royal coach to the king's lodging in Minster Yard in Colonel Pownall's house (now No. 10 Pottergate). The whole civic company was entertained to a banquet at the king's expense.[3]

Before William left for Welbeck the next morning he granted the mayor and aldermen's request for a new fair to be kept yearly at such time as the city should think fit. They chose September.[4]

The absence of any reference in the records to the accession of Queen Anne cannot have any political significance, for addresses were presented on the union with Scotland, on some of Marlborough's victories, and later she was assured that the city would stand by her and the Established Church and the protestant succession. Rumours of Jacobite activity were reported from time to time, as when Mr Disney of Lincoln wrote that private levies of men were suspected of being made, and that horsemen were lately discovered about midnight not far from Tattershall.[5] There were rumours about Sir John Bolles, who first became a member for the city in 1690.[6] He said that when the king went to Lincoln he tried to prevent the return of Bolles at the election a few days later, but the latter had been elected in the king's teeth. Some of the gentry warned him that such talk would bring him to the gallows, to which he replied that he hoped to see the king there first. He had been drinking heavily, and boasting that he could have been lord high treasurer or a duke if he had wished.

[1] He was said not to have above £10 or £12 a year (A. Gordon, *Freedom after Ejection* (1917), pp. 70, 255).

[2] See above, p. 182.

[3] De la Pryme says that the king was so merry and drank so freely when he was the guest of Sir John Brownlow that when he came to Lincoln he could eat nothing but a mess of milk (*Diary*, ed. C. Jackson (Surtees Society, 1870), p. 73).

[4] Birch, p. 290. This is the last of the long series of royal charters of Lincoln.

[5] *C.S.P.D. 1700-2*, p. 269.

[6] In October 1695 twenty-five freemen were admitted by birth and twenty-three by servitude. In July 1698 there were twenty-three by birth and fourteen by servitude. There was no rush before the elections of 1701 and 1702, and soon after the record ceases.

It is not to be supposed that incidents of this kind would cause the government much disquiet.[1]

At the turn of the century there emerged a decisive influence in county affairs in the person of Lord Willoughby de Eresby, who sat for Boston in 1685 and 1688, supported William of Orange, and was called up to the House of Lords. He followed his father as lord lieutenant in 1700 and as earl of Lindsey in 1701.[2] Like all his family he had been on the tory side, but in 1705 he was declaring himself a whig,[3] and supporting his brother Albemarle Bertie and Colonel Whichcote for the county; they were successful.[4] The duke of Newcastle reported the result to Harley, saying he believed the latter would not be sorry for the defeat of 'lofty Sir John' Thorold, evidently a high tory.[5] Meres sat for the city until the parliament of 1708, being joined by Thomas Lister in 1705. In 1713 Lister was joined by John Sibthorp, the first of a long line of representatives of that family.[6]

In the life of the city the bishops of Lincoln played no part. They lived mostly at Buckden or in London, seldom visiting their cathedral city, in which they had no home; even at an enthronement the bishop might be represented by proxy.[7]

---

[1] C.S.P.D. 1700–2, pp. 499, 501, 505. He was involved in a remarkable incident at Lincoln assizes in 1695. A prisoner asked for delay, which Gould J. was willing to grant, but Bolles, who was sitting on the Bench, told the prisoner he must have his witnesses ready by the afternoon. When the judge overruled him Bolles replied that he too was in the commission, and he was an M.P. of years' standing and understood the laws as well as the judge. The judge quieted him, but later he spoke so loudly as to disturb the court on the other side of the hall where Lord Chief Justice Holt sat, saying 'that he was a parliament man, the representative of the corporation, and in them of all the people of England, that the judge on the other side was a better man than Gould, that he himself was a better man than Holt, that he would maintain the liberties of the subject, and in fine more than once threatened to bring Gould upon his knees at the Bar of the House of Commons. A gentle rebuke having failed to silence Bolles, the judge imposed a fine of £100 on him, which was afterwards taken. Bolles soon afterwards kicked one who told him a man without wished to speak with him. The judge then ordered the sheriff to take him into custody, and the disorder was so great that the court had to adjourn (L.A.O. Monson, 7/8).

[2] Bishop Burnet described him as a fine gentleman with both wit and learning; upon which Dean Swift commented 'I never saw a grain of either' (Complete Peerage, I, 127 n.). He seems to have had a great sense of his own importance, expecting, as his mother said, his younger brothers to keep at a distance from him (Verney Letters of the Eighteenth Century, ed. M. M. Verney (1930), I, 309).

[3] H.M.C. Rutland, IV, 231.

[4] H.M.C. Bath, I, 70.

[5] H.M.C. Portland, IV, 201.

[6] He presented to the city the portrait of Queen Anne that hangs in the Guildhall.

[7] His throne was so frequently left vacant by its holder that the Lincoln ladies were accustomed to intrude upon it. In 1705 Mr Precentor Inett excused this encroachment as being 'the common claim of that sex to do what they please', but added the more serious argument that 'they very much wanted room in the quire for women, who in the

Whilst the services at the Minster were chiefly carried on by the canon in residence and the priest vicars, the many parishes in the city were served by two or three clergy. The returns to the articles of inquiry issued by Bishops Wake and Gibson have been well summarised by Canon Cole:

St Peter at Arches was the only one in which Divine Service was regularly and decently performed. Here under the incumbency of Mr Gilbert Bennet, who himself was non-resident, living at Reepham, which he held in plurality with Cherry Willingham, but who had a curate at St Peter at Arches, there were prayers on Sunday morning, and every day in the year twice; also on Sunday afternoon there was a sermon, and a great concourse of people to it, because there was no other sermon below hill. At St Mary le Wigford there was service once every Sunday, except that once a month they went to St Peter's, probably St Peter at Gowts, where their vicar officiated monthly. On the other hand, at St Benedict's, there was service only once a month, which later was reduced to eight times a year; at St Mark's only three or four times a year; while at St Margaret's it is returned, 'Divine Service never celebrated here, nor within the memory of man.' At St Martin's there was Service three times a year when the Eucharist was administered, so that the parishioners might comply with the requirements of the law. At St Mary Magdalen there was Service every Sunday afternoon, but only three times a year in the morning for the celebration of the Eucharist. At St Paul's also there was Service every Sunday afternoon, and at St Peter at Gowts once a month. But at St Botolph's, St Michael's, St Nicholas, St John's, and St Peter in Eastgate, the return is 'No Church here', while at St Swithin's the earlier return which says 'The Church unfit' is altered later into 'None'. It was this churchless condition of so many of the city parishes, together with their diminished population, which enabled Mr Anthony Reid, who was also Priest-Vicar and Master of the Grammar School, to take charge at once of St Mark's, St Margaret's, St Mary Magdalen, St Mary le Wigford, St Peter at Gowts' and St Swithin's; while Mr James Debia, who was Prebendary of Crakepole, served the cures of St Botolph, St Martin, St Michael, St Paul, and St Peter in Eastgate, and in addition held the rectory of Boultham and the vicarage of Skellingthorpe. It is fair to add that Mr Debia's income from his numerous benefices seems to have been little more than £53 per annum, and Mr Anthony Reid's about £60.[1]

Unless they were exceptional they preached the fashionable doctrine of non-resistance and denounced schism: though they may not have gone so far as Mr Samuel Wesley, the rector of Epworth, who wrote books against the dissenters, and told Colonel Whichcote, the whig candidate for the

___

heat of the year were very much straitened and incommoded; and upon that ground at assizes and other public times the bishop's seat had been commonly used'. Attempts to stop the practice by fixing a lock to the seat had been resented as an affront, but Bishop Wake ordered that means should be tried again (Norman Sykes, 'Episcopal Administration in England in the 18th Century', in *E.H.R.* XLVII (1932), 417).

[1] *Speculum Dioeceseos Lincolniensis...1705–1723*, ed. R. E. G. Cole (L.R.S. 1913), pp. xvii–xviii.

county, why he must vote against him. Wesley thereupon found himself a prisoner for debt in Lincoln castle, dismissed from a regimental chaplaincy, his flax crop burnt in the night, and his three cows, which were a great part of his numerous family's subsistence, stabbed.[1]

On his part Whichcote commented upon the heats of the high churchmen in a letter to Newcastle in 1710. Writing from his house at Harpswell he said: 'I find all the parsons, who endeavour to incite the people, in greater heats here than the Oxonian parsons in London. And indeed they press their non-resistance doctrines so far that they rather excite the people against themselves than the Government, which I tell all my friends they are only angry at because they cannot have the administration of it themselves: and I do not doubt my arguments out of the pulpit will be as prevailing as theirs in it.'[2]

Some idea of the confusion of mind of ordinary folk is given in a report sent to Harley by his agent Daniel Defoe from Lincoln in 1712.

What strange things they are made to believe, what wild inconsistent notions they have infused into the minds of one another, what preposterous ridiculous incongruous things take up their heads is incredible, and but for the novelty of them are not worth repeating. Such as, the Queen is for the Pretender, the ministry under the protection of France; that Popery is to be tolerated; that as soon as a peace is declared the war with the Dutch will be proclaimed; that the French are to keep their trade to the South Seas...the poison is unhappily spread from London, and especially among the Dissenters, who are made everywhere to believe that the ministry is for the Pretender, and that French government and Popery is the design.[3]

[1] *H.M.C. Kenyon*, pp. 434–5.   [2] *H.M.C. Portland*, ii, 210.
[3] Ibid. v, 224.

CHAPTER X

THE LATER STUARTS: ECONOMIC AND SOCIAL AFFAIRS

THE unproductive expenditure of the war, crushing taxation, fines upon royalists, and the dislocation of trade and transport resulted in an impoverished countryside. The gentry were heavily incumbered, many of them owing money in London, and low prices made recovery more difficult. Dymock Walpole, a Louth attorney, summed up the matter in 1672 when he wrote that 'all our country concerns, as cattle, wool and the like fall so low that we have no other coin. Although these be staple commodities yet are they not current pay in Cheapside...so soon as cattle will melt into money the annual payments will be made good.' Three years later he referred to his London agent a gentleman who wanted £2000 to defray debts, including the expense of an election at Grimsby:

He is troubled with our country disease, which is an abundance of wool and stock that will not sell. And I do assure you that it is not any bad husbandry that puts him to this....I wish you could help him to a rich and a good wife. We have not one in these parts...you have all the money and women at London, and have considerable portions.[1]

Charles Dymoke was in touch with the London scrivener Alderman John Morris, a partner of the more famous Sir Robert Clayton. He wrote in 1673 that he was getting his tenants settled, mostly at the same rents, though with some small abatements, though he found general complaints of the scarcity of money. Later (1674) he wrote that he could not pay his mortgage interest as he dared not press his tenants lest they throw their farms on his hands as had happened to several other landlords: 50 tenants were 1½ to 2 years behind with their rents.[2]

The steward of the Monson estates told a like tale. He wrote in 1677 that

we have above £120 per annum thrown up now in Burton and South Carlton; and I wish I can but let it, the times are so bad, for every one is afraid of a new Parliament and warres that they are very unwilling to hold or take anything.... And we have a great rot of sheep among us hereabouts although it hath not taken us as yet, and money is extraordinary dead hereabouts...[3]

One Crane, who had started a woolcombing enterprise at Blankney, found himself in difficulties, and applied to Clayton both to take up a bond

[1] Clayton MSS. in my possession. [2] L.P.L. MS. 5226 (7, 12).
[3] L.A.O. Monson 10/3/1.

for him and to draw up a case to induce parliament to aid so public a work. He thought that if he were able to carry on he would in three years work out nearly 5000 tods a year at so small a town as Blankney.[1] Most of the wool grown in the county was however bought and sent off to the manufacturing areas in the West Riding or East Anglia. Sir Thomas Browne mentioned in 1682 that one of his patients, Mr Payne of Norwich, had gone into Lincolnshire, where he bought wool, whereby he had got a fair estate.[2] By Defoe's time the vast consumption of wool in Norfolk and Suffolk was supplied chiefly out of Lincolnshire, 'a county famous for the large sheep bred up for the supply of the London markets'; it also supplied them with cattle.[3]

Agricultural recovery was hampered by the fall of prices, which came soon after the political settlement of the Restoration, as the following summary of the Lincoln leet jury returns shows:

	Wheat		Peas		Oats		Barley		Rye	
	s.	d.	s.	d.	s.	d.	s.	d.	s.	d.
Mich. 1656–62	46	3	22	7	11	7	24	6	32	1
1665–80	29		16	6	9	0	12	5	22	0
1681–1700	32	9	18	3	9	7	17	5	22	5
1701–12	30	7	16	4	10	10	19	0	22	3

In almost all cases these prices are below Thorold Rogers's decennial averages. Poverty at home and the cost of transport to other markets no doubt kept prices down. The war with Louis XIV, however, brought some increase. De la Pryme noted in 1696 that all sorts of commodities had sold very well since the war began. Wool was 19–20s. a stone, barley 22s. a quarter, and in Yorkshire 28s.[4]

A poor countryside meant a poor city of Lincoln, and made it all the more difficult to make good the immense material damage of the Civil War. The churches suffered severely, and they were more durable than the houses, though of course they may have been singled out for violence. St Nicholas, St Peter in Eastgate and St Botolph were in ruins; St Swithin had been burnt down; the nave of St Benedict was in such a state that it was demolished and the tower rebuilt across the chancel arch; St Michael presently collapsed; and to judge from rebuilding operations undertaken later others must have been in poor condition.

Already before the war the cathedral was in bad repair,[5] and it was to be long before the damage done to roof, windows, carvings and furniture could be made good. The houses round it suffered severely. In the castle

---

[1] L.P.L. MS. 5225 (7).
[2] *Letters of Sir Thomas Browne*, ed. G. Keynes (1931), p. 256.
[3] Defoe, *Complete English Tradesman* (1841 ed.), II, 73, 189–90.
[4] De la Pryme, *Diary*, ed. C. Jackson (Surtees Society, 1870), p. 79.
[5] *C.S.P.D. 1637*, p. 152; see above, p. 123.

the gaol was destroyed and the shire house not fit for the judges to sit in. The palace was described in 1726 as utterly ruinous and uninhabitable, and the stone was given to the dean and chapter for repair of the cathedral.[1] The vicars declared in a petition to the chapter that their houses were 'by the sons of violence in the late times of devastation reduced to confusion and heaps of rubbish, so that they are now destitute of dwellings.' A Commonwealth survey of dean and chapter property refers repeatedly to war damaged buildings: a dwellinghouse pulled down in the wars, a tenement pulled down in the late wars, a dwellinghouse whereof some part was pulled down and some part fired, a new house just built, a tenement whereof the lease was lost in the storming of the town. The 'Cardinal's Hat' was in an extremely ruinous condition; St Martin's vicarage house was very ruinous; St Mary's Guildhall was much in decay; heavy repairs had to be carried out to the Bluecoat School, which had ceased to be inhabited, partly because rents could not be got in during the war to maintain the boys. The grammar school house too needed repair.

Quarter Sessions records present a different aspect of the same sad tale. Houses in St Nicholas parish which were chargeable to serve the office of constable had been demolished, and no new houses built, so that the office had devolved on cottagers and the poorer sort; and the owners of the ruined homesteads were ordered either to serve the office or find deputies. In 1656 the laws against rogues and vagabonds and sturdy beggars were so ill enforced that a marshal was appointed to report defaults of parish officers. There was such an increase of poor in St Martin's parish that nine other parishes were ordered to help; Bracebridge was ordered to help St Botolph, and St Margaret to maintain a poor child in St Michael. The Lindsey justices, with jurisdiction in Bail and Close, ordered St Mary Magdalene to contribute to the poor of St Paul. The city grand jury presented all twelve aldermen, who 'ought to take care to set the poor on work, neglect the same, and suffer the Jersey School within this city to be laid aside and wholly neglect, to the great damage of the poor and detriment of this whole city'; though perhaps it is not surprising that the aldermen were exonerated at a subsequent sessions. A house of correction was urgently needed, and at last in 1697 the council found a fit place in the house of one of the city sergeants at the 'Black Goat' in St Benedict's parish.

A new burden was imposed for the relief of poor and maimed officers and soldiers who had faithfully served the king and his royal father. The parishes were assessed to bring in £29. 6s. 0d. yearly, and pensions of 26s. 8d. or 20s. a year were granted.

[1] L.A.O. Episcopal Register 38, p. 132; D. & C. Ciii/2/5a.

Everything needed doing at once. For purposes of house repair the common council agreed first with alderman Ward the brickmaker, and then with his widow, for the provision of brick and tile to all freemen according to their needs. The chamberlains of the wards were presented for not repairing roads, like those at Newland gate and part of Pottergate, which were chargeable to the city and not to the parishes, and frontagers were presented where they were liable, as Sir Thomas Meres was in Pottergate and Francis Manby at Bracebridge in respect of St Katharines. In 1665 the commissioners of sewers caused the river from Brayford head right through the town and so forward to be cut 2½ feet deeper than it was, at the cost of the frontagers.[1]

Several observers have recorded their impressions of the city about this time. John Evelyn found it an old confused town, very long, uneven, steep and ragged, formerly full of good houses, especially churches and abbeys.[2] The naturalist John Ray viewed it from the cathedral tower in 1661, and saw that it consisted only of one long street. 'It is a mean and poor place, not well built, of little trade; many of the churches fallen down; of no strength.... The town being full of tumult, by reason that the assizes were there that day, we stayed not all night, but rode on 10 miles further to the Spittle.'[3] Celia Fiennes noted that 'the streetes are but little...the houses are but small and not lofty nor the streets of any breadth'.[4] Abraham de la Pryme was prompted to the reflection that it is a strange thing that great towns should so decay and be eaten up with time; several stately houses and churches were falling, and of what had been such a famous city, there was scarce anything worth seeing in it but the high street, it being indeed a most stately and excellent structure, and the chief ornament of the town. The old bounds of the city were pointed out to him in 1696, and he found corn growing where once the city stood.[5] Its reputation as a decayed town is illustrated by the comment of a statistician that though the population of the country was increasing that of Lincoln and Winchester was decreasing; and he attributes their decline to the growth of London.[6]

Less is heard of plague in this period than in earlier ones, and it seems that it did not break out even in 1665, at the time of the great plague in London. Warning, however, was given by the county justices. In July 1665

---

[1] L.P.L. MS. 4938. [2] Diary, 19 August 1654.
[3] *Lincolnshire Naturalist Union Transactions*, VII (1927–30), 172.
[4] *Journeys of Celia Fiennes*, ed. C. Morris (1947), p. 71.
[5] De la Pryme, *Diary*, ed. Jackson, pp. 19, 87.
[6] 'Observations upon Bills of Mortality', in *Economic Writings of Sir William Petty*, ed. C. H. Hull (1899), II, 370, 372. John Ogilby wrote that for all its misfortunes Lincoln was a large, well-built and well-inhabited city (*Britannia* (1675), p. 82). Licence to exaggerate is often assumed by writers of guide books.

magistrates were ordered by quarter sessions to see that constables restrained vagrants who might carry it, and to prevent unnecessary meetings at petty fairs, feasts and wakes. In October the justices declared the city to be in imminent danger from travellers from London and other infected places, and ordered guards in open places in the city, Bail and Close.[1]

The upper city recovered first. In 1688 the judges of assize imposed a fine of £1000 on the county which was assigned for the building of a shire house and gaol.[2] St Mary Magdalene's church was rebuilt by the parishioners in 1695 and the chancel of St Paul's in 1700. It was to be another generation before any such move was made downhill. The richer gentry had their town houses in the Close, and in the Bail were some of the principal inns, which filled up for assizes, quarter sessions, musters and visitations. As the establishment of clergy was restored, the tradesmen of the Bail recovered their old custom. Here were the routs and balls to which the wives and daughters of the squires looked forward during long months of dullness in their manor houses: for their festivities they had to make do with the quarters at the Angel until the Assembly Rooms were built.

With the shrinking of the lower city into one long street most of the markets were gathered there. From old St Martin's, at the top of High Street, as far south as St Lawrence Lane (now Clasketgate) was the butcher market, though killing in the street became such a nuisance that it was forbidden. Below it, in the churchyard of St Peter at Arches, was the butter market; it was brought here from Newland, where the Butter Cross once stood—it was taken down in 1572—and the market was to remain in the open until the butter market house was built in 1736. Between the Stonebow and the High Bridge was the fish market, which, wrote Thomas Sympson in 1737, 'is well and plentifully furnished twice a week for the most part, that is, with sea fish on Wednesdays and fresh water fish on Fridays, the former being brought chiefly from the Yorkshire coasts, the latter taken from the Witham, which affords plenty of pike, carp, tench, eels, barbotts &c., and those the best of their kind'. The market for all grain save oats and ground meal was moved from St Mary le Wigford to the churchyard of St John the Evangelist, it thus becoming (as it is still called) the Cornhill in 1598, leaving oats by the churchyard wall of St Mary's. The swine market was moved from St Rumbold's to the lower end of Pottergate, which means the south end of the present Lindum Road, perhaps the Jobbers Square which was to become, in compliment to the

[1] Lindsey Sessions Minutes, I, 525, 534 b. Apparently they thought the city justices not alive to the danger. In November the holding of Boston fair was forbidden (*C.S.P.D. 1665–66*, p. 50).

[2] *Cal. Treasury Books 1685–89*, p. 2006.

Manchester Unity of Oddfellows, Unity Square. The sheep market was also held to the east of the High Street, in the yard before the Greyfriars, where St Swithin's church now stands, and the horse fairs were held in Newland.[1] The fish market once held near the top of Steep Hill was no more. Perhaps the Reformation had extinguished the clerical demand for fish. The sale of pit coal was regulated in the same way: it must only be sold in High Street.

One of the first duties of the common council after the Restoration was to protect the markets against their old enemies the forestallers and regrators. 'Whereas complaint is made unto us of the great abuse of His Majesty's Market within this city by setting up corn and grain and selling it in private houses and in boats upon the water before it come to market, contrary to the laws and statutes of this nation, not bringing the same to public view in the market as it ought to be, whereby the poor and other His Majesty's subjects are very much injured in this time of dearth and scarcity', proclamation was ordered that the law would be enforced, and citizens and other inhabitants were warned not to permit anybody to sell in their houses or other private places, upon penalty of 3s. 4d. for every quarter of grain so sold. The opening market bell was to ring at 11 o'clock weekly, and the corn measures were prescribed.

The annual fairs were also the concern of the council, who were roused by the threat of competition from Wragby. In 1668 the inhabitants of that township were seeking a grant from the king of several fairs which might prejudice the interests of the city, and when a writ of *ad quod damnum* was to be executed there—to inquire whether anyone's rights would be injured by the grant of a market—the recorder and some of the aldermen were sent over, armed with the charter of Henry IV, to show to the sheriff and the jurors what damage it might be to the city. The city's case was that it had two annual fairs, one on St John the Baptist (24 June) and the other on St Hugh in winter (17 November), and a Friday market for beasts, sheep, cattle and other things; the fee farm of £80 was principally raised out of the tolls, and a beast market in Wragby on Thursday would injure, if not destroy, the Lincoln Friday market; and the trade of Lincoln citizens much depended on the buyers and sellers of cattle. A Wragby market would draw tradesmen there, perhaps from Lincoln.

It may have been this matter that decided the mayor and citizens to ask William III for a new fair when he visited the city in 1695.[2] The request was granted in the last of the royal charters in the city series. It was to be a three-day fair in September, the first two days for horses, the last for

---

[1] Thomas Sympson, 'Adversaria', Bodleian Library, Gough MS. Linc. I.
[2] See above, p. 194.

beasts and goods.[1] New regulations defined the places in which the markets were to be held, specifying that stalls and booths for wood and earthenware, cloth and all other goods were to be set up on the Corn market and up to the Stonebow. Later (in 1706) it was ordered that the April and September fairs should be kept in upper High Street for all merchandise except horse, beast and sheep; Midsummer fair in Newland only, and St Hugh's fair on the Friars.

The protection of the tradesmen who provided the main body of citizens was bound up with the old rules giving them a monopoly of retail trade, to the exclusion of 'foreigners', and the control of the companies over the craftsmen. It is evident that during the interregnum these rules, like much else, had not been effectively enforced, and a general tightening up was called for. In 1667 the cordwainers company consulted counsel about the renewal of their charter and the indictment of persons offending against the company's rights. It was no doubt on counsel's advice that the country cordwainers, who were the offenders, were indicted.[2]

In 1679 the ordinances of the tailors were overhauled, they having been 'discontinued and not observed, to the great decay and hurt of the city'. The draft statutes were examined by the common council several times before they were sealed: they followed the usual lines. At the same time the council resolved that a non-resident freeman could not make his apprentice a freeman: the full term of apprenticeship must be spent in the city. The rule was that only freemen might open a shop in the city or county of the city; but weakness crept in with the addendum that if a non-freeman took an apprentice he was not to be enrolled or admitted. Doubts about enforcement of monopoly appeared in the decision that if there was a suit at law against a non-freeman the city should bear the charge of the first trial, but no more.

The old rule, even in its fullness, was no protection to the freeman against competitors who bought the freedom, and so it was decided in 1685 that automatic admission by purchase must cease, and that each application must be considered by the council after due notice, with time allowed for objections. A recent practice of enrolling apprentices and admitting freemen at the Court of Burghmanmote before the mayor and sheriffs was abolished, and the former practice of doing these things publicly at the common council was restored.

In 1686, after signs of wavering, the battle against unfreemen was resumed: they were selling their wares openly, 'to the great detriment and

---

[1] *C.S.P.D. 1696*, pp. 77, 88; Birch, p. 290.

[2] Among the costs of the suit is an item 'ale expended against the country shoemakers, 2s. 1d.' Waiting at assizes has always been a thirsty business.

hurt of the city and the citizens thereof, who bear offices and undergo other charges which strangers and others not free are not chargeable withal nor will perform'. Such practices were positively forbidden, on penalty of 20*s.* for every time a shop was opened for retail trade. The by-laws were solemnly approved by the judges of assize. In 1687 writs were ordered against a plumber and a tentmaker, who being unfree, were carrying on their trades in the city. In 1693 the sheriffs had levied 40*s.*—in accordance with a fine imposed by the mayor and justices—upon Robert Allen, a Scotsman who traded as a linendraper. Allen then brought an action against the sheriffs, who were told to consult counsel as to their defence, and also as to how best to punish such Scotsmen and other unfreemen. Two more Scots linendrapers were indicted at the assizes about 1695. The repetition of these proceedings suggests that the city was successful, but that nevertheless the unfreemen persisted. In 1706 and 1707 counsel were again being consulted upon the enforcement of the by-law against un-franchised tradesmen. The times were moving against these ancient privileges.

It is notable moreover that whereas in the Elizabethan period more free-men qualified by apprenticeship than by patrimony, in the years following the Restoration the position was reversed. All the sons of a father who was free at the time of their birth were entitled to the freedom on coming of age; the companies having for the most part disappeared they might trade without serving an apprenticeship; and as the apprenticeship system declined in the eighteenth century there was coming into being the largely hereditary distinction between freemen and non-freemen which the reformers of the nineteenth century found indefensible as a basis of civic government. The rush of eligible men to take up their freedom before parliamentary elections suggests that the freedom was not so greatly valued for other reasons, and that many people were able to get a living without it.

Some of the tradesmen on whose behalf these battles were being fought have left memorials peculiar to periods of disturbance. The disorder and interruption of communications during the Civil War and the years that followed resulted in a shortage of small coin. All over the country, therefore, tradesmen began to issue their own halfpenny and farthing tokens. The issue began about 1656, when conditions were beginning to improve, and lasted until 1670. By then the need had passed, and the citizens were conscious only of the trouble of getting the tokens changed, some owners having refused to honour them, and others having died or gone away. In 1669 the common council had resolved to issue a city halfpenny changeable by the mayor. They began with £20 worth, and after their receipt the crier was bidden to decry all other halfpennies and farthings. A further £50 was laid out by instalments. In 1674, however, the king forbade the issue of private tokens, and the common council ordered the sale of the city stock of halfpennies and farthings. Twenty-five tradesmen had issued their own tokens, fifteen in the city and ten in the Bail. Among them were William Marshall, a mercer and doubtless the alderman of that name, Bartholomew Yorke of the Bail, and the innkeepers of the Falcon and the Two Dolphins; and there were vintners, tallowchandlers, fishmongers, an ironmonger, and an apothecary.[1]

The prosperity of the city was bound up with that of the countryside, which in turn depended largely upon corn and wool. As their principal market, of increasing importance, lay in the West Riding, the maintenance of the Fossdyke navigation was vital. The upkeep of waterways had been neglected during the war and after, and so there was an outburst of interest in new river schemes at the Restoration. In 1662 a bill was introduced in parliament to provide water passage from Great Yarmouth to York by way of the Waveney, the Little Ouse, the Great Ouse, the Witham, the Fossdyke, the Trent and the Yorkshire Ouse, but it did not become law.[2]

The common council were thinking on a much smaller scale. They were alarmed—on a warning given in 1663 by Sir Robert Bolles—by the possible effect which the drainage of the Lindsey Level, on the lower Witham, might have on the city's river lands and low grounds; and they feared that if a bill for draining the fens from Kyme Eau (the river Slea, a tributary of the Witham) to the Trent was carried without provision for the continuance of 'our river' the Fossdyke, their river would in all likelihood be totally lost.

The fear for the continuance of the Fossdyke seems not to have been exaggerated, for a French observer, visiting the city about this time, wrote:

Here are several rich merchants; for Lincoln has always been a trading town, by means of the canal which joins the river of Whitham to that of the Trent, one of the principal branches of the Humber, whereon the largest vessels may come with the tide, from whence the barks bring their lading to Lincoln by the canal, which enters that town with the river of Whitham. I do not say that they do not use this conveniency at present; it is however but seldom, and with little success.[3]

---

[1] Arthur Smith, *A Catalogue of the Town and Trade Tokens of Lincolnshire issued in the Seventeenth Century* (1931), pp. 25–34.

[2] *C.J.* VIII, 370; *C.S.P.D. 1661–62*, pp. 306–7; T. S. Willan, *River Navigation in England 1600–1750* (1936), p. 9.

[3] Jorevin, 'Description of England and Ireland in the seventeenth century', translated in *Antiquarian Repertory*, IV (1809), 617. He mentions that in Lincoln there were a few manufacturers of cloth and other woollen goods.

His book was published in 1672. Two years earlier the common council had decided that they must in the city's trading interests seek power to improve the Fossdyke and the Witham themselves. They no doubt had before them the example of statutes passed since 1660 for the improvement of other rivers, the Stour, the Wye, the Medway and the Wiltshire Avon, and there had been at least talk of making the Great Ouse and the Welland navigable. Perhaps they already had the advice of Samuel Fortrey, with whom they were to go into partnership later. Fortrey was the son of a London merchant, who acquired some reputation as a statistician by his tract *England's Interest and Improvement, consisting in the Increase of the Store and Trade of this Kingdom.*[1] By 1650 he had gone to live at Oakington near Cambridge; and he pledged his interest in the fenland and problems of drainage by building himself a house in Byall Fen, which for lightness— necessary in building on fenland—was of studwork with turf between. He was appointed a jurat by the participants and adventurers of the Great Level in 1656, a commissioner of sewers of the Level in 1662, and was frequently a bailiff or conservator of the Board of the Great Level during the two decades after 1663. Clearly he was regarded as an authority on matters of water engineering: later he became director of the Wiltshire Avon undertaking.[2]

The council asked Sir John Monson and Sir Thomas Meres, the city's burgesses in parliament, to try to procure an act for making the channels navigable between the Trent and Boston, whereby the city corporation should have the first right to become undertaker of the work. Means were to be found of raising not more than £100 to procure an act, and it was resolved to borrow this sum from the Master and Governors of Christ's Hospital, to collect city rents half yearly, and to fine chamberlains who omitted to return the names of tenants in arrears with their rents. This lack of capital did not bode well for the enterprise.

If, as was usually provided, the undertakers were to operate under the supervision of commissioners, the first question to be settled was the relation of those commissioners to the commissioners of sewers who had jurisdiction over the rivers within their sphere. There had always been one commission for the whole of Lincolnshire. It seems that the city thought in the light of experience that the commissioners of sewers would not be sympathetic towards the navigation project, and would put before it the interests of land drainage, for it was apparently first proposed that the new com-

[1] Cambridge, 1663; he describes himself on the title page as 'one of the Gentlemen of His Majesty's Most Honorable Privy Chamber'.

[2] Samuel Wells, *History of the Drainage of the Great Level of the Fens, called the Bedford Level* (1830), I, 303–464; *Fenland Notes and Queries*, IV (1898–1900), 352–8; Willan, op. cit. p. 79.

missioners should become the commissioners of sewers for the Witham and the Fossdyke. A clause to this effect was however opposed on several grounds: it would create a new jurisdiction within the county, and there would be difficulties about the limits of the old and new; and further, the Crown would lose the power of appointing commissioners, as the nobility and gentry appointed by the act would maintain their ranks by co-option. It was also pointed out that in other acts for making rivers navigable, the works of navigation were carried on without affecting the ancient sewers commission.[1] The clause was dropped.

The Act was passed in 1671.[2] The preamble recited that for some hundreds of years there had been a good navigation between Boston and the River Trent through the city of Lincoln, and that great and beneficial trade had been carried on by means of this navigation with those parts of Lincolnshire and some parts of Nottinghamshire and Yorkshire, affording an honest employment and livelihood to great numbers of people. The channels were much silted and landed up, and thereby not passable with boats and lighters as formerly, to the great decay of trade and intercourse of the city and all market and other towns near any of the said rivers, which had produced in them much poverty and depopulation. In order to remedy these evils, the Act empowered the city within two years to make the channels or either or any part of them navigable, or on their neglect or refusal, such other persons as the commissioners appointed by the Act should nominate. A large number of the nobility and gentry of the county, the mayor and three senior aldermen of Lincoln, and the mayor of Boston, or any six of them, were appointed commissioners to settle all differences, to treat with the undertakers and any landowners affected; and to fix tolls to be charged for the carriage of pit coals, sea coals, lead, corn, timber and other things. Vacancies among the commissioners could be filled by the survivors of them or any six of them, by appointment of persons residing in the county and having a freehold estate of 300 acres of land at least within ten miles of the navigation. The undertakers were empowered to mortgage their profits by assigning part of them as security for loans. A last section in the Act was added as an afterthought: it is written in a different hand on parchment sewn to the statute roll. It provided that Fossdyke tolls must be spent on the Fossdyke, and Witham tolls on the Witham, save by direction of the commissioners for the benefit of the whole navigation.

It was evidently known that the city's real interest was in the Fossdyke,

[1] 'Reasons for the Conference upon Lincoln River', in Braye MSS. Lot 110, no. 86, from photographs in the House of Lords Record Office.

[2] 22 and 23 Charles II, c. 25, private act: 'An Act for improving the Navigation between the Town of Boston and the River Trent.'

PLATE 17

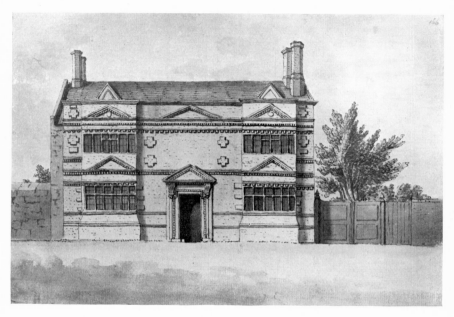

THE BROMHEAD HOUSE, built in 1646

From a drawing by S. H. Grimm in the British Museum

and it was not intended that tolls should be taken on the Witham for its benefit. The common council decided to concentrate on it, and they allowed their option of dealing with the Witham to run out. On 4 October 1671 they declared themselves undertakers of 'that part of the navigation which lieth or runneth between the Bridge commonly called the High Bridge in the said city and the River Trent'. (They later declared themselves undertakers of the Witham between High Bridge and Sincil dyke end.) Money was ordered to be raised for the necessary works by mortgage of the rectory and manor of Belton, the rectory of Hemswell and the hall of St Mary's gild. The sum of £900 was so raised. Samuel Fortrey came in as a joint undertaker. After the corporation had spent £500, Fortrey was to bear one-third of the expense and receive one-third of the profit, and he was to afford his best advice, direction and assistance according to the best of his skill and knowledge.[1]

Work seems to have begun at once, for in August 1672 compensation was ordered to be paid to a farm tenant at Torksey for damage done by cutting through his land and throwing dirt and silt upon it. A tollkeeper was appointed for one year in the following November.

The improvement of the navigation was at least effective enough to produce complaints that keeping water at a high level in the Fossdyke meant the flooding of the adjoining low lands. In 1680 divers persons in the county riotously opened the sluices at Torksey, and then tried to keep them open 'to the intent to lay the said river almost dry and not passable for boats, to the great damage of the city and several other persons'. In the following year Henry Stone of Skellingthorpe began a suit against the mayor and others for hindering the water from passing to the Trent, thereby flooding several of his grounds at Skellingthorpe. The interests of land drainage and navigation clashed as usual.

The surviving accounts of the navigation begin in 1714–15. They show that the chief cargoes from Lincoln were corn, wool, ale and poles (no doubt for pitprops), and from the Trent, coal. In that year there was a credit balance of £77. 10s. 11d. of which a third belonged to Robert Peart, an attorney, who had succeeded to Fortrey's interest. It was noted in 1728 that plenty of both pitcoal and seacoal was brought along the canal.[2] Meanwhile river works in Yorkshire had much increased the value of the Fossdyke to Lincoln. The Aire and Calder Navigation was undertaken in 1699 by the aldermen of Wakefield and Leeds, where were Lincolnshire's

[1] Appeals for aid were sent to interested places (*Calendar of Ancient Deeds and Charters, Hull* (1951), L826.

[2] Nathaniel Salmon, *New Survey of England* (1731), p. 268. By 1700 coke or crude coal from Derbyshire was being used for drying malt along the Lincolnshire coast (*Philosophical Transactions Royal Society*, XX (1695–7), p. 343).

principal markets for corn and wool, and water communication with them from Lincoln was thus completed. Presently the need for maintenance works began to grow, and a new search for capital began.

Perhaps the Fossdyke works contributed to an increase of population, of which there are clear indications during the period. The returns to the hearth tax of 1662, Archbishop Sheldon's religious census of 1676, and the returns to the enquiries of Bishops Wake and Gibson are not all complete, nor should they be assumed to be accurate or strictly comparable. Nevertheless there is no mistaking the general trend in the following figures:[1]

	Houses assessed to hearth tax 1662	Population over 16 1676	Families 1705	Families 1721
St Benedict	50	188	60	69
St Botolph	45	114	26	50
St Margaret	32	—	32	32
St Mark	24	73	30	24
St Martin	57	372	80	160
St Mary Magdalene	—	308	100+	107
St Mary le Wigford	33	141	40	48
St Michael	31	173	25	80
St Nicholas	9	80	16	21
St Paul	—	168	30	60
St Peter in Eastgate	18	134	26	42
St Peter at Gowts	42	161	60	60
St Peter at Arches	58	224	60	60
St Swithin	71	325	150	168
Total	470	2461	635+	981

The conclusion suggested that the increase became more marked after the turn of the century is confirmed by the register of St Peter at Gowts parish: there, until 1699, the numbers of burials exceeded the numbers of baptisms, but in the following fifteen years the number of baptisms was the greater. In the estimates prepared for the population returns of 1800 it was computed that in Lincoln in 1700 there were 176 baptisms and 158 burials; in 1710, 166 and 132; in 1720, 150 and 151.[2]

The dwellings of the great majority were miserably poor. In the hearth tax returns of 1662, out of 470 houses 130 had only one hearth; 97 had two; 73 had three; 64 had four; 49 had five; 48 had from six to ten; and 9 had more than ten. Francis Manby, who had followed the Granthams at St Katharines, had 15, Sir Adrian Scrope in Pottergate had 20, Sir Charles Dalison 16, Robert Mellish in what remained of the Palace, 13. Several of

---

[1] The hearth tax returns are contained in the city quarter sessions minutes, the religious census is printed in *Lincs. N. & Q.* xvi (1920–1), 34–50, and the returns of Wake and Gibson in *Speculum Dioceseos Lincolniensis...1705–23*, ed. R. E. G. Cole (L.R.S. 1913), pp. 80–93. Figures for various liberties in the city have been added to those of neighbouring parishes.

[2] *Abstract of Answers and Returns to Population Act 41 George III, 1800*, p. 174.

the aldermen had only one or two hearths, but most of them had five or more.

Houses had generally been built of stone and wood with roofs of tile or thatch. The stone quarries were still in use, and the Sibthorps rebuilt part of their town house in St Marks parish of stone. The new houses however were mostly being built in brick, as John Loveday noticed in 1732.[1] The common council agreed with the city brickmaker that he should provide brick to freemen at 13s. 4d. a thousand and tile at 20s. a thousand. The brickyard east of Monks Leys was regularly let. A house built in 1646 opposite the present Unitarian chapel was supposed to have been the first in Lincoln to be built wholly of brick, presumably in modern times. It had been built by alderman Original Peart and devised by him to his daughter Mary, who was assessed for nine hearths: it later became the home of the Bromhead family, whose memorials survive in St Peter at Gowts church.[2]

There were other signs of improvement besides the building of houses. In 1706 Pottergate head was repaired, and the new causeway from St Marks church to Bargate was made, no doubt on the initiative of the gentry, handsome contributions being made by Meres and Thomas Lister, the city's representatives in parliament.[3] These were roads beyond the resources of the parishes. In the following year the common council declared that the cleansing of the high streets was not only commendable but necessary, and tended to the general good; and it ordered that a common scavenger be appointed for the lower city by the mayor and the justices of the peace, and that a rate be levied on householders at a parish meeting or by the overseers of the highways for the parishes concerned, in proportion to the lengths of their pavements. The steep ascents of Pottergate[4] and Cross Cliff Hill, both of much steeper gradients then than now, gave constant trouble, and were often repaired at the city's costs.

By the end of the period there was marked recovery at the grammar school. When deans and chapters had been abolished in 1649 and their revenues impounded there had been a saving clause for all payments to schools and other charitable objects. In order to secure the benefit of this provision the mayor and citizens petitioned the parliamentary committee for the removal of obstructions in the sale of chapter lands, asking that the

[1] *Diary of a Tour in 1732*, ed. J. E. T. Loveday (Roxburghe Club, 1890), p. 210.
[2] L.P.L. MS. 696. There was a story that the bricks had been made at Newark and brought to Lincoln by horse loads in panniers. It was recorded but doubted by E. J. Willson (notes in Drury's *History of Lincoln* (1816), p. 151; B.M. 1430, h. 19). About 1640 Thomas Grantham was repairing the brick church at Goltho (L.A.O. Andr. 1, loose mem. at f. 137).
[3] L.P.L. MS. 4938.
[4] Now represented by Pottergate and Lindum Road.

£20 hitherto paid out of chapter houses in the Bail for the schoolmaster should be restored. The lands had been sold without reservation of the fee, and 'the present schoolmaster is very much disheartened and will be necessitated to leave the school for want of maintenance'. The committee made an order for payment of the £20.

The condition of the school must have given ground for dissatisfaction, for in 1668 the common council recalled that the bishop had formerly been moved to visit it, but had not done so, and it was resolved to make further address to him and to the dean and chapter to desire their care and pains in visiting the school. After several masters had reigned for short periods, Samuel Garmston was elected in 1683. He had kept school at Nuneaton so successfully that the chapter pressed him to come, and he was dispensed from six terms' residence at Oxford so that he could at once proceed M.A.[1] At the visitation of the following year statutes were made by the visitors for regulating the respective spheres of master and usher and other purposes. The city was asked to provide a place for the boys in St Peter's church. School was to begin at 7 a.m. from October to February, and 6 a.m. during the rest of the year. Some bad old practices were to be abolished: one, the custom of barring out the master at Christmas; another, the pretended custom of playing at the assizes was to be reduced to a day or two at the most. There should be a public exercise at Christmas. There being only 15 boys in the upper and 40 or 50 in the lower school, the numbers were to be made equal; and the master was to have authority over the whole school as his predecessors had done, and as in other schools. It was for him to prescribe teaching methods to the usher. When he removed the boys to the upper part of the school, he ought not simply to take those that would pay him best, but take them 'according to the books they learn or the classes in which they are'. Both master and usher must use their utmost care to improve the boys in Latin and Greek, teach them the true science of religion towards God, conformity to the church, obedience to their prince, and good manners towards their betters; and that city and county might have public testimony of the flourishing state of the school, two boys every Michaelmas day should congratulate the choice of the city (as mayor) in two orations, one Latin and one Greek.[2]

The school evidently prospered under Garmston and his successor John Garmston, a pupil and no doubt a kinsman. It received the sons of lesser gentry, clergy, citizens and countrymen alike, and it sent a succession of boys to Cambridge, mostly to Magdalene, where scholarships had been

[1] *H.M.C. Ormonde*, IV, 634. He was curate of Boultham in 1690 and a prebendary in 1693.
[2] L.A.O. Lincoln School MSS.

founded by Lord Chief Justice Wray and Lady Frances Wray, for which scholars from Kirton in Lindsey were to be preferred, then those from Lincoln school, and then generally.[1] Among them were Daniel Waterland the divine and Penistan Booth, who became usher at the school and was later to be dean of Windsor. Gervase Disney was a pupil, and he mentions as schoolfellows of his brother there John Reyner, son of the Puritan divine, Jonathan Robinson, who became a bookseller in London, Thomas Peachell, who became an attorney, and others.[2] On 30 January 1712, the anniversary of the martyrdom of Charles I, a sermon was preached by John Garmston before the mayor and corporation; it was printed in London for John Knight, bookseller in Lincoln, the city paying £10 towards the cost. It was a statement of the current doctrine of non-resistance.

For a generation after the Restoration the Governors of the Bluecoat School were in debt, and they had constant trouble with their schoolmasters. Hugh Walter has already been mentioned.[3] When he was finally disposed of, the new master, Thomas Nevile, was warned that he and the dame should take care honestly to employ the boys according to their strengths at such times as they were not in school, so that they should not be so much bred up in idleness. Perhaps Nevile was one of the founder's kin, a clan which gave the Governors much trouble. Richard Smith, the founder, had wished to provide for his own kindred, and in particular directed that George and Katharine Nevile and their issue should have leases of Potterhanworth manor house on the expiration of the then existing lease. In 1640 the manor house was leased to John Nevile their son for 21 years at a rent of £16. 13s. 4d. Claims for renewal were honoured from time to time until 1770, when the existing lease was bought and the claims of the kin at last extinguished. Among the poorer kindred were the Cussons, two of whose boys were admitted after 1660. The Governors showed unusual patience in dealing with them. In 1672 John Cusson ran away, and 'was detained by his mother Elizabeth Cusson and not suffered to reside in the house with the rest of the boys. And now the Master and Governors having sent for the said Elizabeth Cusson and her said son, and having tried by all the best means they could to persuade her to let her said son continue in the said house she refused to condescend thereunto and did furiously strike the messenger that was sent after her to bring her said son back to this hospital.' The boy was thereupon discharged and another of the kin admitted in his place; but even then the Governors were still willing to pay a premium if Cusson were bound apprentice.

[1] *Report of Charity Commissioners* (1839), 'Lincolnshire', p. 453.
[2] *Some Remarkable Passages in the Holy Life and Death of Gervase Disney Esq.* ed. D. Disney (1692), p. 15.   [3] See above, p. 176.

Besides these two schools there were the charity schools, in which religion went hand in hand with philanthropy in an attempt to raise the children of the poor from their ignorance. In 1710 orders were made by the trustees, those present being the precentor, the subdean and John Disney, providing for the appointment of visitors to the schools, and enjoining the mistresses to cause their children to attend constantly at church every Sunday and holy day and every Wednesday and Saturday, and to prepare them for catechism at St Peter at Arches and St Paul in the Bail every Saturday, except at times of breaking up. Later the visitors were bidden to visit twice a week, and to inquire as to proficiency in reading, and attendance and behaviour at school and in church.[1]

In the same year John Disney wrote to Bishop Wake reporting that 120 poor children were taught by four poor clergymen's widows, each having a salary of £10 per annum, house rent paid, and a load of coals yearly. Attempts to teach the boys were thwarted by their irregular attendance, as parents found it more profitable to send their children out to beg 'or worse'. The best way to prevent this, said Disney, would be to create some inducement to attend. They therefore intended each year to set up as an apprentice one child from each school as an encouragement to attendance and industry, and for that purpose were inviting subscriptions.[2]

The Jersey School appears again in 1661, when the master, on giving security, was handed the stock to use to the best advantage for employment of the poor in such work as they had usually been employed in. He was to pay spinners 5d. apiece and knitters 4d. apiece weekly during their first six months in work and afterwards according to agreed rates. The most notable event in the history of the school was a bequest by Henry Stone of Skellingthorpe of £700 to be invested in land and the rent applied for the support of the school. Apparently this gift led to some expansion, for by 1705 the master's salary had risen from £20 to £35, and in 1708 the mayor and senior aldermen were bidden to treat with the dean and chapter and gentlemen above hill about making an addition to the school.

Few but the clergy and schoolmasters can have been interested in books. For the former, or at least some of them, there was the cathedral library, Wren's new building housing a collection much enlarged by Dean Honywood. Below hill, adjoining the grammar school, was 'a fair library for the use of the Masters and Ministers of the town', given by Mr Swift, the

---

[1] Lincoln School MSS.
[2] Christchurch Library, Oxford, Letter no. 237, Wake's Lincoln Letters, per Mr R. H. Evans; Cox, *Magna Britannia*, p. 1496, mentions that the annual subscription to the schools was £73.

rector of Waddington, whose father, a draper, had been mayor of the city.[1]

During the Civil War there had been a great output of tracts by Royalists and Roundheads alike for propaganda purposes, but however limited and local their interest they were mostly printed in London. The first Lincolnshire newspaper appeared, as might be expected, at Stamford. The *Stamford Mercury* was in existence in 1714, and though the claim that it was established in 1695 is probably unfounded, there was a *Stamford Post* in 1711 and probably a year earlier.[2] It could still be said in 1726 that the London *Evening Post* was the only printed paper that came to Lincoln;[3] though in 1728 the *Lincoln Gazette or Weekly Intelligencer*, a half sheet of paper folded in four leaves, made a brief appearance. It was printed by William Wood, who is variously described as a printer, bookseller and bookbinder. He unsuccessfully sought to purchase the freedom of the city in 1728, and twice in 1729, but was at last elected in 1741. He published the *Lincoln Journal* in 1744.[4]

Booksellers appear much sooner. Augustine Waitman was a Lincoln bookseller; when he died in 1617 he had a book stock worth over £200.[5] Samuel Williams, who is so described, lived in High Street in St Martin's parish in 1676, and in 1682 Joseph Lawson of the Bail, bookseller, had printed for him in London *A General Discourse of Simony* by James Mitford, the rector of Bassingham.[6]

Though the economic progress of the city was to become marked during the eighteenth century, the horizons of the citizens were to be little widened until the nineteenth was well advanced.

[1] Corpus Christi College, Oxford, MS. 390, vol. 2, f. 49, per Rev. R. P. Baker.
[2] Information kindly supplied by Mr C. L. Exley. For the *Stamford Mercury* see *Lincolnshire Magazine*, II (1934–6), 326–31.
[3] P.R.O. State Papers Domestic George I, vol. LXIII, no. 34.
[4] See notes by E. J. Willson in his copy of Drury's *History of Lincoln* (1816), in the British Museum.
[5] L.A.O. Lincoln Inventories, 120/72.
[6] Per Mr C. L. Exley. Thomas Walker, bookseller, of the Chequer, died in 1694, and was followed by Thomas Knight.

APPENDIX I

THE OLD PROCLAMATION OF THE CITY OF LINCOLN CALLED THE MAYOR'S CRY

[From *An Historical Account of Lincoln and the Cathedral* (1802)]

Mr Mayor and his brethren do, in His Majesty's Name, strictly charge and command all Manner of Persons, who are in any wise concerned in the Laws and Ordinances now to be proclaimed, that they truly observe and perform the same, upon Pain and Penalty hereafter expressed, and such further Punishments to their Deserts, as the Law requires.

1. That all Manner of Foreign fishers, or other persons whatsoever, which bringeth any fresh Herrings, Oysters or other Shell Fish, into the Market to sell, that they do not put the same to Sale till Mr Mayor has set a Price thereupon, upon Pain of Forfeiture of the same, and Fine.   6s. 8d.

2. That no Fisherman of the City of Lincoln, nor any other Person do buy any Fish of any Foreign Fishermen, coming to the City, with Intent to sell the same again, until eleven o'clock in the Forenoon, upon Pain of Forfeiture of   6s. 8d.

3. That no Man of the City or County, buy any Pigs, Geese, Poultry, Wild Fowls, or Conies, to sell again by Retail, till one o'clock in the Afternoon of any Market-Day upon Pain of   6s. 8d.

4. That all Manner of Men or Women that bringeth any Pigs, Geese, Wild Fowls, or Poultry Ware, to the Market, or Conies to be Sold, that they bring them into the Market to sell them openly in the Market Place, and in no other Place, upon Pain or Forfeiture thereof, and Fine   6s. 8d.

5. That no Alehouse-keeper, Victualler, or Tipler do keep any Men-Servants, Apprentices, or other Persons in their House, Tipling or drinking at any Time, especially on Sundays in the Time of Divine Service, upon Pain for every Time,   6s. 8d.

6. That all Manner of Butchers of the County, that bringeth any Manner of Flesh to the City for to sell on the Market Day, that they bring it into St Laurence's Parish, and there sell the same, and in no other Place, upon Pain of Forfeiture for every Default,   6s. 8d.

7. That all Foreign Butchers shall sell their Flesh on the Market-Days in the Winter, from Ten o'Clock in the morning till Four in the Afternoon, and in Summer Time, from Nine o'Clock in the morning till Five o'Clock in the Afternoon, and shall not leave their Flesh with any other to be sold after, upon Pain, for every Default, to the Sheriffs,   6s. 8d.

8. That no Person of the City receive any such Flesh, of any such Foreign Butcher, into their Houses to sell for them, upon Pain of Imprisonment for Three Days and Three Nights, and Fine for every Default,   6s. 8d.

9. That all Foreign Butchers do bring their Tallow and Skins, of all such Beasts and Sheep as they bring to sell on any Market-Day, upon Pain of   6s. 8d.

10. That whatsoever Butcher that bringeth any Mutton to this City for to sell, betwixt Michaelmas and Shrovetide, that the Heart and the Liver hang in the Carcase, till Mr Mayor hath seen it, or his Deputy, on Pain of Forfeiture of the Carcase, and Fine to the Sheriffs   6s. 8d.

11. That no Foreign Butcher coming to this City on the Market-Day do hawk his Flesh from House to House, or sell the same privately, but openly in the Market, upon Pain of .... 6s. 8d.

12. That no Butcher, or any other Man, have or hold any great Dog, going loose in the Street unmuzzled, so that he may do harm, on Pain of .... 1s. 8d.

And as oftentime as he is found unmuzzled, and that any Harm be done, then the Owner shall pay .... 6s. 8d.

And as oftentime as it is so found, that such Dogs be kept untied in the Night, so often the Owner shall pay to the Sheriffs a Fine of .... 3s. 4d.

13. That no Butcher slay any beasts in the Streets, whose Blood and Corruption may displease Men going in the Ways or Streets; and that they cast no Blood nor Corruption in any Highways, or in the Water of the City, on Pain of .... 3s. 4d.

And that they wash no Inmeats of Beasts, but between the Stamp End and the Hermitage, and in no other Place, on Pain of .... 3s. 4d.

14. That no Butcher sell any Tallow to any Stranger Regrater, till the City be fully served, (some Tallow only excepted) upon Pain of Forfeiture of .... 3s. 4d.

15. That every Chandler do make his own Candles, in clear Cotton and Winter Tallow, and sell the same as Mr Mayor and His Brethren shall fix, at a reasonable Price, upon Pain of Forfeiture, for every Default, ... 6s. 8d.

16. That all manner of Men and Women that bringeth any Butter, Eggs, Cheese, Capons, Hens, Chickens, Turkeys, Oatmeal, Flax, or Fruit; that they bring the same to the Market-Place assigned, at St Peter's Churchside, on Forfeiture of .... 6s. 8d.

17. That no Huxtor nor any other Person for them, buy any Eggs, Butter, Cheese, or Oatmeal, for to sell again by Retail, before Twelve o'Clock, on Pain of .... 1s. 0d.

18. That all Manner of Men that bringeth any Hides or Sheep Skins to this City for to sell on the Market-Day, that they bring them to the Rails at the Corn-Market Hill, and there sell them openly, and in no other Place, upon Pain of Forfeiture of the said Hides or Sheep-Skins to the Sheriffs, and Fine .... 1s. 0d.

19. That all Manner of Men that bringeth any Corn or Grain on the Market-Day, to the City to sell, that they bring the same to sell to the Market-Place assigned, and not to sell any Corn by Sample on the Market-Day, on Pain of .... 6s. 8d.

20. That no Baker or Cadger buy any Corn on the Market-Day, in any Time of the Year, before one o'Clock, upon Pain to the Sheriffs for every Default .... 3s. 4d.

21. That no Man in the Country buy any Corn in the Market on the Market-Day, to sell again Retail, upon Pain of .... 3s. 4d.

And that no Man of the City or County buy any Corn under Colour for the Use of any Baker of the City, upon Pain to the Sheriffs, for every Default .... 3s. 4d.

22. That no Man of the City or County, set their Horses in the Street on the Market Days, on Pain for every Default, ... 0s. 1d.

23. That no Man has any Swine walking in the Streets in Nuisance of the People, upon Pain of Forfeiture, for every Foot of such Swine, ... 0s. 1d.

And if any Man put Swine in the Street, by Night or by Day, and be not before the Herd, he shall for Trespass of the said Swine, forfeit to the Sheriffs, for every one, ... 0s. 4d.

24. That no Man of the City let his Oxen or Kine go about in the City, but that they be put before the Keeper of the City for them ordained, on Pain of   *0s. 4d.*

25. That every one of the City or of the County, coming with any Carriage, giving his Beasts Hay or other Fodder, defouling the City, shall make it clean again, on Pain of   *0s. 4d.*

26. That no Man cast any Filth or Dirt in any of the common Waters, nor that any Fisherman or other Man have any Privy in his House, descending into the Waters upon Pain (as oftentimes as the Contrary is done) of   *20s. 0d.*

27. That no Man suffer or have any Midding, Storks, or Trees, lying in the common Ways, in Annoyance of the People, but that they be removed within eight Days, on Pain of Forfeiture, to the Sheriffs, of   *3s. 4d.*

28. That no Man or Woman lay or cast any Dirt within the City, or without, but where it is assigned to be laid, that is to say at the Stamp, Badgerholm, and Besom-Park, and in no other Place, in Nuisance of the People, on Pain to the Sheriffs, as often as committed,   *3s. 4d.*

29. That no Man or Child of Discretion, cast any Dirt or Ashes, or any Manner of Filth, into the common Waters of the City, or any Manner of Corruption, on Pain of   *6s. 8d.*

30. That no Man or Woman, or Child of Discretion, put any Sweepings of the Streets into the Channel in Time of Rain, to let it run into the Waters, on Pain of   *3s. 4d.*

31. That no Manner of Man or Woman dwelling in the Parish of St Benedict, St John, St Mary, or St Peter at Arches, lay or cast any Dirt against the Holdings in the King's Stream of Brayford, neither on one Side nor the other, upon Pain of   *1s. 8d.*

That all Men that have any Middings, Dirt-Hills, or any other Filth at the Garth-Ends, that they remove and carry them away, within Ten Days after Notice, on Pain of   *20s. 0d.*

That no Man or Woman shall burn any Middings upon Pain of   *20s. 0d.*

32. That every Citizen of this City, do cause the Ways to be made clean in the King's Street, one Day every Week, against their Holdings, upon Pain of Forfeiture to the Sheriffs, as oftentime as neglected   *0s. 6d.*

33. That no man set any Turf or Thatch between the High-Bridge and Thorn-Bridge, upon either Side of the Water, to the Annoyance of the People, on Pain of Forfeiture to the Sheriffs, as often as committed,   *1s. 8d.*

34. That no Man of the City buy any Charcoal for to lead out of the City until it hath stood twelve Hours in the Market, upon Pain of   *3s. 4d.*

And that no Man buy any Charcoal but by Measure, on Pain of   *6s. 8d.*

35. That no Man nor Woman buy any Turf or Thatch, or put Thatch to sell again by Retail, until it hath stood on the Water a Day and a Night, on Pain of   *3s. 4d.*

And that no Man buy any Turf or Thatch in great, to Retail the same, on Pain of   *3s. 4d.*

36. That no Man or Child fish in any common Waters, by Night or by Day, (the which is Let) nor to flow any Dykes with Fish so taken, on Pain of   *3s. 4d.*

37. That no Man draw any Sean in the said Waters, or with any Manner of Nets but with such as a Man may cast, or throw; and that no unfranchised Man fish in any of the common Waters with any Manner of Angle-Rod, or with any Manner of Implement, in any Wise or Manner on Pain of   3s. 4d.

38. That no Man or Woman lay any Hemp or Flax in the King's Stream in any Place, but beneath the Stamp End, on pain of   3s. 4d.

And that People dwelling on the East Side of Wigford, lay none but in the East Dyke, on Pain of   3s. 4d.

39. That no man wash any Sheep or Skins, or lay stinking Skins in the Water of the City, from Synshall Dyke, West Ward, on Pain of   3s. 4d.

40. That all Bakers sell their Bread according to the Assize, and put no Bran into Household Bread, on Pain of   3s. 4d.

41. That no Tanner or Craftsman whatsoever, or any other Person of this City, buy or sell by any Manner of Mets or Measures, but by such as be sealed after the King's Standard of this City, on Pain of   3s. 4d.

42. That every Franchiseman, of what Degree soever, dwelling in the County, shall take no Benefit by his Franchise, except he had a Dwelling-Place, and is Couchant and Levant within the City, and to pay and bear Scot and Lot as a Franchiseman ought to do.

FINIS

GOD SAVE THE KING

and the Right Worshipful
The Mayor of this City

APPENDIX II

CERTIFICATE OF THE MAYOR AND JUSTICES OF THE CITY AND COUNTY OF THE CITY OF LINCOLN, MADE 12 JUNE 1563, UPON WAGE RATES AND ASSESSMENTS, UNDER THE STATUTE OF ARTIFICERS

[Common Council Minutes, 1541–64, f. 181.]

They the said mayor and justices before not only conferring with other discreet persons of the said city, suburbs and county in the premises, but also having understanding and respect to the scarcity and dearth of all kinds of grain and victuals there at this time, that is to say, the quarter of wheat sold for 40s., the quarter of rye sold for 36s. 8d., the quarter of malt sold for 22s., the quarter of beans, peasen and barley sold for 26s. 8d., the quarter of mutton and veal sold for 20d., the quarter of beef sold for 16d. and white meat after 5 eggs a penny, the buttercake weighing one lb. and three quarters 5d., and the stone of cheese after 20d., and other necessary victuals very dear.

	With meat and drink	Without meat and drink
Freemason, shipwright or botewright, master carpenter, rough mason, sawyer, plowwright, thakker stonewaller, bricklyer, master tiler, plumber, glasier, joiner and carver		
By the day mid-Sept.–mid-March	4d.	8d.
Mid-March–mid-Sept.	5d.	10d.
Their servants and labourers		
By the day, mid-Sept.–mid-March	3d.	6d.
Mid-March–mid-Sept.	4d.	7d.
Every servant being a		
glasier	26s. 8d.	
tailor	26s. 8d.	53s. 4d.
baker	33s. 4d.	
sherman, walker or fuller	20s.	
dyer	40s.	
milner	26s. 8d.	
weaver	26s. 8d.	
sadaler	26s. 8d.	
parchmentmaker	33s. 4d.	
cutler or armourer	26s. 8d.	
waterman, fishmonger, fisher or fishdrier	33s. 4d.	
tilemaker, brickmaker, limemaker	40s.	
currier	26s. 8d.	
beer brewer or cooper	30s.	

	With meat and drink	Without meat and drink
shoemaker	26s. 8d.	
(or by the day)	4d.	8d.
smith	33s. 4d.	£4
fletcher and bowyer	26s. 8d.	£3. 6s. 8d.
butcher	40s.	
tanner	40s.	£4
mercer	26s. 8d.	
draper	26s. 8d.	
glover	40s.	£4
Bailey of husbandry, other servant of husbandry and shepherd	26s. 8d.	£4
Apprentice or other servant		
16 to 23	20s.	
10 to 16	10s.	
Mower		
by the day	5d.	10d.
per acre of meadow or hay		8d.
per acre of barley and oats		5d.
Shearing		
per acre of wheat or rye		14d.
or by the day	3d.	8d.
Thrashing		
qr wheat or rye		12d.
barley, peas, beans, oats		5d.
Reaping		
per acres beans and peas		6d.
Making hay	2d.	5d.
Dyking, setting, hedging of new dyke, 6 ft. broad and 4 ft. deep per rood		6d.
Plashing and hedging per day (Sept.–Mar.)	2d.	5d.

APPENDIX III

CORN PRICES RETURNED BY LEET JURIES,
1513–1712

Mich.	1513	8s.
	1515	6s.
	1516	5s.
	1518	8s. 6d.
27 June	1520	12s. 6d.
Mich.	1520	15s. 6d.
	1521	7s. 6d.
	1522	5s.
	1523	—
	1524	5s. 6d.
	1525	5s., 4s. 6d., 4s.
	1526	4s. 6d.
	1527–29	—
	1530	6s.
15 Dec.	1531	13s. 6d.
6 Feb.	1532	12s.
3 Mar.	1532	11s. 6d.
Mich.	1532	7s.
9 May	1533	7s. 6d.

		Wheat	Beans and/or peas	Oats
Mich.	1539	7s., 6s. 6d., 6s.	4s.	3s.
Mich.	1543	15s., 14s. 6d.	8s. (?), 6s.	
	1544	11s., 10s. 6d., 10s.	4s. 8d.	2s. 8d.
	1545	17s., 16s. 6d., 16s.	5s. 8d.	3s. 4d.
Easter	1546	20s., 19s. 6d., 19s.	8s.	5s.
Mich.	1546	10s. 6d., 10s., 9s. 6d.	4s.	3s.
Mich.	1547	6s., 5s. 6d., 5s.	4s.	2s. 8d.
Easter	1548	5s. 4d., 4s. 10d., 4s.	4s.	3s.
Mich.	1548	6s., 5s. 6d., 5s.	3s. 4d.	2s. 8d.
Easter	1549	7s., 6s. 6d., 6s.	4s.	3s.
Mich.	1549	12s., 11s. 6d., 11s.	5s. 4d.	4s.
19 Nov.	1549	13s.	—	—
19 Nov.	1549	14s. 6d.	—	—
Easter	1550	15s., 14s. 6d., 14s.	8s.	6s.
Mich.	1550	21s., 20s. 6d., 20s.	14s.	8s.
Mich.	1551	20s., 17s. 6d., 15s. 6d.	8s.	5s.
22 Nov.	1551	22s. 6d.	—	—
Easter	1552	17s., 16s. 6d., 16s.	8s.	4s.
Mich.	1552	12s., 11s., 10s.	10s.	6s.
Easter	1553	10s., 9s. 6d., 9s.	6s. 8d.	4s. 8d.
Mich.	1553	9s., 8s. 6d., 8s.	4s.	3s. 4d.
Easter	1554	10s. 6d., 10s., 9s. 6d.	5s. 8d.	4s.
Mich.	1554	14s., 13s. 6d., 13s.	12s.	8s.

		Wheat	Beans and/or peas	Oats
Mich.	1555	15s., 14s. 6d., 14s.	10s.	6s. 8d.
Easter	1556	22s., 21s. 6d., 21s.	18s.	7s.
Mich.	1556	24s., 23s. 6d., 23s.	18s.	8s.
Easter	1557	37s. 4d., 36s. 10d., 36s. 4d.	30s.	12s.
Mich.	1557	—	—	—
Mich.	1558	11s., 10s. 6d., 10s.	5s. 4d.	3s. 4d.
Easter	1559	12s., 11s. 6d., 11s.	5s. 4d.	4s.
Mich.	1559	16s., 15s., 15s.	6s.	4s. 6d.
Easter	1560	18s., 17s. 6d., 17s.	8s.	5s. 4d.
Mich.	1560	16s., 15s. 6d., 15s.	6s. 8d.	4s.
Easter	1561	19s., 18s. 6d., 18s.	9s.	5s. 4d.
Mich.	1561	20s., 19s. 6d., 19s.	14s.	8s.
Easter	1562	20s., 19s. 6d., 19s.	15s.	8s.
Mich.	1562	21s., 20s. 6d., 20s.	14s.	6s. 8d.
Easter	1563	30s., 29s. 6d., 29s.	15s.	6s. 8d.
Mich.	1563	16s., 15s. 6d., 15s.	12s.	5s.
Easter	1564	16s., 15s. 6d., 15s.	8s.	4s. 8d.
Mich.	1564	—	—	—
Easter	1565	10s., 9s. 6d., 9s.	4s. 8d.	3s.
Mich.	1565	18s., 17s. 6d., 17s.	6s.	4s.
Easter	1566	26s. 8d., 25s. 6d., 20s.	8s.	6s. 8d.
Mich.	1566	14s., 13s. 6d., 13s.	8s.	5s. 4d.
3 Oct.	1566	16s.	—	—
Easter	1567	12s., 11s. 6d., 11s.	7s. 6d.	5s. 4d.
Mich.	1567	14s., 13s. 6d., 13s.	10s.	6s. 8d.
Easter	1568	13s., 12s. 6d., 12s.	10s.	6s.
Mich.	1568	12s. 6d., 12s., 11s. 6d.	9s.	6s.
29 Nov.	1568	15s., 14s., 13s.	9s.	8s. 8d.
Easter	1569	18s., 17s. 6d., 17s.	11s.	8s.
Mich.	1569	14s., 13s. 6d., 13s.	8s.	4s.
Easter	1570	15s. 6d., 15s., 14s. 6d.	8s	4s. 8d.
Mich.	1570	12s., 11s. 6d., 11s.	5s. 4d.	4s.
Easter	1571	13s., 12s. 6d., 12s.	6s. 8d.	5s.
Mich.	1571	14s., 13s. 6d., 13s.	6s.	4s. 8d.
Easter	1572	20s., 19s. 6d., 18s. 6d.	8s.	5s.
Mich.	1572	18s. 6d., 18s., 17s. 6d.	7s.	5s. 4d.
Easter	1573	20s., 19s. 6d., 19s.	9s.	6s.
Mich.	1573	26s., 25s. 6d., 25s.	12s.	6s.
Easter	1574	28s., 27s. 6d., 27s.	13s. 4d.	8s.
Mich.	1574	19s., 18s. 6d., 17s. 6d.	13s. 4d.	7s.
Easter	1575	20s., 19s. 6d., 19s.	12s.	6s.
Mich.	1575	14s., 13s. 6d., 13s.	8s.	5s. 4d.
Easter	1576	18s., 17s. 6d., 17s.	10s.	7s.
Mich.	1576	23s., 22s. 6d., 22s.	9s.	6s.
Easter	1577	27s., 26s. 6d., 26s.	9s.	6s. 8d.
Mich.	1577	18s. 6d., 18s., 17s. 6d.	8s.	6s. 4d.
Easter	1578	24s., 23s. 6d., 23s.	9s.	6s.
Mich.	1578	17s., 16s. 6d., 16s.	9s.	6s.
Easter	1579	20s., 19s. 6d., 19s.	10s.	6s. 8d.
Mich.	1579	17s., 16s. 6d., 16s.	8s.	7s.
Easter	1580	17s., 16s. 6d., 16s.	9s. 4d.	8s.

		Wheat	Beans and/or peas	Oats
Mich.	1580	17s., 16s. 6d., 16s.	9s. 4d.	8s.
Easter	1581	27s., 26s. 6d., 26s.	8s.	6s.
Mich.	1581	18s., 17s. 6d., 17s.	8s.	6s.
Easter	1582	20s. 6d., 20s., 19s. 6d.	10s. 8d.	8s.
Mich.	1582	16s., 15s. 6d., 15s.	10s.	6s.
Easter	1583	18s., 17s. 6d., 17s.	10s.	6s.
Mich.	1583	16s. 6d., 16s., 15s. 6d.	9s.	6s.
Easter	1584	17s., 16s. 6d., 16s.	9s. 6d.	6s.
Mich.	1584	16s., 15s. 6d., 15s.	10s.	6s.
Easter	1585	19s. 6d., 19s., 18s. 6d.	10s.	7s.
Mich.	1585	18s., 17s. 6d., 17s.	9s.	6s.
Easter	1586	26s., 25s. 6d., 25s.	16s.	9s.
Mich.	1586	36s. 8d., 36s., 35s. 6d.	—	—
Easter	1587	55s., 54s. 6d., 54s.	22s.	13s. 4d.
Mich.	1587	22s., 21s. 6d., 21s.	13s. 4d.	6s.
Easter	1588	22s., 21s. 6d., 20s.	10s.	6s.
Mich.	1588	18s., 17s. 6d., 17s.	10s.	5s. 8d.
Easter	1589	22s., 21s. 6d., 21s.	16s.	10s.
Mich.	1589	28s., 27s., 25s.	10s.	6s. 8d.
Easter	1590	32s. 6d., 32s., 31s. 6d.	15s.	8s.
Mich.	1590	22s., 21s. 6d., 21s.	22s.	11s.
Easter	1591	29s., 28s. 6d., 28s.	24s.	14s.
Mich.	1591	20s., 19s. 6d., 19s.	20s.	9s.
Easter	1592	16s. 6d., 16s., 15s. 6d.	16s.	16s.
Mich.	1592	13s. 6d., 13s., 12s. 6d.	10s.	6s.
Easter	1593	16s., 15s. 6d., 15s.	12s.	6s.
Mich.	1593	21s. 6d., 21s., 20s. 6d.	10s.	6s.
Easter	1594	22s., 21s. 6d., 21s.	10s.	6s. 8d.
Mich.	1594	33s. 6d., 33s., 32s. 6d.	10s.	6s. 8d.
Easter	1595	42s., 38s., 32s.	21s. 4d.	16s.
Mich.	1595	40s., 36s., 32s.	16s.	7s.
	1596	—	—	—*
Mich.	1597	44s., 40s., 36s.	20s.	8s.
Easter	1598	48s., 47s. 6d., 47s.	20s.	9s.
Mich.	1598	30s., 29s. 6d., 28s.	—	—†
Easter	1599	24s. 6d., 24s., 23s. 6d.	10s.	8s.
	1600	—	—	
	1601	—	—	—‡
Mich.	1602	30s., 24s., 20s.	22s.	6s.
Easter	1603	24s., 22s., 20s.	12s.	6s.
Mich.	1604	26s. 8d., 24s., 21s. 4d.	12s.	8s.
Easter	1605	32s., 28s., 24s.	10s.	7s.
	1606–8	—	—	—
Mich.	1609	32s., 31s. 6d., 30s.	—	—
Easter	1610	28s. 2d., 24s., 21s.	17s.	10s. ‖

* Justices of victuals elected.
† 'And beyond nothing to say. Justices of victuals elected.'
‡ Two assistants to Mr Mayor in the pricing of victuals because he is a victualler.
‖ 25 Sept. Associates to Mayor elect for pricing victuals.

	Wheat	Beans and/or peas	Oats	Malt	Barley	Rye
Easter 1611	40s., 36s., 32s.	13s. 4d.	10s.	17s.	—	—
1612	—	—	—	—	—	—
Mich. 1613	44s., 40s., 36s.	21s. 4d.	9s.	23s. 4d.	20s.	—
1614	—	—	—	—	—	—
Mich. 1615	44s., 40s., 36s.	32s.	14s.	24s.	—	—
Mich. 1616	36s., 30s., 20s.	20s.	13s. 4d.	24s.	20s.	—
Easter 1617	46s., 44s., 28s.	20s.	10s.	20s.	20s.	—
Mich. 1617	40s., 37s., 32s.	14s.	10s.	24s.	20s.	26s.
Mich. 1618	40s., 36s., 30s.	10s.	9s.	22s.	17s.	23s.
Mich. 1619	34s., 30s., 26s.	13s. 4d.	10s.	16s.	13s. 4d.	—
Mich. 1620	25s., 23s., 20s.	13s. 3d.	9s.	14s.	10s.	—
Mich. 1621	34s. 8d., 30s. 4d., 24s.	16s.	8s.	14s.	13s. 4d.	—
Easter 1622	48s., 43s. 4d., 40s.	34s.	—	26s. 8d.	—	—
Mich. 1622	53s. 4d., 48s., 40s.	24s.	8s.	28s.	23s.	—
Mich. 1623	32s., 26s. 8d., 24s.	16s.	8s.	25s.	18s.	—
Easter 1624	34s. 8d., 30s., 26s. 8d.	13s. 4d.	8s.	20s.	16s.	—
Mich. 1624	34s., 32s., 26s. 8d.	12s. 8d.	8s.	16s.	16s.	24s.
Mich. 1625	36s., 32s.	16s. 8d.⎱ 13s. 4d.⎰	10s. 8d.⎱ 8s. 4d.⎰	20s. —	18s. 4d.⎱ 16s.⎰	28s. ⎱ 25s. 4d.⎰
Mich. 1626	36s., 32s.	13s. 4d.	8s.	25s.	16s.	26s. 8d.
Easter 1627	30s., 26s. 8d.	12s.	6s. 8d.	16s.	13s.	22s. 8d.
Mich. 1628	36s., 32s.	18s. 8d.	12s.	18s.	21s.	28s., 34s.
Mich. 1629	30s., 26s. 8d.	23s.	10s.	—	22s.	25s.
1630–31	—	—	—	—	—	—
Mich. 1632	43s. 4d., 36s.	16s.	10s.	26s. 8d.	24s.	36s.
Mich. 1633	40s., 36s.	16s.	10s.	24s.	18s.	26s. 8d.
Mich. 1634	40s., 36s.	26s.	12s.	28s.	26s. 8d.	32s.
1635	—	—	—	—	—	—
Mich. 1636	44s., 36s., 32s.	26s.	10s.	24s.	20s.	26s. 8d.
Mich. 1637	47s., 43s., 38s.	36s.	18s.	38s.	34s.	40s.

	Wheat	Peas	Beans	Oats	Malt	Barley	Rye
Mich. 1656	38s., 34s.	21s.	21s.	12s.	24s.	20s.	26s.
1657	42s., 40s., 30s. 6d.	20s.	—	10s.	—	30s.	30s.
1658	48s., 46s.	24s.	24s.	12s.	26s.	22s.	30s.
April 1659	50s., 44s.	—	—	—	24s.	22s. 6d.	—
Mich. 1659	48s., 40s.	—	—	16s.	—	29s. 4d.	—
1660	44s., 40s., 24s.	20s.	20s.	8s.	28s.	20s.	26s. 8d.
1661	64s., 60s., 53s. 4d.	26s. 8d.	—	13s. 4d.	34s.	28s.	48s.
1662	40s., 36s., 32s.	24s.	24s.	10s.	24s.	22s.	32s.
1663	No entry						
1664	No entry						
1665	32s., 26s. 8d.	13s. 4d.	13s. 4d.	12s.	—	16s.	24s.
1666	20s., 18s., 16s.	13s. 4d.	13s. 4d.	8s.	—	10s. 8d.	13s. 4d.
1667	22s., 20s., 18s.	—	—	8s.	—	15s.	15s.
1668	20s., 17s.	7s.	12s.	—	16s.	12s.	17s.
1669	32s., 28s., 24s.	18s.	20s.	10s.	25s.	20s.	24s.
1670	32s., 28s., 24s.	20s.	24s.	10s.	25s.	19s.	24s.
1671	No entry						
1672	No entry						

	Wheat	Peas	Beans	Oats	Malt	Barley	Rye
1673	32s., 30s.	—	—	8s.	—	17s.	28s.
1674	40s., 37s. 4d., 34s. 8d.	30s.	—	11s.	—	24s.	37s. 4d.
1675	32s., 30s., 28s.	14s.	15s.	8s.	—	16s.	26s.
1676	22s., 21s., 20s.	16s.	—	7s.	—	13s. 6d.	18s.
1677	34s., 28s., 26s. 8d.	—	20s.	10s. 6d.	—	22s.	26s. 8d.
1678	29s., 26s.	13s. 4d.	—	7s. 6d.	—	15s.	20s.
1679	32s., 26s. 8d.	18s.	18s.	8s.	—	16s.	18s.
Easter 1680	28s., 24s.	18s. 8d.	—	8s. 6d.	—	14s.	16s.
Mich. 1680	30s., 26s. 8d.	16s.	16s.	8s.	—	14s.	16s.
1681	35s., 33s.	16s.	20s.	10s.	—	16s.	32s.
1682	29s., 27s.	18s.	22s.	12s.	—	23s.	26s. 8d.
1683	25s., 22s. 6d.	—	16s.	8s.	—	14s.	20s.
Easter 1684	32s., 29s.	16s.	—	9s.	—	17s.	26s.
Mich. 1684	38s., 34s.	—	28s.	14s.	—	22s.	26s. 8d.
1685	28s., 22s.	24s.	28s.	8s.	—	16s.	20s.
1686	40s., 32s.	20s.	20s.	9s.	—	22s.	28s.
1687	24s., 20s.	12s. 8d.	12s. 8d.	8s. 6d.	—	15s. 6d.	16s.
1688	24s., 18s.	—	16s.	8s.	—	15s.	16s.
1689	25s., 22s.	12s.	12s.	8s.	—	13s.	18s.
1690	24s., 21s.	13s. 4d.	13s. 4d.	8s.	—	12s.	18s.
1691	21s., 17s.	13s.	16s.	8s.	—	10s.	18s.
1692	34s., 35s.	13s.	16s.	10s.	—	13s. 4d.	21s. 6d.
1693	38s., 34s.	20s.	22s.	12s.	—	24s.	24s.
1694	32s., 24s.	18s.	—	8s.	—	16s.	24s.
1695	39s., 34s.	20s.	24s.	10s.	—	17s.	22s.
1696	38s., 36s. 8d.	20s.	20s.	9s.	—	15s.	20s.
1697	43s., 40s.	20s.	20s.	9s.	—	20s.	32s.
Easter 1698	50s., 48s.	22s.	22s.	15s.	—	32s. 6d.	30s.
Mich. 1698	50s., 47s. 6d.	32s.	32s.	13s. 4d.	—	24s.	40s.
1699	36s., 30s.	22s.	22s.	8s. 6d.	—	22s. 6d.	24s.
1700	32s., 28s.	20s.	20s.	10s.	—	18s.	22s.
1701	24s., 20s.	12s.	12s.	8s.	—	17s.	16s.
1702	20s.	16s.	16s.	10s.	—	15s.	15s.
1703	20s.	16s.	16s.	10s.	—	12s.	15s.
1704	3s. a st.	1s. 8d. a measure	1s. 8d. a measure	10s.	—	12s.	2s. 3d. a st.
1705	No entry						
1706	No entry						
1707	24s.	14s.	—	8s.	—	16s.	16s.
1708	No entry						
1709	52s.	28s.	—	12s.	—	24s.	40s.
1710	40s.	30s.	—	12s.	—	24s.	30s.
1711	40s.	—	—	12s. 6d.	—	24s.	28s.
1712	25s.	—	—	15s.	—	15s.	18s.
1713–21	No entries						

APPENDIX IV

THE STRUGGLES OF 1584–1588

AT the mayoral election on Holyrood day 1584 alderman Hanson received 78 votes plus 3 on the aldermanic bench—the mayor (Rishworth), Mason and Winterburn; William Yates, an alderman elect, received 72 votes plus 4 on the bench—Kent, Scolfield, Dawson and Emonson. Yates was therefore declared elected by the votes of the bench. This was in accord with rule; the aldermen chose between the two candidates who had received the highest number of votes in the outer chamber (see above, p. 36). At first the mayor refused to consent to the election of Yates, and it seems that he only agreed after lord chief justice Wray, Sir Anthony Thorold and the recorder, on the orders of the privy council, had intervened, and adjudged the election to be good. (The privy council register is missing for the period between January 1580 and February 1586.) Here was a junior alderman elected over the head of one of his seniors.

The following year Henry Blow, who had become an alderman at the preceding Easter leet, received 108 votes plus 4 on the bench—the mayor (Yates), Emonson, Scolfield and Dawson—and he was declared elected by the votes of the bench because the mayor was one of them. At the Michaelmas leet that followed he was sworn as mayor, and at the election of justices his four supporters were chosen. The voting indicates the strength of the reaction against Rishworth and his party: Yates 126, Dawson 115, Scolfield 114, Emonson 112, Mason 17, Hanson 26, Winterburn 10 and Rishworth 7.

A letter from the privy council, dated 18 October, over the august names of Burghley, Leicester, Hunsdon, Hatton and Walsingham, indicates that in electing Blow they had defied the direction of the privy council and the bishop's advice to choose a man able in discretion to govern the city, and well affected in religion. They had since added a second contempt, savouring of mere wilfulness, in electing as justices the four ringleaders in the election of the mayor, who had already been punished therefor, 'whereat we do not a little marvel'. As they held the four unfit for office, and especially Dawson and Emonson, they sequestered these two, and ordered the common council to appoint two persons well given in religion to assist in their places. The mayor was warned that at the end of his year of office he would have to answer for his contemptuous dealing and receive the punishment he deserved. The privy council assured themselves that this double contempt had not grown by default of the commonalty, of whom they held a better opinion, but 'of you, the mayor, and the rest of your factious brethren'. (The letter is entered in the common council minutes.)

The common council hastened to comply with this order, and to elect two justices in place of Dawson and Emonson. To ensure compliance the privy council sent Thorold to attend their meeting. All the candidates were of Rishworth's party, Mason and Winterburn being elected with 22 votes and 17 respectively. Hanson polled 12 and Rishworth himself only 5. Clearly the mayor's large majority abstained from voting.

These dissensions were too much for the city preacher, Mr Jermyne, who resigned and departed. The dominant party then resolved, perhaps with a view to finding a friend in higher places, that the stipend should be paid to Dean Griffin so long as it should please his worship to take pains therein.

Having attained the mayoralty, Blow, in defiance of the warning of the privy council, made the most of his opportunities. He wrote to Lord Rutland that the bishop would soon be in Lincoln to hold an inquiry. Rishworth having drafted articles against Blow and his party (perhaps the manifesto referred to on p. 104), Blow asked Rutland whether he advised the production of articles already prepared against Rishworth (*H.M.C. Rutland*, i, 190). Whether Rutland committed himself does not appear, but Blow and his party attacked Rishworth and tried to disfranchise him. Rishworth appealed to Sir Francis Walsingham, who wrote to the mayor and aldermen desiring them to appease the factions in the city by coming to terms among themselves; and he warned them that the attempt to disgrace Rishworth would be ill taken by the lords of her Majesty's council. The same day he wrote to Sir Edward Dymoke asking him to use his credit and ability to appease the factions and to see that no wrong was offered to Rishworth (State Papers Domestic, Eliz., CLXXXVII, no. 70). But Dymoke was on the other side. He replied that he had dealt therein with Mr Dean, 'an honest grave and reverend gentleman' called in by the town as an umpire, as religion was a colour to faction. He added that Rishworth and his party had refused arbitration, and that 'if he had as good a mind to peace as the Mayor hath a will, his religion would bear much more credit with it' (ibid. CLXXXVIII, no. 25). The dean sent Burghley a letter by Rishworth's hand, saying 'I have found the bearer in his answer to the things wherewith he hath been charged very reasonable and in his doings so far as he hath been by me moved, very Christian': his zeal was sufficiently known, and his ability to govern honestly in life was admitted by his enemies. The dean added that he had done his best to keep the peace, but that 'offence many times is given when a man purposeth not', which suggests that Rishworth was tactless. Unity could not be reached by persuasion, and would have to be enforced. Griffin sat firmly on the fence: he accused neither side, both being his good friends (ibid. no. 24).

If the dean temporised, Bishop Wickham's views were pronounced. He supported Rishworth on grounds of principle and policy; and he commended him to Walsingham, saying that he advanced the cause of religion and all other good things in the city of Lincoln, and that if he were not assisted against his enemies, the grief and ill thereof would touch all the well affected in the city (ibid. no. 28).

Meanwhile Blow and his justices had given Rishworth a copy of the articles against him, appointed a time to receive his answer, and so informed Walsingham. When the appointed time came Rishworth produced a letter from Walsingham, and the proceedings were adjourned. Blow and four aldermen then wrote to Walsingham asking that the matter might be referred to Rutland and lord chief justice Wray for settlement—suitable because sympathetic arbitrators. (Ibid. no. 27. Blow, Dawson and Yates signed their names, Scolfield and Hodgson made their marks.)

Burghley and Walsingham addressed a letter to the bishop, Thorold and the recorder Thimbleby, or any two of them, ordering them to report on the whole matter, to advise the mayor to study for the peace of the city, and to see that no ill course should be taken to molest or disgrace Rishworth, 'who in the year of his mayoralty did many good things'. A postscript added the dean to the committee in place of Thimbleby, who was not available. Dymoke was not included, but Walsingham wrote to him to ask him to use his good offices. (Ibid. no. 39. Thimbleby wrote to Rutland saying that the latter was to be umpire if they could not end the dispute (*H.M.C. Rutland*, 1, 199).)

In a letter to the mayor, Walsingham pointed out that though his letter had been addressed to the mayor and all the aldermen, the reply was subscribed only by the mayor and four of them; and he doubted the mayor had not imparted it to all his brethren. He was surprised that they had proceeded on the articles against Rishworth, and had only been stopped by Walsingham's previous letter: 'to be short, it will not be well thought of here that such persons as the bishop and the rest chosen by assent of the parties should be thought by you unmeet and insufficient to hear and order your controversies, yea, and greater matters if need were'.

It appears that the dean, a man of peace, had not thought fit to accept the duties and stipend of city preacher amidst the civic violence. The common council therefore resolved that as the city was destitute of a preacher, the archbishop of Canterbury should have the nomination for this turn, and that a salary of 40 marks should be paid. Whitgift had been dean of Lincoln from 1571 to 1577: either this was a bid for support or the decision was made under pressure.

As the proceedings against Rishworth were held up, the mayor's party prepared charges against two of his friends, Laythorpe and Dobson, aldermen elect. It was charged against Laythorpe that he was elected in a disorderly way on the very day of his predecessor's funeral, when most of the senior aldermen were out of town; that he had tried to further the election of Hanson as mayor the year before, though he knew it was illegal; that penance had been enjoined on him for failing to pay moneys to the poor as he should have done; that being an attorney and an officer to the sheriff of the shire and clerk of the county he could not attend to his city duties as by his oath he was bound to do; that he had been impeached for forgery in the Star Chamber; and there were other counts. Against Dobson it was claimed that he being a mercer had sold his shop and stock in trade, let his house and left the city without the mayor's consent. When Mr Mayor moved him that being an alderman he should stay in the city he replied that he was not of sufficient ability or wealth to do so.

When the articles were duly read in the inner chamber, the mayor and three other aldermen voted in favour of disaldering the defendants, and four aldermen voted against: 'whereupon...it was thought convenient according to the usage of the place, Mr Mayor having three votes besides his own, that the said articles' should be referred to the common council in the outer hall. All save four agreed that the two men be disaldered. But when the next day it was intended to elect two new aldermen the mayor and his brethren could not agree upon the calendar, and the election was adjourned. The privy council later commanded that the vacancies should not be filled.

The inquiry dragged on, and Rishworth petitioned Walsingham to expedite the findings of the bishop and his colleagues, and he sent up his reply to the charges against him (State Papers Domestic, Eliz., cxcii, nos. 68, 69).

Holyrood day, when a new mayor must be elected, was approaching, and on

10 September 1586 the privy council wrote letters to the mayor and his brethren. They ordered that the displaced aldermen be allowed their places and voices until the bishop and the rest had reported (*A.P.C. 1586–87*, pp. 220–1). Nevertheless the mayor and three aldermen adjudged that Dobson and Laythorpe, not then being aldermen, were not eligible for election as mayor. Five aldermen thought otherwise, and refused to consent to the calendar prepared by the mayor's party; whereupon the calendar was delivered to the common council, who proceeded to election. The three candidates were Scolfield, who was elected with 85 votes plus 3 on the bench, Hodgson with 81 and Dennis with 32. The five dissentient aldermen refused to vote in the outer house.

The official record is not the whole story. Walsingham obtained a full report. When the mayor and his brethren were sitting for the election, Laythorpe came to the chamber door to deliver the privy council letters, whereupon William Milner, a sheriff's peer, took him by the coat collar and threw him down under the feet of himself and Abraham Metcalfe, where he was bunched by one or both of them, and threatened by Milner to be thrown out of the hall window. He was so ill used that he was forced to throw down their honours' letters, which Rishworth took up lest they be torn or taken away. Then followed the dispute about the calendar. According to his version the five aldermen prepared a calendar, and the mayor and his adherents called a common council, ostensibly to restore Laythorpe and Dobson to their offices, thinking 'to colour their contempt and to give a counterfeit show of obedience to their lordships' letters.' The council refused to restore them. Milner told one of the five aldermen that if their calendar came out from the inner chamber it would be rejected.

It appears that it was on the advice of Thimbleby, who had come to the hall, that the mayor had put out his calendar, saying that he would answer for the doing of it, and that the privy council did not mean that the displaced men should be aldermen. After Scolfield had been chosen by the outer house, and sworn mayor, the five aldermen in the inner house, where they had been kept nine hours, heard a great noise in the outer house, to wit, 'Bring them out to us, bring them out to us', whereunto one Peter Wilson, a sheriff's officer, added that if they would not come out he and others would fetch them out by the ears, and Dawson said the commoners would burst in upon them. The five desired the mayor that their lives should be preserved, and that they might have the peace of all those outrageous commons; but this being refused they durst not come out until the mayor and his adherents had gotten what they wanted and gone (State Papers Domestic, Eliz., cxciii, no. 36).

Blow and others wrote to the privy council that they had intended to restore Laythorpe, but that the common council refused; and that he and his brethren stayed upon the matter all day until sunset with no calendar made, whereupon the citizens and freemen began earnestly to exclaim upon them, saying that they had small regard to the customary and charter, until they were forced to send out their calendar. The man chosen was universally well thought of in the shire both for his religion and government (ibid. no. 41).

Thimbleby also wrote to Walsingham. To prevent uproar he had advised the mayor to make a calendar, after which they quietly proceeded to elect a very honest man: he begged Walsingham not to be persuaded that their strivings were for a matter of religion, but a matter of faction with religion as a cloak, as he could prove (ibid. no. 39). He wrote in like terms to Rutland (*H.M.C. Rutland*, I, 207).

The bishop disagreed. He wrote to Walsingham's secretary:

The letters sent from their lordships took small effect, as by the report of this bearer you may understand. Notwithstanding the men to whom I stand of my credit and conscience have the part of good citizens, of honest men, of zealous Christians, and of faithful subjects, the man that is now chosen to be mayor (if his election be real) is one of the corruptest in all the town for his religion, and such a one, as if his day served, would think it a great glory to be accounted a papist. These contempts of authority and disgraces of the godly, if they be not prevented, we may well put up our pipes and fall to mourning.... The Lord bless and preserve the Queen's Majestie and defend her Church from the paw of the Lion. (State Papers Domestic, Eliz., cxciii, no. 51.)

The plague was raging in Lincoln in the summer of 1586. Scolfield, elected mayor on 14 September, was dead before he could be installed on the 29th. Another election was held on the 26th. Hodgson, one of Rishworth's party, was elected, though the aldermanic vacancy went to Blow's party. When the justices were elected at the Michaelmas leet, Blow and two of his friends were elected and Winterburn, one of Rishworth's party. Winterburn refused to take the oath, though after much persuasion he did so. A few weeks later the justices were sent for one Sunday to take examinations; and the day after, summoned again to take order for the relief of the poor suffering from plague, demanded sight of the examinations. The mayor commanded one of his officers to read them, whereupon Winterburn replied 'that he could and would read them himself, and drawing out his spectacles, and seeming to put them on, espying his hand in the latter end of the examination, he most violently and contemptuously before Mr Mayor, the justices and some other of his brethren there present, in great fury and madness, rent and tore in pieces the said examinations using this or the like speeches: "There you are, do with them what you list",' for which contemptuous dealing, after time being given him to relent, he was disaldered. Meanwhile Blow's party had charged the town clerk, Leonard Carr, with supporting the other faction, and with forging a signature to a petition, and he was displaced. He appealed to Lord Chancellor Hatton, who intervened, to be told that he was too late and the place was filled.

At some time before 1587 the report of the bishop was laid before the privy council, in consequence of which Dawson, Emonson and Yates were called before the lords of the council to answer (among other things) for contempts committed against the bishop's discretion at the time of Blow's election to the mayoralty in 1585. Blow himself had escaped, for he was dead. The others were committed to the Marshalsea during their lordships' pleasure, and remained there some five or six weeks. The common council resolved that, the action of the aldermen being in accordance with the customary of the city, their expenses should be borne by the common chamber; but the allowance should not be paid until Blow's election, which was in issue, had been proved lawful and warranted by the customary.

The mayor, Hodgson, died on 10 September, and Milner held office until Michaelmas. Dennis, apparently a member of Blow's party, was elected for the ensuing year, being the fifth man to be elected or to hold office within a twelvemonth.

At the New Year 1588 Walsingham wrote again about the displacement of Laythorpe and Dobson. He awarded that Dobson should retain the place of an honest citizen, but should not be restored at present to his aldermanic seat. As to Laythorpe, the Secretary thought he had been treated harshly, and that the evidence against him was weak, and he wished that he might with greater allowance have remained an alderman. He did not, however, wish to risk a disturbance for the sake of an individual, and he contented himself with directing that on the election of two aldermen his name should be included in the calendar. If he were elected, as Walsingham wished, he was to remain an alderman; if not, he must abandon his attempt at restitution. But if he were not elected, a note must be placed in the council book by the articles against him that he was displaced 'rather for common quietude than upon the validity of the articles objected, being a most fit man for those good parts it has pleased God to endow him withal to have government in that city'.

In accordance with this tactful award the common council proceeded to the election of two aldermen. William Gosse and John Becke were elected with 24 and 19 votes respectively, Laythorpe and John Redthorne receiving only 5 votes each. Having got their way, the council solemnly recorded in compliance with Walsingham's award, that Laythorpe should stand disaldered rather for common quietness than upon the validity and sufficient proof of the articles exhibited against him.

Carr, the ejected town clerk, obtained judgment in Chancery against the intruder upon his office; and Hatton directed that he be restored as town clerk, clerk of the peace and clerk of the statutes as the equity of his cause required. He was accordingly restored, and admitted to practise in all the courts held in the Guildhall. It is clear that the sympathy of the common council remained with Parkins, the intruding town clerk, who was granted £10 towards his unsuccessful defence.

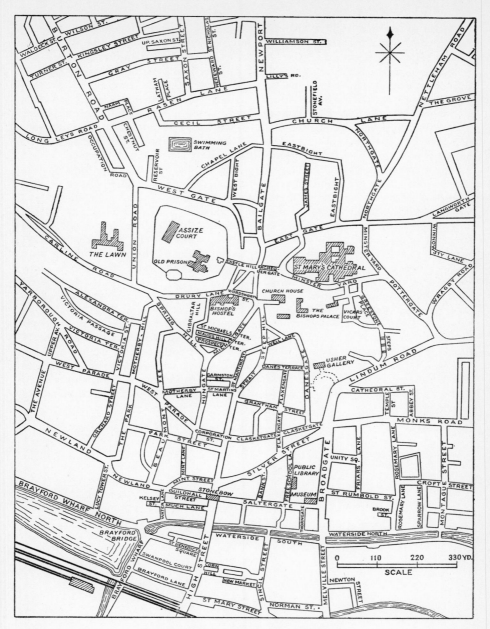

Map 4. Modern street map of Lincoln.

INDEX